— HIGH PRAISE FOR —
M. JOHN FAYHEE

"No one tells more hilarious or thought-provoking stories about living in the West than John Fayhee. It always amazes me that he doesn't make his tales up. This book is a perfect example."

— Devon O'Neil,

Columnist, espn.com

"*Mountain Gazette* is host to many interesting and diverse regional writers, but the numerous letters from readers in each issue are overwhelmingly addressed to whatever editor John Fayhee has last scribbled. Whether the subject is the ultimate meaning of dogs and beer or how to conduct yourself in a lightning storm, Fayhee's 'Smoke Signals' columns somehow come across as a personal letter to each reader, I think in large part because he has, for decades now, remained loyal to his audience of mountain jocks, pundits, poets and thin-air hedonists. This kind of reader rapport is unusual these days."

— Jon Kovash,

Moab correspondent, Utah Public Radio

"As a storyteller Fayhee is not to be trusted. He should be read and savored, then passed on to the next unsuspecting soul willing to be corrupted."

— Vince Welch,

Author of *The Last Voyageur: Amos Burg and The Rivers of the West*

"John Fayhee has for years been an inspiration and one of my literary heroes. As the many longtime devout readers of the *Mountain Gazette* will attest, he is a master of pure storytelling in the most classic American style — it's hard to not imagine him sitting next to you on a barstool as you read his words on the page."

— **Brendan Leonard,**

Contributing editor, *Climbing Magazine*

"*Smoke Signals* has a good deal in common with Ed Abbey's *Desert Solitaire* and Gretel Ehrlich's *Solace of Open Spaces,* with one major difference: M. John Fayhee will make you laugh out loud."

— **Alan Stark,**

Publisher Emeritus,

Colorado Mountain Club Books

"Like the quirky, funny and even brilliant bar conversations that you can never quite reconstruct the next day, John Fayhee's 'Smoke Signals' columns insinuate their way into your system. Sometimes illuminating, sometimes obscure, they are messages from a high ground you should read because they are important and more importantly because they are highly entertaining."

— **Jay Cowan,**

Author of *The Best of the Alps,*

"Hunter S. Thompson"

and *In the Land of Living Dangerously*

"Fayhee's tales are sometimes rambling accounts of a life lived to the fullest. He crafts his language in a way that drives you to a lengthy sentence's conclusion with unconventional twists and clever turns of phrase."

— **Jefferson Dodge,**
Managing Editor, *Boulder Weekly*

"Fayhee is not only a literary signpost for the mountain folks, but an incredible and insightful man who brings the outdoors into every aspect of living."

— **deuter.com**

"M. John Fayhee tells the truth: ugly, surreal, hilarious, entertaining, and heartbreaking truth. Whatever myth still survives of a West swarming with rugged individualists living by their own code, Fayhee keeps that freewheeling romanticism from flat-lining with ropey prose packed with do-your-own-thing, be-your-own-person credos."

— *Matter Daily*

"If there's one thing John Fayhee is, it's honest — even when he's misrepresenting or embellishing the facts."

—**Kimberly Nicoletti,**
Summit Daily News

"Fayhee is a humorous, irreverent raconteur."

—**Katie Klingsport,**
Telluride Daily Planet

"There is in most, if not all, of Fayhee's stories a sincerity and an eye for detail that belie his self-proclaimed tendency to lie and exaggerate. There is a tender core that speaks of his love for the life he has chosen, and this is why he is just so damned compelling to read."

— Joe Foster,
Durango Telegraph

"Nobody understands mountain culture better and where it stands within the larger American culture."

— George Sibley,
Author of *Part of a Winter: A Memory More Like a Dream* and *Dragons in Paradise: On the Edge Between Civilization and Sanity*

"If you moved to Colorado from anywhere else in the United States, or, for that matter, the world, chances are you did it because you wanted to be like M. John Fayhee — whether you knew it or not. And the chances are equally good you're nothing like Fayhee."

— Ted Holteen,
Durango Herald

SMOKE SIGNALS

wayward journeys through
the old heart
of the new west

M. JOHN FAYHEE

foreword by b. frank

—ALSO BY —
M. JOHN FAYHEE

Mexico's Copper Canyon Country

Along the Colorado Trail

Up At Altitude: A Celebration of Life in the High Country

Along Colorado's Continental Divide Trail

Along the Arizona Trail

A Colorado Winter

When In Doubt, Go Higher: A Mountain Gazette *Anthology*
(editor and contributor)

Comeback Wolves (contributor)

Bottoms Up: M. John Fayhee's
Greatest Hits from the Mountain Gazette

The Colorado Mountain Companion

SMOKE SIGNALS

Wayward Journeys Through
the Old Heart of the New West

Published by: Raven's Eye Press, Durango, Colorado
[www.ravenseyepress.com]

Versions of the chapters previously appeared in *Mountain Gazette,*
as noted in the text

Fayhee, M. John. (1955-)

Smoke Signals: Wayward Journeys Through the Old Heart
of the New West
1. American West
2. Humor
3. Adventure / Travel

Library of Congress Control Number: 2012945171 © 2012

ISBN 978-0-9840056-2-8

Foreword by: B. Frank

Cover photo by: Mark Fox

Book layout and design by: Lindsay J. Nyquist, elle jay design
[www.ellejaydesign.com]

Printed in the United States of America

1 3 5 7 9 10 8 6 4

AUTHOR'S NOTE:

I advise you to take these tales with a grain of salt.

Matter of fact, it's probably best for all involved if you consider every syllable herein contained to be either an overt exaggeration, a gross misrepresentation, a poorly recalled memory or a blatant, unrepentant fabrication. Maybe even all of the above.

CLARIFICATION OF PREVIOUS AUTHOR'S NOTE:

On the advice of my attorney, I think I ought to just go ahead and call this entire shebang an unabashed work of fiction. My lawyer further suggests that I attach the following standard work-of-fiction disclaimer: All the events herein described have been pulled from the deepest, darkest recesses of my ass. Any resemblance to real people — alive, dead, brain-dead, falling-down drunk and lying in a ditch, reincarnated, in utero or not yet conceived — is purely coincidental and more than likely the result of a sordid imagination (yours, not mine). Shame on you!

OK, it's time to spill the beans: There really is no such person as M. John Fayhee. He himself is a work of fiction, a joint creation of a disparate group of otherwise innocent, anonymous folks who, with zero in the way of malice aforethought, met over the course of many years in beaucoup bars, on a multitude of wilderness trails, on innumerable front porches, around countless campfires and in scores of smoky living rooms. Once the fictitious character of M. John Fayhee was conceived, fleshed out and decanted, members of this committee each took turns adding their own direct and/or indirect influence to the events related in the herein-contained "Smoke Signals" columns which, were there such a person as M. John Fayhee, would plus-or-minus be like words he would pen, were he, in fact, real.

Law Offices of Thompson, Abbey, Chatwin, Kerouac & Bukowski

LEGAL NOTICE

To whom it may concern:

We, the members of the Committee That Made Fayhee Who He Is, hereby serve notice of our immediate, and somewhat frantic, legal dissolution. We stress none of the individual members of the Committee That Made Fayhee Who He Is admit to concocting, writing or contributing any of the specific material included in this book. Furthermore, we each blame all the other members of the committee for conceiving and executing what from the get-go was clearly a bad idea poorly executed by the wrong people at the wrong time in the wrong place.

All communications, especially of the tort-based variety, to the Committee That Made Fayhee Who He Is should be sent c/o the Sluice Box Saloon in Colorado or the Burro Borracho Cantina in New Mexico. Be forewarned: Responses may be slow in coming.

Signed, this 16 day of May 2012.

N.S. Bame, Lauri Beckwith, Collette Beers, Jean Benzine, Jody Berman, Shawna Bethell, Patrick Brower, Stephen Buhner, Jaxon Burgess, Sean and Mary Cavens, Jen Cooper, Joel Cosper, Allan Cox, Currie Craven, Donald Davis, the Dillon Dam Brewery Old Farts' Club, Joseph and Sally Dischinger, Tara Flanagan, Michael Fleming, Mark Fox, Brad Frank, Gay Gangel-Fayhee, Kris Garnjost, Greg and Tanya Gentry, Heather Glyde, Shawn Gordy, Sahuaripa Gonzales, Glen and Sandra Griffin, Mac Griffith, Paul "Fatty" Guglielmo, Martin B. Hamilton, Chris Hickey, Jim Kolb, Jon Kovash, Peter Kray, Beth Lawler, Bill Lee, Rob Lee, Matt Luhr, Jim Marsh, T. Alex Miller, Luan Mitchell, Ma Moose, Kim Marquis, Julie McIntyre, Hugh Morris, Michele Murray, Aleisha Nelson, Chris and Jamie Nelson, Kimberly Nicoletti, Brad Odekirk, Devon O'Neil, Robert Parlett, William Paxson, Barbie Pollack, Margaret Rhode, Frederick Rivera, Curtis Robinson, Jay Scott, George Sibley, Rob Sickler, Frank and Katherine Smith, Nick Spano, Fosco Spinedi, Bryan Stacey, Margaret Stack, Anne Stafford, Philip Stafford, Cat Stailey, Alan Stark, Russ Titsch, Stacy Towar, Trishuwa, James "JT" Tyler, Marc Weinberger, Alan West, Greg Wright, Randy Wyrick, Harley Youngblood, Ed Zeitz.

P.S.: Despite the fact that we disavow all knowledge of this project and each other, if you were inclined to consider this legal notice to be a formal dedication, we promise not to sue you, as long as you promise not to sue us.

—TABLE OF CONTENTS—

"All roads lead to the end of the world."
— Tom Waits,
"Pay Me" ("Bad As Me")

*"The obvious road is almost always the fool's road, and
beware the middle roads, the roads of moderation,
common sense and careful planning."*
— William Burroughs,
"The Western Lands" ("Material • Seven Souls")

Introduction

M John Fayhee (aka Fayhee, MJF, M. John, John, etc.) loves fire. His eyes wander to the heart of one as he talks. His words drift through camp like smoke, and right now it's tempting to paint him as a noble savage come to share laconic, "Chief Seattle"-voiced wisdoms from his hero journeys, but that would be a sepia-toned, Catlin-esque caricature of the sometimes indelicate raconteur I've come to know. Pretty much, "Smoke Signals" is the way you'd hear these stories if Fayhee were across the fire from you, after a long day walking into a place many would like to say they've been, without having to haul the pack past real and imagined dangers.

The MJF in these pages ambles meandering trails, giving each story enough time to reveal slices of a life well lived. Expect him to suck you in with casual details before dropping hints of just where a story may be headed, whether the subject is basketball/ping-pong diplomacy in China, river and balloon misadventures in Georgia, redneck 4-wheeling in Colorado or meeting Jesus on a mountainside while taking a surreptitious, drunken piss.

Yes, dear reader, more alcohol and other "recreational"

drugs than would perhaps be prudent in these ever-more pro-
hibition-loving times were consumed in the living of some of
these tales, but, like listening to a bearded, sandal-wearing,
beer-drinking visionary telling "shaggy dog" stories down the
bar just far enough away that truth is hard to discern in the
din — you might lean toward your copy of "Smoke Signals"
to catch Fayhee's punch lines, and hear also some insights
into why humans slip free of the leash of social norms just
often enough to keep us interesting.

Not long ago, I came across a photograph of a lone figure silhouetted against a skyline. The figure bends toward a
campfire. Puffs of smoke rise toward the top of the frame.
According to the caption, the noble brave (we know this by
the noble feather plume atop his head) is "Lighting the Signal Fire," in an illustration from *The Vanishing Race* (Joseph
K. Dixon [1909]). Using purplish prose common about a
hundred years ago, Mr. Dixon lamented the passing of a way
of life made impractical by — well, perhaps we should turn
to the author for a short sample: "The country was large and
the tribes were widely separated...The white man came, and
for hundreds of years their contest has been waged against
a superior force. They have disputed every mile of territory
which has been acquired from them. During all that time
they could not make a knife, a rifle or a round of ammunition. Their method of communication was confined to the
smoke signal, signal fires and scouts. They had no telegraph,
no heliograph, no arsenal..." — and the reason I've let this
paragraph digress from what started out to be an examination
of just what the hell John Fayhee means by "Smoke Signals"
is that after reading most of the *Mountain Gazette* columns
that led to this book, I've accepted that I'll never quite figure

out if he thinks a nobly simple way of living on, in and around mountains is being replaced by this century's "superior force" of cell-phoning, emailing, Facebook-friending, smartphone-wielding, Twittering invaders.

According to an ongoing debate among loyal and casual *Mountain Gazette* readers, the Morse code column headers appearing at the top of Fayhee's "Smoke Signals" columns do (or do not) give us clues, but I don't struggle to decipher them. Twelve years into this uncertain century, Fayhee seems comfortable enough juggling nostalgia, modern technologies, changing social mores and the interests of a self-selected tribe of readers to keep a mountain-oriented magazine relevant enough that advertisers still want to buy space, even as print media's obituaries are repeated ad nauseam. I also don't waste energy fact-checking MJF's sometimes fantastical descriptions of human follies and foibles, allowing myself to read his stories for the same reason that a favorite mentor of mine once said he read *Playboy* magazine, "To see places I'll never be."

In over a decade of exchanging emails (and, I'll admit, a few beer-hazed campfire and bar bullshit sessions) about the venerable "art" of writing, my favorite MJF editorial advice is, "Truth always." In the well-told stories Fayhee presents here, facts may be embellished but truth is never compromised, as far as I can tell. As you read, I hope you'll understand just what this means, and perhaps examine where we've been and where mountain lovers may be going from here. You might even find yourself reconsidering whether discomfort, danger and occasional accusations of a lack of social decorum are really enough to keep you a safely productive cog in the group experiment we grandly label "civilization."

Commonly, in a missive to word-pushers like me, Fayhee will briefly toss out an idea or hint at future magazine editorial interests, and sign off with, "There it is. MJF" Much can be said for such brevity in an editor, but the twists and turns of his stories allow glimpses of just what made a British-born, Virginia-raised, border-country educated career journalist into a unique interpreter of all things mountain — long trails, campfires, towns, bars, dogs, misfits, lovers, friends and fools. It is an absolute pleasure to introduce this latest installment in John's lengthening life list of books. Enjoy.

FROM SOMEWHERE
ON THE HOME RANGE,
B. FRANK

Author's Preface

In July 2007, I started writing "Smoke Signals," a monthly column for the *Mountain Gazette*. I wish I could claim clear title to that name, which came about because my friend Mark Fox, a photographer for the Summit Daily News in Frisco, Colorado, was visiting me at my home in Silver City, New Mexico. Mark, camera ever at the ready, took several shots of me puffing on a stogie in my back yard and, upon returning home, proceeded to run one of them (the very one that appears on the cover of the book you now hold) in the Summit Daily, which, despite my current 600-mile remove from the county in which I dwelled for so long, was appropriate enough, since I helped start that particular paper in 1989 and toiled there in a variety of positions for more than a decade, clear up until George Stranahan, Curtis Robinson and I decided to resurrect the *Gazette*.

The accompanying caption said words to the effect of, "We wish we could figure out what Fayhee's trying to convey, but we don't understand smoke signals." I do not know who penned that caption. Might have been Mark. Might have been the janitor. I may not be very creative, but I have always been a more-than-competent hunter/gatherer; I know when to reach out and grab something that may be useful somewhere down the line, sort of, I would guess, like a crocodile does when he/she stores carrion under a submerged log. When it came time for me to launch and, thus, properly name, a regular column for the *Gazette*, "Smoke Signals" seemed as good as anything else I could pull out from under the submerged log as deadline loomed.

After more than five years and more than 60 "Smoke Signals," I have come to feel very comfortable having my column invoke images of a form of communication that boasts a solid connection to the most venerable part of the Old West, a form of communication that can easily be misinterpreted, or interpreted in various ways, or lost entirely if the wind kicks up at an inopportune moment.

"Smoke Signals" has never been subject to externally driven conceptual marching orders any more specific than: Try not to get us sued. We did not engage any focus groups or incorporate its conception and evolution into any sort of targeted, demographic-specific marketing strategy. "Let's use it to try to draw in more ugly, drunk old fat guys" or "This is a perfect opportunity to appeal to young, heavily tattooed female snowboarders" never was part of the organic discussion.

Basically, I have always had creative and stylistic carte blanche influenced only by obvious seasonal considerations (meaning I generally write about warm-weather topics in summer and cold-weather topics in winter).

From the get-go, I decided to mostly make "Smoke Signals" a venue for transcribed versions of the various stories I have been telling in bars and around campfires for well nigh half-a-century, almost all of which, because they have taken place in bars and around campfires in the very areas served by *Mountain Gazette*, were de facto subject appropriate for our pages.

The ability to translate stories from tongue to keyboard is a lot harder than many people would think, even for professional bullshitters and wordsmiths. I know many top-notch storytellers/accomplished writers who have tried (and tried and tried) and failed (and failed and failed) to do just that. There's just some sort of filter in one of the crucial brain interfaces that engages when most people sit down in front of their laptop with the intention of getting the bear tale they just related to a rapt barroom audience 10 minutes prior converted from sound waves to pixels.

Though there are beaucoup types of writing I suck at (such as Author's Prefaces), thankfully, I have always felt comfortable translating my personal verbal stories to the figurative blank white page — to the point that I often have difficulty penning pieces that did not make their first public appearance via the (often-alcohol-enhanced) oral tradition. I know not everyone agrees that bar or campfire stories ought to be taken out of their context. Fair enough. I fully understand that the transition from the oral to the written tradition is not always appropriate and, even when it might be, it's not always acceptably achieved. Grammatical mainstays such as basic subject-verb agreement, verb-tense consistency and even rudimentary sentence and paragraph structure are often sacrificed in the name of narrative expediency (or they are waylaid by the tectonic forces of inebriation) in a spoken story. And, when attempts are made to fit the round pegs of a verbal story into the square holes of the Roman alphabet, something, sometimes something critical to the original telling, is often lost in translation.

Not surprisingly, there have been more than a few failed attempts at making the leap from my vocal chords to a Word document. The "Smoke Signals" I opted to include in this book were examples of more successful attempts. At least in my mind. Such as it is.

———

The only limitation ever placed upon "Smoke Signals" takes the form of pre-determined word counts based solely upon the available space within the *Mountain Gazette*. That space has been somewhat fluid over the years. "Smoke Signals" debuted on two full pages located at the front of the magazine when it was, for reasons I never did quite get a handle on, almost square in shape. Then a regular half-page advertisement was placed upon the second page. Then the column was moved to a single page located at the very back of the magazine. Then the magazine's size was shrunk. Then "Smoke Signals" was moved once again to the front of the magazine. Then the size of the magazine was increased dramatically. So, my word count has fluctuated between 1,200 and 2,400, where, as these sentences are being typed, it now stands.

Any professional writer regularly tasked with filling a very specific amount of acreage utilizes a real-time cranial word-count-o-meter while engaged in the creative process. The goal is always to hit the targeted word count as close as possible while penning the piece. Saves editing time down the road. That's not exactly how I go about creating "Smoke Signals." Not by a long shot.

What I do is pen the story I desire to tell in its fulsome entirety, no matter how many words are birthed as a result. Sure, I keep a basic tally of where I'm at, because I understand full well that I'm going to have to cull the beast down so that it fits into an editorial hole, which, under no circumstances, can be expanded to accommodate my oft-irrepressible natural tendency toward loquaciousness. I know, for instance, as I am writing, that certain tangents likely will have to be axed. I build transitions into my narrative thread that allow entire chunks of text to be seamlessly eliminated. Still, it is not uncommon for the original versions of "Smoke Signals" to top out at 10, 15 or even 20,000 words. (For purposes of comparison, this book contains about 75,000 words.)

This causes far more work than standard column-writing methodology, because, by the time I have sluiced down the final text into printable form, I have gone through as many as 25 drafts. Never less than 15 drafts. I often spend 40 hours on a single "Smoke Signals." (And that does not count the significant thought I give those columns while I am hiking, sitting on the porch with a beer and/or testing out the material on my hapless drinking buddies.) I liken the process to those monster espresso machines you see in Italy, where there's this giant piece of almost Tim-Burton-esque technology, filling an entire wall, with dials and gauges and levers, that grunts and groans and clanks and expresses stream and aroma, all to make one teensy little cup of liquid perfection. I am not saying any of these "Smoke Signals" achieve espresso perfection. I *can* say that I sweat and fret and curse and cry and bleed and, yes, grunt, groan, clank and express steam and aroma, trying mightily to make them so.

Then, for reasons that escape me, I decided to compli-
cate my life by re-packaging my favorite "Smoke Signals" into
book form, which required a considerable amount of reverse-
editing-engineering, a process that consisted of reconciling
the version of "Smoke Signals" that first saw the light of printed day in the *Gazette* with the original, unexpunged version
of the story I very much wanted to tell in the first place.

This would seem easy enough: just use the unabridged
version that existed before the culling process began. Yeah,
right.

Harmonizing the many versions of each story was te-
dious in the extreme. Not surprisingly, the process of editing
the original "Smoke Signals" down to fit into the *Gazette* produced much in the way of improvement and enhancement.
Redundancies were eliminated. Extraneous verbiage was jet-
tisoned. Irrelevancies were sliced away like the fat on a Smith-
field ham.

Yet, few have been the versions of "Smoke Signals"
that have appeared in the pages of *Mountain Gazette* that I
felt were complete and whole. I almost always feel that the
printed "Smoke Signals" are truncated, "Cliff Notes" versions
that end up missing some relevant tangents, critical back stories, amusing asides and over-written descriptions that added
richness to the original bar/campfire stories upon which they
were based in the first place.

So, what I ended up doing was going through every draft
of every single "Smoke Signals" included in this book word
by word, line by line, deciding only then which components
of which version I liked the best. Then, I went through the
process of once again re-molding the resultant iteration into

a form that hopefully resonates with the readers of this book the way a good bar story hopefully resonates with those gathered around pitchers and shots on a cold winter night.

I have a friend who owns a saloon I visit fairly regularly. She said to me just the other night that, whenever she reads "Smoke Signals," she hears me sitting on a barstool and telling the story. She hears my *voice*. I can think of no higher compliment.

I hope you too hear my voice — even if you've never heard my voice — when you read these stories.

And I hope you realize as you do so that the man who first told them, then wrote them, then edited them, then rewrote them 15 or 20 times each understands clean down to his DNA how damned blessed he is for having the opportunity to shovel his unadulterated bullshit into a magazine and between the covers of a book. And he thanks you from the depths of his heart and soul for choosing to sit on a barstool that's within earshot.

— MJF

CHAPTER ONE

The Dandelion Manifesto

"90% of happiness is picking the right ethicist."
— Dilbert

The inhabitants of the Sluice Box Saloon went instantaneously silent as the ostensibly innocuous words flowed from my lips. And, let me assure you, the Sluice Box is not prone to even slight periods of silence. My fellow tiplers could suddenly fall over dead, be carted away to the morgue, autopsied, cremated and reincarnated as dung beetles in China, and, still, somehow, the boisterous interior bullshit factor would not be diminished one decibel. My buddy Milt had reflexively — verily, involuntarily, as though the action were a facial tick he could do nothing about — started to order yet another round.

To the consternation and confusion of all the hapless, hopeless and mostly toothless ne'er-do-wells there gathered, I stated I had had enough and it was time for me to weave my way home. Everyone immediately chugged their beverages and stood up to leave along with me. Then Milt, never one to miss something as obvious as broad daylight, looked toward the open door, squinted and stated, "Hey, the sun's still up; it can't be last-call time. What gives, Fayhee?" He eyed me suspiciously.

"Well, maybe it's tomorrow already," Big Del chimed in, attempting to lend clarity to a chronological interpretation situation that was not exactly setting any new-frontier standards on the quantum physics front.

Truthfully, it was 5 p.m. Dead of summer. Bright as the light at the end of the long white tunnel.

Having an entire bar full of people assuming, simply because yours truly was headed for the exit, it must be last call, even though that horrid time was not due to arrive for another *nine hours*, does not necessarily make me feel good about the direction my life has taken. The worst part, though, was having to explain to my beer-breathed brethren why I was leaving a perfectly workable imbibery while the taps were still flowing and the establishment was still mostly legally open.

"Got yard work to do," I responded, feeling simultaneously responsible beyond comprehension (all things being relative at the Sluice) and DNA-level mortified that such syllables were gestated and birthed in the womb of my vocal cords.

The bar erupted with a volcano of deep-rooted laughter.

"No, really, what's up? Got a meeting with your lawyer? Bail bondsman? Lady of the night?" my dear friend Milt, the asshole, asked.

"No, Milt, I've got a meeting with point-ten acres of weeds, dandelions and all manner of phylum-less green shit growing every place I don't want it to grow, and not growing every place I do want it to grow."

I explained that my neighbors, all of whom would rather

putter in their yards than do anything in the world, except maybe watch *Desperate Housewives* re-runs, are starting to give me stink eye and, Martin-Luther-like, tacking copies of the yard-upkeep part of our subdivision's covenants to my front door. And, I further explained, my wife's growling, because, last winter, as a means of getting out of helping her paint the living room, I made a deal: She takes care of the inside of the Casa de Fayhee, and I take care of the outside. My Faustian pact with the missus has come due.

As 12 jaws dropped, I left and headed directamundo to my yard.

Halfway home, I looked in the rear-view mirror and could not believe my bloodshot eyes: There was a mini-caravan of piece-of-shit pick-up trucks lined up in my wake looking like a cross between the Beverly Hillbillies and *Road Warrior*. When I pulled in the driveway, my bar buddies, who I am usually easily able to escape by merely leaving the bar, pulled in right behind me, which made my yard-puttering neighbors *real* happy as they all gathered up their children, ran inside and started thumbing through the "unsavory visitors" section of our subdivision's regulatory Koran.

"We decided to come and watch you work in your yard," Milt said, pulling out several cases of the warm "emergency beer" he always keeps in his truck, Bud Girl (its true name).

My amigos stood there and waited as I stood there and stared at them. It was like the opening few hours of the Somalia invasion.

"What's the big deal with someone doing yard work?" I finally asked, exasperatedly.

"There's no big deal with SOMEONE doing yard work," Big Del drawled. "But it is a big deal YOU doing yard work.

That we gotta see for ourselves. Some of us think you must have treasure buried in your yard, or some other more reasonable explanation for your suddenly suspect behavior."

Merle even had his video camera with him, which he pointed at me as soon as he egressed his Truck of Many Colors (its true name).

I must admit, the notion of yours truly grabbing hold of rake and shovel for any reason more creative than burying evidence must seem a tad incongruous, even to a bunch of falling-down drunks who could neither define nor spell "incongruous" if they had a dictionary — which they damned sure don't — already opened to "C," which is exactly where they would open it under those circumstances. They have heard me intone enough times over the years about the total, absolute fool-heartiness of yard work, the complete waste of energy and resources better spent doing things like canoeing or mountain biking or, well, solving all the world's problems one beer at a time back at the Sluice.

My macro-enmity toward yard work doubtless comes, as do most of the skeletons in my psychic closet, from the farm I grew up on in the fetid swamp country of eastern Virginia. When it comes to the need to keep atop one's yard work, I would put that area up against any other part of the country. I hear people from Ohio or Kansas piss and moan about how often they had to cut their piddly-assed little suburban lawns back when they were abused kids, and I laugh. Our yard was almost two full acres and, in the dead of summer, had to be cut twice a week just to keep the snake-and-tick-infested jungle from overtaking our house and our people. There was no time for making positive design inroads in one's yard in eastern Virginia; it was nothing more creative than a constant battle against the Mordor-like forces of floral evil. I spent my entire childhood mowing, trimming, weed-hooking, bush-hogging and raking, and I vowed when I left the swamp country to never, ever live in a place requiring so much as a scintilla of yard work unless it could be sufficiently accomplished solely by using gasoline and matches.

I have made entire life-sized decisions based upon avoiding yard work, which is a fairly easy thing to do in Mountain Country, a place where, if you find yourself dwelling in the belly of the yard-work beast, then you've likely got no one to blame but your own dumbass self. Then, my own dumbass self goes and buys a house in, of all things, the High County equivalent of the Stepford Neighborhood. Understand: I certainly don't mind living in a place where yard work is done; I happen to actually like kicking back with a brewski and a stogie and watching all the scantily attired local Stepford Wives bending over and pruning their petunias, or begonias, or whatever the hell it is they prune. But, the thought of actually having to do any pruning *myself*, well, that's where I draw the line. Yard work as a spectator sport, sure; yard work as a participatory activity, negatory.

Yet, there are those pesky covenants, which I may or may not have actually read before buying my house, and which actually say something fairly ambiguous like, "All yards must be kept in such a state as not to be able to harbor undetected rogue elephant herds that may trample our children and cover our shiny new SUVs with massive piles of elephant caca."

As Merle videotaped and Milt gave the play-by-play, I proceeded to don work gloves, get a shovel and rake and stand there scratching my noggin. I mean, where does one start when one feels obligated to prune one's petunias, which one, in this case, does not have, or at least does not think one has, as one would not know a goddamned petunia if it bit one on the pecker, upon which case, one would work tirelessly to upgrade one's flower-identification skills.

One thing one did know was that one's yard was covered with thick dandelions, otherwise known as "easy targets." For some reason, my dandelion crop had as of late begun irking me above and beyond my need to comply with those afore-mentioned draconian covenants. Somewhere along the line, I had picked up a healthy dose of anti-dandelionism. So, without further ado, while listening to Milt say, "and now he's ac-tually bending over, fixin' to wage war on those hapless, inno-cent pretty little yellow flowers that have never done nuthin to him or his," I began my personal dandelion holocaust.

Milt's words did not dissipate into the vapid nothing-ness they usually deserve as quickly as they usually do. Why, I wondered, do we work so hard to eradicate dandelions, while working so hard to get other, often less-qualified flowers, like, I would guess, petunias, to grow in our yards? What is the root of our dandelion bigotry, our cultural dandelion-o-pho-bia? From what I have gleaned from the many, many PhD-level academic treatises I have read dealing with the history of flowers in the High Country, the miners in the old-timey days actually introduced dandelions hereabouts because they are edible, tasty and nutritious in a part of the world seriously short of digestible native green-age. And, well, let's not forget, dandelions can be and often were fermented. A versatile little plant, as it were. Verily, the Swiss Army Knife of foliage.

But once iceberg lettuce and bottled alcohol-bearing beverages started making their way to Mountain Country, I guess dandelions fell out of both culinary and aesthetic favor.

A falling out of favor, however, did nothing to diminish their presence. Au contraire. Dandelions began spreading through every lifezone the High Country has to offer like a bad case of crab lice at a Youth Hostel. And, as they spread, the hatred of them grew. Mountain people, especially those inclined to codify life at altitude into things like subdivision covenants, started looking at dandelions the way Germans look at Turks: once useful, but longer necessary for our way of life. It finally got to the point where dandelions were classified as "noxious" and "invasive" and, worst of all, "non-native." The use of aggressive chemical weapons was not only condoned, but ordered by well-meaning, but undeniably sociopathic, weed final-solutionists.

So, now, we kill dandelions by the millions, and, yet they continue to spread and grow stronger and more resilient. They are the Viet Cong of plants, and, consequently, I respect and admire them, even as I work feverishly and inexplicably to uproot them and exterminate them all, the little hyper-reproducing, yard-despoiling bastards! Curse their active little pistils and stamens!

That I suddenly found myself maniacally pulling dandelions up by the handful — while being videoed by Merle, no less! — made me question my motives not just as a nascent yard-worker, but as a human being. As it often does during rare moments of self-examination, my mind tangented off toward the wilderness, the eternal conceptual safety valve for those seeking philosophical vindication, absolution or rationalization. My attitude about wilderness management tends toward "even though our wilderness areas are not ecologically the way they would be if White Folk had never come to these parts, I still would prefer we now leave them to the devices of

Mother Nature, rather than try to manipulate them, the way many otherwise smart folks want to, in an attempt to recreate pre-White-Folk conditions," because, well, our species' track record of not screwing up the stuff we are trying to improve is pretty damned abysmal. When in doubt, let Nature take her course.

Why then, would I not take that land-management philosophy with me into my very own yard, especially when, by adopting that argument, I would have to do less yard work? Well, there's the covenant thing, but, you know, if a full-time professional writer can't get the argumentative upper hand when it comes to ambiguously worded document interpretation — especially when he's dealing with nothing more threatening than trowel-wielding, petunia-pruning Stepford Wives — then why go on living?

So, I relinquished my dandelion-killing equipage and accepted one of Milt's warm emergency beers. My yard work career was over as quickly as it started. Yes, let Nature take her own course. I'll tell my neighbors I'm now an adherent of the cutting-edge *nouveau gauche* school of landscaping. And, every couple years, when things start getting out of hand, I'll forget to pay close attention to my barbecue, and let fire sweep through my yard, like it occasionally does up high in the wilderness areas I love so much. I'll call it a prescribed domestic burn.

"He has seen the light," Milt said, seconds before Merle's camera faded to black.

— MOUNTAIN GAZETTE #133

CHAPTER TWO

A Beautiful
Mountain Funset

"People must not do things for fun. We are not here for fun.
There is no reference to fun in any Act of Parliament."
— A.P. Herbert

"Better to have loafed and lost,
then never to have loafed at all."
— James Thurber

"If someone tells you not to do something
— that's a clue to do it."
— Artist Mark Innerst,
as quoted by Laren Stover in *Bohemian*
Manifesto: A Field Guide to Living on the Edge

Road-tripping had caused me to miss a couple weeks of slow death in the Sluice Box, but, since, according to my buddy Milt's highly scientific understanding and interpretation of all matters space/time-continuum related ("There is no passage of time in the Sluice, because there is no time in the Sluice," Milt proclaims, far too often, generally to people who are thinking maybe it's time to go drink elsewhere), I knew I wouldn't miss a beat. I fully expected the half glass of beer I had left on the bar (Merle had mistaken it for his spit cup, rendering it rather unpalatable) to still be there, flat and warm as ever, like the whole near-month I had been on the road, some cosmic pause button had been pressed.

I could tell something was way way wrong before I even stepped past the pearly gates of the front door. Generally, the volume factor of the Sluice is such that, from two counties away, you need to be thinking in terms of earplugs, immersion therapy and Valium. From out on the sidewalk, you already know what arguments are taking place and who's taking what side, which, in all likelihood, will be exactly the opposite side of the exact same argument they were having yesterday, except no one remembers either the argument or the side they were on, discourse in the Sluice being a combination of a feedback loop, a Mobius strip, an echo chamber, a perpetual-motion machine and a triple dose of Nyquil.

The palpable wrongness slapped me upside the head even before my senses maladjusted to the perplexingly din-less dimness. Instead of 29 slovenly ne'er-do-wells crammed in front of a bar specifically designed in 1881 to hold only 15 slovenly ne'er-do-wells, all the usual suspects were sitting about as far as humanly possible away from each other at the tables scattered about the premises. I mean, it was as though Pattycakes had hired a Nobel Laureate in trigonometry to specifically perform the calculations necessary to determine how you could get "x" number of stinky drunk people into "y" amount of space with the most distance possible between said stinky drunks.

Everyone was sitting there staring purposefully at their

individual bottles of bottom-shelf suds as the bubbles made their myopic way toward atmospheric reunification. I went over, sat at Milt's table and noticed his can of Old Toothache Ale was clothed in a koozie, an apparatus specifically designed to keep one's beverage cold. This was a sure sign something was badly askew, as I've never known Milt to possess a beer long enough for it to get warm. I looked around and noticed that everyone's beers were thus sheathed, condom-like.

"Milt, what's wrong? Who died?" I posited, knowing full well no one had died, because, if someone had, that would have been an excuse for even more raucousness than usual, as the dearly departed's health would have been toasted ad infinitum. Milt almost imperceptibly scooted his chair away from me, like it was being conveyed by cilia.

"Shhh ... they'll hear you," he responded, almost inaudibly, with lips that did not move, like he was working on his ventriloquism act and I was the dummy. It was the first time in two-plus decades of acquaintanceship I had heard so much as a syllable spew from Milt's mouth that did not set off some sort of decibel-recognition alarm at the closest OSHA office. Fortunately, I was too parched to ponder, so I turned and halfway bellowed for Pattycakes to bring me a Fat Tire. The look on her face brought to mind some sort of silly simile about having seen a ghost, except, when you've slung drinks in the Sluice for 21 years, ghosts are all you ever see. Pattycakes long ago made peace with the inhabitants of the hereafter, whether they were here or after. As the words left my lips, Milt scooted his chair ever farther away from me and angled it toward the big-screen, upon which, instead of the Nuggets or the Avalanche, was playing an old "Brady Bunch" re-run, with the sound turned down, I guess so as not to drown out the

... shit, I just noticed, instead of the usual classic '70s rock, they're playing what sounds like a freakin' all-Tony-Bennett station! As Pattycakes brought me my beverage (which was also in a koozie), I saw her eyes darting all around the gloom-ily lit interior of the Sluice. I simply could not suss out what on earth was going on.

I took a few quick sips and asked Milt if he wanted to shoot a little 8-ball, figuring the act of him liberating my pock-et change would break whatever ice had glaciated its way over the Sluice while I had been out of town. From the look on his butt-ugly face, I might as well have asked him if he wanted to have dinner in public with his third wife. Mortification, pure and simple, was what I saw on Milt's mug, and this from a man who I have long considered unmortifiable.

"I gotta go," he muttered fast, leaving nearly a full can of the Toothache Brewery's finest on the table. I had never seen Milt leave alcohol unconsumed. And I don't just mean his. A last-call devotee of the first magnitude, you could always rely on Milt to polish off the contents of every unfinished bev-erage left on the bar as the patrons were being ushered out into the 2 a.m. darkness. "Waste not, want not," is Milt's op-erational slogan in all circumstances, except as they directly relate to money and words.

There was only one conclusion: Aliens had taken over the bodies of all the regular Sluice Box patrons. My old chum Milt had probably already changed his name to Zorp, and was heading home to finalize the invasion plans.

It was only after Milt left, with sweat dot-dotting his fur-rowed brow, that I looked around and noticed the strangers. There were four of them, all wearing matching brown shirts, sitting off by their lonesomes in each of the Sluice's heretofore cobwebbed corners, which, stunningly, now looked like components of a Formula 409 TV commercial set. They had notebooks and, though they were not looking down, they were scribbling madly, their pens twitching across the paper like digit-borne lie-detector needles. And they were all staring directly at … me. No matter which way I turned, and I turned every way I could think of, including inside and out, there was either one of these very strange strangers directly in my view line, or two of them dominating the haziness of my peripheral vision. I quickly about-faced toward the bar, where I noticed that the Broncos betting pool had been replaced by a whole series of neatly framed governmental notices about how alcohol can cause blurred vision, slurred speech, inane babbling, zeroed-out bank accounts and pissed-off spouses. I also noticed the back bar was now stocked top-to-bottom with wine coolers, wine spritzers and every variety of alcohol-free "beer" ever concocted by whatever mirthless souls suck the very essence from that which God legally and rightfully gave us so we can be happy. Gone were the dusty bottles of Jack Black, Jim Beam, Patrón and Jagermeister.

On the back wall, which had always been adorned with an impressive array of donated bras and panties and a full set of vintage, "Beer — helping ugly people have sex since 1876" and "Beer — helping white people dance since 1912" placards, were now found framed versions of those vapid inspirational posters adorned with superficial dogshit like, as but one random example, which was right then before my very eyes: COURAGE IS NOT THE ABSENCE OF FEAR, BUT RATHER THE JUDGMENT THAT SOMETHING ELSE IS MORE IMPORTANT THAN FEAR. (This particular poster boasted a photograph of a suitably inspired, courage-filled penguin jumping off an iceberg into the Antarctic Sea, where, doubtless, seconds after the photo was shot, he was consumed lock, stock and courageous barrel by a voracious leopard seal.)

I suddenly felt like I was drowning. I needed room to think, and to breathe, and to try and figure out a way to exorcize whatever demons had descended upon this little bar I love so much, so I moseyed back to the pool room and, well, I was shocked so badly I almost dropped my beverage. Gone was the antique pool table, the geographic center of the Sluice universe, the very table upon which Dusty McClain and his spouse-du-jour Sassy had "honeymooned" (after hours, I should note, lest anyone think they lacked suitable decorum), giving new meaning, Sassy said later, to calling your shots. In the pool table/honeymoon bed's stead were a couple of new couches, and the proximate walls were lined with bookshelves, which were filled with titles like, *Wild Sobriety* and *The Bar Manager's Guide to Good Clean Fun: Charades, Pictionary and Other Socially Acceptable Forms of Leisure.*

Hell, maybe it was *me* who had been taken over by the aliens. Just as I was about to pull out my pocket knife to see if I still bled red, I heard a "Psst ..." coming out of the kitchen. It was Big Del. He motioned me back, which was a first, because Big Del considers the Sluice Box kitchen to be his personal domain. "None save me are allowed into the Kingdom of Grease," he has said, many times, to many people, including local health department officials, who happen by every few years and who feel anyone who eats food prepared at the Sluice deserves whatever happens on the pathogen front.

Big Del pulled me into his Kingdom of Grease, then closed the door.

"You've been gone for a few weeks, huh?"

"Yeah," I responded. "What's up here?"

"You knew there was an anti-smoking ordinance on the ballot, right?" Big Del asked.

I nodded, biting my lower lip, preemptively fearing the words to come.

"Well, it passed. Which was bad enough, but the exact instant the election results were announced, it was like the goddamned German panzer divisions moving on Poland in '39. The people behind the anti-smoking ordinance did not even wait for the smoke to clear before they unfurled their new incarnation. They are now known as the 'High Country Anti-Fun League.' They began circulating literature filled with anti-fun facts. They said playing pool causes both bad language and bad backs. They said those who have to clean drink spills off the pool tables are susceptible to dust inhalation from the chalk residue. And sports on TV at bars? They had literature showing how that causes near-bipolar mood swings, as well as causing cocktail waitresses to carry more trays of drinks, which in turn causes repetitive bar stress disorder."

"Jeez. And what about the Broncos betting pool?" I asked.

"Man, that's gambling," Big Del said, shaking his head slowly and seriously, like a man on the verge of being simultaneously born again and dying, like Paul Winfield in *The Wrath of Khan*, just before he phasered his own ass. "Because people who gamble hoot and holler when they win, it results in fight-or-flight-based adrenalin-gland releases among those within earshot. After 30 or 40 years of exposure to this particular verbalization of fun, patrons and bartenders can get high blood pressure. And, for those who lose, there's a tendency to want to have a drink, which causes all manner of problems for society, including increased belching and flatulence. We were told, if we don't police ourselves on these issues, then we run the risk of having anti-fun petitions circulated throughout the county. We've got to voluntarily tone things down a bit on the fun front."

"And who are those people sitting in the corners with the notebooks?"

"They're the Fun Monitors," Big Del said. "They're bad news. Don't cross 'em! We had to install fun vents in each corner of our bar, just so they could sit there, observing our behavior to make certain it falls within acceptable parameters, without any risk of being contaminated by second-hand fun. Cost us $12,000, and, even then, we figure it'll end up being a waste of money because we all know, sooner or later, no matter what we do, there's gonna be a local election over fun, and fun will be outlawed inside the bar. People will have to go outside and stand a minimum of 15 feet from the front door in order to have fun."

It was too much to digest at one time. As I was getting ready to leave, my knees shaking and my spirit shaken, a light-bulb went on over my head: There was no rancid smell in the Kingdom of Grease. I looked around, and what I saw stunned me: The counters were piled with lettuce, tomatoes, cucumbers and avocados.

"What, are you guys now putting vegetable matter on your world-famous Cholesterol Burgers?" I asked Big Del.

"No, we don't serve Cholesterol Burgers any more," he said. "Cholesterol is bad, and, well, it's fun. We now only serve salads and rice cakes. Goes great with wine coolers."

As I walked out of the once-proud Kingdom of Grease,

Big Del ran after me, yelling.

"And don't you dare come back here until you realize the unhealthful effects of beer and burgers and pool and sports and betting and bullshitting! We don't need your kind in Mountain Country anymore. There's a new wind blowing!"

I made eye contact with one of the Fun Monitors as I weaved my way through a subdued game of charades taking place where the pool table once stood. There was a smirk on her face as I walked out into the glorious brightness of a High Country spring evening, where the last tendrils of alpenglow illuminated the summits of peaks towering above town like guardian angels, their avalanche chutes aimed directly at targets never identified until it's way too late.

— MOUNTAIN GAZETTE #134

CHAPTER THREE

Dearly Departed

"If you give up possession, if you give up trying to possess what attracts you, a lovely thrilling happiness flows through you and you feel you're in touch with the secret of everything. There are only two mortal sins in the world; one of these is to be cruel and the other is to possess, and they are both destructive of happiness."
— John Cowper Powys, *A Glastonbury Romance*

Photographer Mark Fox has been my buddy for enough years that entire volumes of communication can be transmitted between us via a couple well-intonated syllables, grunts or even the great unsaid. The phone rang. It was Mark. And the conversation began, "Well, pard ..." I knew instantly that someone or something was no longer tromping around on terra viva.

"You heard about the windstorm we had the other night?" Mark asked. "It was terrible. Hundreds of trees went down. Ma Moose's house got whacked. Guisto's pick-up got flattened. A ponderosa came down in my yard and destroyed part of my roof. It glanced off and landed directly on ... your ... canoe."

I had stored my canoe at Mark's house last fall, and one of the grim realities of High Country life is, due to rooftop-high annual snowfall averages, anything left outside come autumn will be still outside come spring, unless you're a lot more enthusiastic about your digging-out than I have ever been. I was due to pick up the canoe, which I have owned forever and ever, in a week. Mark lives in what Frisco, Colorado, residents call the "Mount Royal Shadow," which, true to both the literalness and figurativeness of its appellation, is not like a shadow cast by a wispy passing cloud or a lone tree at certain times of day, but one of mountainous, geologic-level proportions. An Old Testament-kinda shadow. Thus, the substantial snow that falls in Mark's 9,100-foot-altitude yard stays almost until barbecue season is in full swing. My canoe had finally melted out, and I was laying plans to retrieve it. Then the windstorm came, and my canoe, which, truth be told, was getting a bit long of tooth anyhow, took a death blow to the rib cage and spinal column.

Pretty much DOA.

The news ought to have hit me like a falling tree. After all, this is the very same canoe my wife and I took with us when we drove all the way to Central America on what remains one of the biggest adventures of my life. The canoe, which lately had been relegated mostly to leisurely beer paddles on Dillon Reservoir's flaccid Frisco Bay, took us down the Sittee River, just outside Belize's Jaguar Sanctuary, where is found the highest concentrations of jaguars (weighing as much as 300 pounds, the world's third-largest species of kitty-cat) on the planet. It took us through Belize's Baboon Sanctuary to a lake, we found out upon arrival from our guide in a most-casual and matter-of-fact manner, chock full of monster-sized crocodiles. It took us across Guatemala's massive Lake Peten Izta, the back door to Tikal. It took us across Lago Atitlán, which was surrounded by towering volcanoes covered in "Heart of Darkness"-like jungle thick with well-armed and serious-business insurgents with a shitty attitude toward tourists, jungle where the erstwhile ubiquitous bleatings of toucans had been replaced by the near-constant rat-tat-tat of automatic weapons fire. It carried us across Lago Yajoa in Honduras on an all-night paddle from which we were afraid to return because the camp where we were staying was filled-to-brimming with shadowy CIA operatives and Honduran soldiers who did not seem to believe we were just vacationing in that particular sordid part of the world at that particular menacing time in history. And it had taken us under the radar across a little-known lake in southern Mexico to an island no one seems to know about, which was home to a large population of darty-eyed imported Asian monkeys being "studied" by scientists for reasons we never could quite get a grasp on.

In short, with the exception of the long-gone (RIP) Toyota truck upon which it was tied during that 5,000-mile journey, my canoe was likely the bearer of more adventure tales than any other piece of gear I have ever owned. I am still wrestling with how I feel about that boat's demise, since I essentially abandoned it when I moved south last year. It was an Old Town Discovery, 14½ feet long. One of the seats served as a poster child for the utilitarianism and flexibility of duct tape. The bottom was permanently undulated due to the effects of being covered with about 15 feet of snow for six straight months a couple winters back. It cost me about $350. Better money I have never spent. Though I often eyeballed various canoe-gear catalogues, thinking in terms of procuring some bona fide "accessories," all I ever bought on the canoe-ensemble-front were two basic paddles, one good PFD for my wife and a doggie PFD for my cur. I liberated another PFD for me from a pile my buddy Bernie, who ran the Frisco Marina for many years, was going to donate to some worthy cause populated by, I guess, future surprised drowning victims.

For too many years now, my canoe has resided in a particularly onerous gear category: One where the stories based upon it were getting a tad stale. One where it got pulled out only a couple times a year. One where I kept saying, "Man, I gotta load that old canoe up again and take another drive to Central America!" But the Toyota truck was long gone, replaced by an almost-new, shiny 4Runner, which is far more at home in LoDo than it would be in some steamy Central American jungle. And Central America is now pretty much civilized — to the degree that many well-groomed people I know are starting to make "real estate investments" in places like Nicaragua, places that used to be home to real adventure, not just the bullshit manufactured kind you find advertised in *Men's Journal* and *Outside*. And, besides, I fear the bulk of my hard-core adventure days are behind me; sadly, I now find myself scrutinizing the faux-adventure sections of glossy magazines with an attitude more acquisitive than derisive.

I do not know how old, trusty, dear gear is supposed to die. Most of it, of course, just fades away, like most people. Ideally, gear goes out doing the thing it was designed to do. In this case, a crocodile attack or a tropical waterfall would have been perfect launch platforms into the next realm, except, of course, either of those scenarios would likely have included not just canoe, but canoe paddlers as well. The canoe was

definitely suffering from extended UV damage (as is its owner), as all plastic boats eventually do. Its days were numbered
under any circumstance. Maybe as early as this summer I
would have had to make the decision that it was no longer
safe to take out, even onto flaccid Frisco Bay. I had already
considered bequeathing it to someone for use as a planter or
a wall decoration. I had already started asking if anyone knew
whether canoes could be recycled, which I guess would be a
decent enough way for a boat filled with stories to journey
into the hereafter — especially if there would be any chance
of those recycled parts making their way back into the struc-
ture of a new boat, like Patagonia does when it recycles well-
storied old polypro long johns into new "functional inner
layers."

Far as I know, my canoe still lies twisted under the tree;
I will arrive at the place of its demise in a couple weeks. I have
long wondered if old gear is like felled trees, if, unlike animals, whose mortal coil can be snuffed out in the snap of a
finger, its life force does not linger on until, like the "Termi-
nator," its red power light finally goes dimmer and dimmer
and dimmer, to the point where you can't tell after a while if
it is on or off. I would like to give my canoe last rites. I would
like to whisper into its ear a reminder about the time, down
in Guatemala, when, due to continuous potholes from hell, it
was jostled loose from its moorings atop my truck and I had
to get out and re-tie it right in the middle of guerilla-move-
ment ground zero, and, while I was doing so, a whole bunch
of extremely drunk, uniformed, rifle-toting young men of indeterminate political lineage and moral inclinations stepped
out of the jungle and began simultaneously eyeballing the canoe, the truck and my wife, while I went into husbandly save-

the-day mode (run away! run away!), dunked the notion of tying the boat down under those circumstances, asked the canoe to hold on for dear life (which it dutifully did), got into the faces of those young men, which surprised the shit out of them (as it did me), and calmly (though not really) got back into my truck and drove off into the misty tropical evening at a rate of speed unjustified by the atrocious condition of the road. I would like to whisper into its ear a reminder of the time we went around a bend and found ourselves face-to-face with a fearsome-looking river-wide sweeper and I literally had to reflexively jump out of the back into neck-deep water and hold onto the stern while my wife, who was so attuned to parrot-watching that she was oblivious to our impending doom, merrily continued paddling in the bow while wondering aloud why we weren't making any progress as I was gulping down tepid water and staring down imminent catastrophe a mere 14½ feet behind her. (When she finally did turn around, she asked, "How did you manage to fall out in water this calm?" "Glug … spit … glug … sweeper … glug … BACKPADDLE … BACKPADDLE glug … you … stupid … glug … glug …" was my response." "Don't talk to me like that," was her response.) We would get a good chuckle out of those stories, my old canoe and me. I wonder if it has been lying there wounded, wondering where daddy has been all these months, wondering why I am not there frantically removing the tree and performing fiberglass CPR and telling it everything will be OK, we'll be paddling together again soon.

I have posed this query many times before: It is possible for the denotatively inanimate to possess life force or even soul? — a pantheistic question asked in many ways in philosophy and literature, most recently in the otherwise uninspiring movie, *I, Robot.* It will come as no surprise that, though I am sometimes able to ask the Big Questions, I have never been able to even come close to answering them. When I arrive at the place of my canoe's demise, I will have to make a choice. The Klingons believe the body is nothing more than a temporary vessel for the soul, and, thus, when the soul has moved on (which I believe is now the case with my canoe), you need not worry at all about the manner by which you dispose of the corpse. "Do with the body what you will, it no longer matters," Worf always said when a comrade fell in battle. No taps or 21-gun salutes for Worf. Just more blood wine and endless tales told around a blazingly hot campfire.

It's my guess I will tip a beer to my fallen comrade, and I will maybe tell a few stories, as is my way no matter the circumstances. Then I will seek out a proper burial place, even if that place turns out to be a dumpster or a recycling bin or a flower bed in some High Country yard.

Good journeys down the river of life, old Old Town! We will once again paddle together on the other side, where we will this time keep our eyes very peeled for falling trees, even as we seek out the river-wide sweepers and the crocodiles and the jaguars of our youth.

— MOUNTAIN GAZETTE #135

CHAPTER FOUR

Holiness
by the Gallon

OK, I understand it's a case of blatant Monday-morning quarterbacking; nevertheless, in retrospect, I think it's fair to say, had there had been a few less visible firearms in the possession of people who, on their best day, look like a cross between Che Guevara and Elmer Fudd, the misunderstanding would likely have been averted altogether. There we were, innocently making our way up Peru Creek Road toward Horseshoe Basin, with the goal of instigating a little recreational firearm mayhem, when, without warning, through no fault of our own, an interface with, of all strange and terrible things, the Real World (which is getting more surreal by the day) jumped unbidden right into our Here & Now.

On the way in, we had noticed six cars parked at the trailhead, and all six of those cars were shiny bright Toyota Priuses, and all six of those shiny bright Priuses sported Front Range license plates.

"Must be a yuppie convention going on," Merle growled once we pulled off the pavement onto the joy and rapture of rutted, rocky and potholed Peru Creek Road.

"Least we'll have something to shoot at besides beer cans," chimed in Big Del.

About two miles in, with Milt's venerable F-350, Bud Girl, about 30 yards ahead of Merle's Truck of Many Colors, we noticed, standing on the far side of a tight curve, 12 hikers — six men, six women — who looked as though they had recently finished working as models for a glossy outdoor magazine advertising shoot. They were each and every one attired head-to-toe in a veritable REI catalogue's worth of trendy backwoods duds, all of which looked to be straight off the shelf. And, as of about point-two seconds prior to our decidedly disheveled arrival, nary a molecule of organic matter had interfaced with said natty duds. Then up motors Milt at a rate of speed best described as "borderline reckless," in a rusted-out truck the size of a battleship. Peru Creek Road at that point is narrow, and an early-season snowstorm had left in its wake a fair amount of mud, slush and deep puddles.

Milt drove through a combination of all three of those earthly delights as he passed the hikers, and their flashy ensembles suddenly were no longer so flashy. Milt said later, if they had given him the slightest opportunity to do so, he would have apologized profusely. Such opportunity was not given. Quite the opposite. Before the mud, slush and water even had the chance to start dripping off those heretofore virginal vestments, one of the men in the group, a particularly smart-ass-looking punk who was doubtless working on his Masters Degree in multi-dimensional organic self-righteousness down at Naropa, yelled out, "You could park your goddamned truck and walk! ASSHOLE!!!" Milt, still thinking he was about to beg the pardon of the people he unintentionally drenched, had by then started applying the brakes. Wet as those already suspect brakes were, they did not stop Bud Girl until the bed of the pick-up was right exactly even with the

guy who had called the six-foot-six Milt an ASSHOLE. Regret-
tably, the pick-up truck bed contained five fairly inebriated
flannel- and Carhartt-clad fashion disasters, each of whom
possessed, cradled very obviously in the crook of their arms,
either a rifle or a shotgun.

We're still sitting back in the Truck of Many Colors, so
we didn't see the actual dousing of the hikers, and we didn't
hear what the by-then very-ashen-faced Naropa puke had
yelled at Milt. Just as Merle was saying, "Guess that's who
owns all those yuppie cars," we see Milt bounding out of Bud
Girl, his visage verily defined by a double dose of miffed-ness,
because, when his boots hit terra-not-so-firma, he slipped on
some ice and went down on his ass like a sack of spuds into
the very quagmire he had recently splattered onto the cloth-
ing of those 12 hikers. So, even before those poor hikers had
digested a situation defined by five gun barrels pretty much
demarcating their immediate viewshed, a mud-covered giant lurches his way around the back of Bud Girl, hurling an
astoundingly comprehensive lexicon of invectives in their
direction. Worse, since his beloved Colt .45 had fallen out of
his holster into the muck, Milt entered the field-of-vision of
those hikers not only holding, but vigorously shaking, a very
impressive sidearm.

"What the *fuck*?" Merle asked, as we all started egressing
the Truck of Many Colors, meaning nine more people, four
of whom were also carrying a hodgepodge of weaponry, were
making their way toward a young man who, scant seconds
before, was defiant in his body language, in an if-you-mess-
with-me-I'll-call-my-daddy's-lawyer sort of way. At the sight
of the approaching reinforcements, the young man's dignity
dissipated much the same way I suspect a soul does when one

dies. This poor sap actually yelped the words "don't shoot!" as 12 hikers all raised their hands like they were being robbed by highway banditos.

Milt started laughing. By the time he composed himself enough to talk, the hikers were likewise laughing, though there might have been elements of spontaneous Stockholm-Syndrome-meets-insane-asylum at play.

"Here's the thing," Milt said contemplatively to the entire group, as he reached through Bud Girl's open passenger window into the glove compartment, held shut by a very soiled strap from a D-cup bra of unknown origin, an act that caused an immediate cessation of the hikers' nervous laughter, like they were wondering, "what could possibly be next?" Milt pulled out not a knife or another gun or a can of mace, but, rather, his trusty abacas, which he carries with him everywhere, and which he not only comprehends, but comprehends with aplomb (a bar trick he picked up while stationed in Japan). "Am I to assume those Priuses parked back at the trailhead are yours?" One of the men answered in a falsetto affirmative. "And all 12 of you drove up from the Front Range?" Again, a tepid "yes." "So, you get, what, 50 miles to the gallon in each of those hybrids?" "Yes/squeak."

"So that's about 90 miles one way for six cars getting 50 miles per gallon," Milt said mainly to himself as his sausage-sized fingers slid clacking abacas disks around in seeming willy-nilly fashion. "That's 1,080 total miles traveled, divided by 50, which comes to 21.6 gallons of gas, divided by 12 people, which gives us 1.8 gallons used for each one of you to drive all the way up here to give me shit about driving instead of hiking.

"And, let's see here," Milt continued theatrically, while

stroking a goatee that makes one wonder what a yeti would look like with mange. "I'd guess both Bud Girl here and Merle's Truck of Many Colors each get about eight miles to the gallon. We drove about 30 miles one way to get here. That's 120 total vehicle miles round-trip, divided by eight, which means we, being people who choose to recreate in our own back yard, will use about 15 gallons of gas. And, since there are 15 of us using that amount of gas, that means we are using one gallon each. So, we are using both less total gas and less gas per person than you are," Milt proclaimed triumphantly.

For a moment, the entire world was totally quiet, as this bit of rudimentary roadside ciphering sunk into the thought processes of 12 mystified hikers, who were likely wondering if the penalty in these parts for using more gas than Milt was death by a firing squad that was obviously in its cups enough that its aim might be suspect.

"Who wants a beer?" Milt chirped. The hikers stood there, frozen like fleece-bedecked Otzis, hands still raised toward the heavens all this time, faces contorting in abject bewilderment, like it was beginning to register that they had been granted a reprieve, unless, of course, this mud-soaked monster liked to get his victims drunk before dispatching them.

"Wait a goddamned minute!" Merle, who's as big and ugly as Milt, bellowed, right when those 24 hiker arms were starting to wilt, fatigue likely coming into play. As 24 paws shot back up, even higher than before, Merle stared directly down into the very wide eyes of the once-belligerent multidimensional organic self-righteousness Naropa student, who, most assuredly, will soon be changing his major to criminal justice, and asked, pointedly, "What ... I ... want ... to ...

understand ... is ... this ... " [lengthy pause, intended to increase dramatic effect] [intention achieved] " ... what is the correct plural form of 'Prius', which, if I'm not mistaken, means 'to go before," a word that, in Latin, is treated as an adverb? I mean, how the *fuck* do you pluralize an adverb?"

"Good questions," chimed in Milt. "And germane to the conversation, since you folks own so many of the goddamned things."

"Oh, shit ... here we go," said Big Del, who, understanding fully that our departure was no longer imminent, wandered down to the side of Peru Creek, where he commenced throwing rocks at a long-deserted beaver dam. Instantly, he was joined by the rest of our motley crew, which disconcerted the hikers even more, as they now found themselves with highly suspect characters both in front of and behind them. While trying mightily to focus on Merle's adverb-pluralization interrogative, their concentration was being compromised by a gaggle of projectile-tossing reprobates slightly outside the sphere of their peripheral vision whose rock-lobbing inaccuracy was only exceeded by their foul tongues.

"If 'Prius' is treated grammatically as a purely English word — and there's ample precedent for that argument — there are two likely possibilities: either the regular, 'Priuses,' or the same word 'Prius' is used for the singular and the plural, like 'deer'. I personally hate the word 'Priuses' because it looks both unfinished and unnecessarily gaudy at the same time. Wouldn't you agree?" Merle asked the soon-to-be-criminal-justice major, whose knees were audibly knocking together.

What that erstwhile truculent young man did not know — could not have known — could not have even *guessed* in his wildest chardonnay-fueled nightmares — was that Merle is, rough-hewn appearances notwithstanding, actually a born-again redneck who had achieved his current standing as a chaw-chewing frequent discharger of large weapons only after serving a long apprenticeship under Milt — a born-and-raised redneck good-ol'-boy — who, conversely, had studied under Merle in hopes of one day achieving what he called the zenith of human evolution: an erudite bubba. While Milt was the drawlin' spawn of junkyard owners down in Commerce City, Merle (whose full given name was, believe it or not, "Merlin" ... named after guess which legendary magician?) was the scion of a long line of immodest academics. His parents both (both!!!) held PhDs in Medieval Lit and retired after distinguished careers at Cal-Berkley. While Milt's proudest achievement was building a working riding lawnmower from scrap parts, none of which originally came from a lawnmower, Merle came within a whisker of receiving a doctorate in Comparative Linguistics from Arizona State, with a specialization in the nebulous interface era between late-Etruscan and early-Latin. When Milt and Merle met one day at the Sluice Box — literally two weeks before Merle was set to defend his dissertation — it was like a high-speed head-on collision, with both parties emerging not only unscathed, but better for having been in the crash. Before long, Milt had taught Merle how to play pool and how to re-build a carburetor and Merle had taught Milt about obscure verb tenses like future perfect continuous and how to apply appropriate Proust-isms to barroom disagreements. Their mutual devolution was a sight to behold, though it often resulted in a social conundrum Big Del once described as "not knowing which one to shoot and simultaneously not knowing which one's gonna shoot you." It was a suds-based symbiotic personality transformation, the result of which, according to Milt, was that they were both broker than ever, got laid less than ever, and they'd been pretty much disowned by their respective families.

"I've also seen the word 'Prii' used for the plural," Milt then said, adding fuel to Merle's holy etymological fire.

"Yeah, but that would either look to Greek grammatical roots for applicable lessons for modern-day English — the cactus/cacti pluralization conundrum" — continued Merle, "or it would suggest that the word 'Prius' is less an adverb and more a second-declension Latin noun, because it's clear from context that the pluralized forms are simply using the nominative case form without regard to placement in the sentence in their English-language usage, a habit, I gotta admit, that has a long and respectable academic history.

"However, if 'Prius' is used as a *fourth*-declension Latin noun," Merle continued, taking a long and well-deserved sip of beer, "then it's masculine in gender and, consequently, the plural form is the same as the singular: 'Prius.' But, if the plural is 'Prius', we may never understand if the word is a fourth-declension Latin noun, or simply an English word with an irregular plural form."

Both Milt and Merle then sighed, grinned and shrugged their shoulders the way they do when a bone of contention is gnawed down to the marrow before a conclusion is reached, which covers about 99-percent of the words passing their lips.

"What do you think, cupcake," Merle asked the same man who had so recently called Milt an ASSHOLE. "Second declension or fourth? Noun or adverb?"

The question was received with an awkward silence finally broken not by syllables birthed by human vocal cords, but, rather, by the first tenuous squeaks of flatulence put forth by one of the women hikers, a low-intensity high-pitched soprano poot my late English mother would have called, "popping off." Merle recoiled in feigned horror. "Who farted?" he barked. No one so much as flinched. Merle looked at each of the hikers as though he was studying a line-up of suspected felons down at the police station. Each of those 12 hikers bore clenched-teeth grimaces and reddened cheeks, indicating, in this particular context, that, though there was only one party guilty of the opening methane salvo, the entire clan was getting ready to let loose a noxious gastrointestinal fusillade doubtless brought on by what must surely have been an understandably nerve-wracking previous few minutes. It's my guess that an exercise physiologist could right then have penned an entire how-to book chapter on glute-tightening. As Merle was getting ready to let his face break out into a bright smile, a second fart discharged. This one was deeper, more resonant, than the first. Before Merle could even formulate a witty retort, a veritable symphony of flatulence erupted from the hikers. It was like the intestinal dyke had been breeched and, soon, we were entertained by what sounded for all the world like "The 1812 Overture" of wind-breaking. There were soprano farts, tenor farts, baritone farts, bass farts and even impressive hints of countertenor farts. There were woodwind farts and brass farts and string farts and percussion farts. It was truly glorious in its own malodorous way, a near-perfect diatonic homage to the human digestive system, the sort of thing you'd half-expect to see on Letterman.

In a textbook case of the chamber pot calling the kettle black, Merle, whose own infamous, and frequent, stink bombs could be used by Middle Eastern despots to disperse pro-democracy riots, said simply, "Gauche."

Once the fart crescendo had come and gone, Milt applauded loudly while shouting "bravo," which drew quizzical looks from Big Del and the rest of the rock-throwers down the hill. Milt then gave each of the seriously befuddled hikers two beers, which, we realized later as we were shooting empties up at Horseshoe Basin, amounted to 20-percent of our supply.

We then left the hikers standing in the cracked rearview mirrors of Bud Girl and the Truck of Many Colors. It was probably my imagination, but I thought I heard one of them yell "ASSHOLES" as we drove away.

By the time we started making our way back out toward dusk, shortly after a squall hit, the hikers were long gone, likely to never again leave the safe confines of their closest REI store. What was not long gone, however, were the three Sheriff's Department cars up shit's creek near the trailhead. The first one was stuck up to its axles, as was the third one, meaning the one in the middle, though not stuck, was going nowhere fast.

"Need some help?" Merle asked, with a hint of a smirk.

It took more than an hour of crawling through the cold mud to free the vehicles. When we were done, Deputy Schneider said, off-handedly, "You gentlemen wouldn't have any information about some hikers getting accosted by a couple pick-up truck loads of drunk gun fanatics."

"Well ... "

Milt proceeded to relate the story. When he finished, we had arrived at one of those cusp moments when you can tell the cops-at-hand were pondering the Next Step, which could have gone either way. All it would have taken was one peek into either truck, where there were piled mounds of weaponry, ammunition and beer cans, both of the full and empty varieties, and an otherwise pleasant day would have been ruined. We held our collective breath, concerned, but feeling it would be mighty hard to arrest a group of men who spent an hour wallowing around in the icy ooze helping to get your dumbass selves unstuck, except that, of course, the only reason their dumbass selves were stuck in the first place was a complaint had been lodged by a group of well-groomed folks driving shiny, environmentally responsible vehicles against, well, us.

"Maybe next time you ought to keep your guns better hidden," Deputy Schneider suggested before fishtailing his way back out toward pavement.

Exhale, followed by a series of decidedly unmelodic farts.

"Always good advice," Milt said, waiting for their taillights to disappear — discretion being the better part of valor and all — before reaching into the cooler for one more beer.

As we crested Swan Mountain, Milt suddenly pulled Bud Girl onto the shoulder. He walked back to the Truck of Many Colors, which Merle had pulled over behind him.

"Shit, I think I ran out of gas," Milt said, dejectedly. And, as he did so, right then, like God was wagging a middle finger directly at us, six Priuses/Prii/Prius drove by at such a high rate of speed, I thought they were going to fly off the road. Milt got sprayed stem to stern with slush. He quickly turned and shook his massive fist at the passing Priuses/Prii/Prius, all of which were by then well on their way back down the mountain, where they all belong.

— **MOUNTAIN GAZETTE #150**

CHAPTER FIVE

And Woof To You, Old Girl

The headline on the Yahoo News home page jumped out at me: "Majority of pet owners say they can understand … woofs." It linked to a cutesy two-minute video wherein canine owners at some unidentified dog park contended their pets understand them, and they, in turn, understand their pets. Well, hold the presses on that one! Despite protestations to the contrary by behavioral biologists who contend inter-species communication is nothing more than personality projection and/or anthropomorphism (could you imagine being that fucking stupid?), those of us who are pet owners know the true story: Hell yes! Serious communication takes place between pets and their human companions on several distinct levels, planes and dimensions.

Motivated by that video, I did something I'd long considered: I put together a list of the human/English words that my dog of 13 years, Cali, understood. Though I'm certain as I put this list together there are words that escape me, at this point, I figure the vocabulary my dog developed hovers somewhere around 50 words, which is more than I can say for a great many of the people I have consumed beer with during my long and storied drinking career.

Here is a list of the words/phrases my dog has long understood, with a bit of annotation. Cali. Mother. (I don't remember when/why I started referring to my wife to my dog as her mother, rather than Gay, but, there it is.) Uncle Tom and Aunt Cathy. (My brother-in-law and sister-in-law, who have functioned essentially as Cali's godparents.) Uncle Mark, Uncle Currie and Aunt Stacy. (Three close friends of mine and Cali's.) Tucker the Kitty Cat. (Our cat.) Car's coming! (An indication as we were walking alongside a roadway that she needed to stay very close to me.)

Sit. Stay. Down. Heel. Move. Look (usually in the wrong direction; she never did quite get this one down, as it was a little too theoretical). Go (used whenever she was in front of me while we were skiing and we began a downhill). Drop (as in something in her mouth). Careful (watch out for that cliff!). Close (remain within sight). Back (get behind me). Come. And, of course, no, which I was lucky enough to never have to use very often, as this dog was her whole life as close to perfect as a dog could be.

Outside. Drink. Doggie (whenever there was another mutt approaching that she did not see, which started becoming more often as her vision began to fail with age). Toy and New Toy (she always knew the difference). Stick. Ball. Potty (a friend once told me I had the only dog he ever saw who would relieve herself on command). Pill (for most of her life, she was on several meds … this word was always greeted with ears down and an aw-fuck, not-again look). Dinner (even if it was breakfast). Snack. Swim. Snow. Deer (Cali had seen several bears, come nose-to-nose with numerous bull elk, interacted with several coyotes, but the only animal that drove her crazy was deer. Generally, however, if I said "deer" while we were driving, she would invariably look out the wrong window.). Ride in the car. Park (as in "dog park"). Bath (though she loved to swim as much as any dog I have ever known, the idea of taking a bath caused her much in the way of consternation). Veterinarian (this one wasn't a personal favorite). Bad girl (used only a few times when she was a puppy). Good girl (used very often, with justification). And the second-most-important word: walk. I have long regretted that I did not keep a log of the time and distance Cali and I spent on the trail, but it amounted to thousands of miles and thousands of hours. Before she saw her first birthday, we spent 62 days out on the Continental Divide Trail. Several years after that, we spent more than a month on the Colorado Trail. And this does not count our near-daily jaunts into the woods of Colorado and New Mexico.

And the most-important word in Cali's lexicon: John, used mainly by my wife whenever I was returning home from wherever. You've never seen a tail wag as fast and furiously as when Gay said my name to my dog.

This was not a one-way communicative street, though. My friends Rob and Heather, who own Sawatch Backcountry in Leadville, once told me their dog was well capable of speaking to them in perfect English, but, sadly, did not sport the proper vocal-chord apparatus. Ditto Cali. She, like her dad, was always a blabber, and she was able to communicate with me using dog words as well as I was able to communicate to her using English. I mean, we didn't dissect Shakespeare or anything — at least partially because I don't comprehend the Bard's work — but we could certainly shoot the breeze about hiking, skiing and the overall state of our little lives as they related to a wide and often confusing world.

Cali's inflection-laden dog-vocabulary consisted of a long, coyote-like yowl that indicated general excitement and happiness; a double-bark that was part of the play dialogue; a series of rapid-fire, short barks that meant, "What the fuck?" (like during those many times during our off-trail forays that we found ourselves cliffed-out); a loud, smiling three-bark series that could be repeated forever, which almost always accompanied one of those great dog experiences, like standing chest-deep in the San Francisco River while I tossed sticks into the water and which, translated, meant, "I am the mighty, invincible Cali, and I am with John in the river, and we are having fun and, wait — did he just throw another stick over my head while I was busy barking?"; a frustrated snorting sigh indicating irritation (such as whenever we pulled into the Moose Jaw parking lot, and she knew she'd likely end up sitting by herself in the car while I imbibed); a long high-pitched whine she, looking for sympathy, would use with my wife whenever, as a random example, her mean old master took her to the vet, and she was saying, "And the horrible man with the stethoscope stuck a cold thermometer up my ass and gave me a shot!"; and, most interestingly, a little short "woof," which covered much communicative ground. It could mean I was really, really starting to piss her off playing, as a random example, pinch the dog's nose while I made a honking sound. It could mean she was disapproving of the way I was driving and that maybe she should take the wheel. (See above: Moose Jaw.) And it could mean, even though the riverbank just gave out from under her and she slid 10 feet into a pool and went completely under and came up with her entire head covered in pond slime, "woof": "It's cool. I'm OK."

The day after Cali died, I walked by myself to her favorite local swimming hole, up on Little Cherry Creek. I have never felt so disconsolate in my life, not even when my mom died or my when dad died. And try though I might (and I did not try very hard), I could not stop blubbering as I made my way along the trail to the swimming hole, where, only three days before, I sat on a rock smoking a cigar while my beloved dog — by that time so arthritically lame, deaf and near-bouts blind, she could scarcely function — frolicked as only dogs can, debilitating physical circumstances be damned.

And then, just as I turned away, tears burning my eyes so badly I could not see the trail, my heart so broken I could scarcely draw air into my lungs, these words came into my head in a voice close to mine, but not mine. "I just want you to be happy," the voice said.

It was Cali.

It always bothered my dear dog that her daddy basically made his way through life unhappily, and, however those words came into my head (don't ask me to explain, for I cannot), they amounted to a parting gift nonpareil. And just as I came to understand clear down to the depths of my soul that this was no trick of the mind, that I had heard those words as clearly as if someone standing right next to me had uttered them, just as I started to say something back, a man came down the trail in the opposite direction, and, as a result of his inopportune presence, the connection with my dog wherever she is now was lost. Though I have many times since admonished the cosmos to give me one more chance to hear Cali's disembodied voice, no encore appearance was forthcoming. I really wanted that short example of inter-species/inter-realm communication to continue, because I think she was getting ready to tell me how to go about being happy. Because, if there's one thing Cali knew more than anything else, it was how to be happy. It came as naturally to her as unhappiness does to me.

There's this big mural in the lobby of the animal shelter in Summit County, Colorado (the very shelter where I first met Cali). In the mural is an embedded poem, the exact words of which escape me. It lets people who have lost their pet know all is well, that their dog is up there in heaven playing stick and going for swims and, one day, your dog will look up and you'll be walking toward him or her over a grassy hill, and he or she will bound over to you and jump in your arms and lick your face, and you will be rejoined forever in a place where the ball-throwing will never be interrupted by corporeal mundanities such as employment and yard work. A vision of heaven I find appealing, of course, though it is a vision of heaven I don't believe in. I can offer no theological basis for this, but I don't think Cali is just running around waiting for me to arrive on the hereafter scene, where we would presumably restart our relationship as if mortality issues had never reared their dispassionate heads. That's a bit too anthropocentric for me. I don't know whether that which we call our "soul" moves directamundo onto its next incarnation or whether the base elements of a soul dissipate and spread themselves out into the greater cosmos, where they find homes in many new venues. Either way, Cali's moved on to her next adventure, and now she's got bigger fish to fry than sitting up there with a stick in her mouth fretting constantly about my well-being.

After that man passed by on the trail, after Cali's few words came to me, and after those words evanesced into the ether, there was only one thing I could say in response:

"Woof, Old Girl." It's cool. I'm maybe not OK right now at this very moment (far from it), but I will be. I promise you, I will be. Because of you. Thanks for caring. Thanks for everything.

— MOUNTAIN GAZETTE #151

CHAPTER SIX

The Greater Depression

Ever since the long-overdue karmic meltdown of the world's financial scene began to dominate not only the news, but, simultaneously, every-waking-minute of a whole lot of people who are now nervously making their way through life pondering the possibility of spending their golden years toiling at the Golden Arches rather than kicking back on the Gold Coast, the media has been expectorating variations on the theme of "little ways" average schmucks can save stunning amounts of cash by making lifestyle adjustments so minor they do not in and of themselves inspire thoughts of class warfare and/or out-and-out revolution. Before venturing any further, let me state, for those of you whose life savings began evaporating during the last glorious months of the Bush administration, a high percentage of the people I hang with are experts on the subject of "making it" with retirement accounts consisting of nothing more than change-jar-dominated pecuniary portfolios. I will be happy to hook you up with a personal consultation with one of my buddies. You'll have to buy the beer, which, you'll realize some hours later, as you're staring into an empty wallet, is Lesson Number One.

Anyhow, you can scarcely swing a dead cat without hitting an advice column in a newspaper or magazine or a money-management segment on CNN informing people apparently unused to the concept of discretionary-income management how to save, as but one random example, $300 a year by shopping around for lower car-insurance rates, which, according to my buddy Milt is easy enough if you just sort of forego the concept of car insurance altogether. (Milt's philosophy there is, if he ever gets to the point where an officer of the law is asking to see his proof-of-insurance card, a lack of insurance would be the least of his problems. "Which means," he told me after a very helpful and pertinent CNN money-management snippet hosted by a perky 20-something (hope you're paying attention to your own advice, young lady, for your time will come) wearing clothes costing more than the cumulative monetary empires of those there gathered was broadcast on the soon-to-be-obsolete analog TV set that has adorned the corner of the Sluice Box Saloon since the earliest days of the Great Depression (very soon to be replaced, Big Del recently observed, by the Greater Depression), "if you don't have any insurance, it just gives you one more thing to plea bargain down when you're arm-wrestling with a lazy-assed DA who hates the thought of taking you to trial yet again!" (Now *that's* the type of advice CNN viewers — especially folks who are so broke, they can no longer afford cable TV — are looking for!)

The kinds of personal financial management articles and TV segments focusing more on pinching pennies than they do on, say, taking advantage of low interest rates to acquire vast empires of undervalued real estate holdings, always catch my eye in ways that macro-level asset-management articles in, say, the AARP newsletter or Forbes magazine do not. Part of that, of course, is because I have no macro-level assets to manage. But part is because, even if I did, I do not have the cranial ability to think in big terms. Articles on consolidating your international currency exchange strategies don't really register between these ears. Therefore, I try to make up for that sad personality defect by trying extra hard to comprehend the vagaries, vexations and vicissitudes of the little things.

And there is no doubt, in the realm of personal assets, or lack thereof, the little things *can* add up, as all these articles and TV segments remind us at least once every 25 seconds. For instance, one recent online article stressed, by foregoing a daily visit to your local java emporium, a person can save more than $700 a year. "Man, with all that extra money, I could drink even more beer," observed Merle, who does not even drink coffee, while sitting down at the end of the bar pondering the latest football pool with all the earnestness of Adam Smith proofreading the first chapters of "The Wealth of Nations."

There is of course more. We are told we can save hundreds of dollars a year by going to the local library instead of the local bookstore, by listening to the radio instead of buying CDs, by hosting potlucks at home instead of meeting friends for dinner over at the Gut Bomb, by purchasing six-packs of beer at the liquor store and drinking at home instead of spending night after night after night (after night) holding down the loose end of a suds-stained bar.

We pulled out a couple cocktail napkins and commenced ciphering. Milt figured, if he gave up shots and stuck only to beer, he could likely save $4,735 a year. "Exactly the kind of advice a lot of people could use!" said Milt, so earnestly you would have thought he just invented the concept of trickle-down economics, which, in Milt's case, would be appropriate. What Milt did not say was, every penny of the money he would save by not doing shots would end up going down his gullet anyhow, because he would simply buy more cans of Old Toothache Ale. When I pointed this out to him, 12 people who were sitting nearby nodded their heads solemnly and sighed while they started scratching out Milt's attempt at financial management advice, which, stunningly, they had all written down like Milt had just uttered the Gospel of Lucre.

After a silence long enough it indicated, in all likelihood, Milt's stop-doing-shots advice was probably going to be the best thing any of us could come up, Merle chimed in with: "Well, maybe we could all start bumming beers off rich tourists!" I've never seen so many faces light up. It was as though we had all just won the lottery. Then Big Del killed the buzz by pointing out it had been 14 years since the last rich tourist ventured into the Sluice Box. We all remembered the incident well. A nattily attired (meaning he wasn't from here) elderly gent ran in, red-faced and agitated, and yelled, frantically, "Someone call 9-1 ..." Then he looked around at the interior of the place, eyeballed the inhabitants, and ran back out before even finishing his yell, which, we all concluded was likely to climax with yet another "1." Rarely is someone in need of someone else calling 911 picky about who ends up actually making the call. But this man apparently had mighty high life-threatening emergency standards, which we respected enough that none of us even got up to go outside and see why he needed someone to call 911 in the first place.

So, yet again, we sat in silence, hoping against hope one

of us would come up with a way we could all save $700 over the course of the next year without suffering any negative life-style consequences whatsoever.

"I know," said Drunk Tony (called thus to nomenclatur-ally differentiate him from Stoned Tony), "we could all stop tipping Pattycakes!"

"Yeah," Pattycakes snarled from her well-worn perch be-hind the bar, "that would save you at least a quarter a night, and believe me, it would not be a sound investment."

Slowly, an economic theory began to grow in the deep-est recesses of the least-economic mind in the Sluice Box: mine. "You know what's been bothering me most about a high percentage of the personal finance advice we've all been reading, listening to and completely ignoring lately?" I asked, as all eyes within 200 feet began to roll. "By making the ad-justments these CNN and *Wall Street Journal* people — all of whom are making 20 times more than all of us combined — suggest, we risk adversely affecting the greater economy and those who work in the greater economy! (I was starting to feel like Otter, as he addressed the disciplinary council at Fa-ber College in "Animal House," just before Delta Tau Chi had its charter yanked.)

"If we all start buying six-packs and drinking at home," I continued (and here I stressed I was talking about buying six-packs and drinking at home INSTEAD of going out drink-ing at the bar, not IN ADDITION TO going out drinking at the bar) (an important distinction that was greeted by a room-ful of thoughtful "ahhhs"), "then all the local bar owners who still let us through the front door would suffer as a result of our economic self-interest." ("Don't worry about us!" Pattycakes said, emphatically. "We'll somehow manage to limp along without you.") "Same thing if we decide to brew coffee at home instead of going over to Jitters every morning. How long would it be before Jitters closed simply because we were all sitting in our own kitchens every morning sipping Folgers while counting our newfound cash? And, by the same token, if we all started going to the library instead LuLu's Read Between the Lines Bookstore to get our reading material, then, before long, we wouldn't have a local bookstore!"

"We have a local bookstore?" Drunk Tony asked.

"We have a library?" Stoned Tony asked.

"So, OK, bad example," I continued. "The point being, a lot of the things that make living here so cool would be seriously screwed if we all started hoarding what little money we have just because people's 401(k)s are going down the shitter. Hell, guys, not a one of us even knows how to spell 401(k), much less actually has one." (Pattycakes raised her hand. Damn her.) "If we were all rich, or even if we weren't all destitute as hell, this kind of stuff would matter. But as it is, all we have is each other and each other's limited fiscal assets. So I say, let's continue to spread the wealth, CNN and the *Wall Street Journal* be damned! As long as we're not spending money at chain stores or businesses owned by asshole greedheads, we're good."

"So, the next round is on you, then?" Milt asked.

"Yeah," I said, "as long as I can put it on my tab. I just realized I'm broke."

Pattycakes pointed, for the 45th time, to the new NO MORE TABS sign she had just put up a week before. "Sign of the times," she called it.

"Damn," lamented Milt, "we obviously need ourselves

an economic bailout."

"Yeah," Big Del responded. "Start bailing."

— MOUNTAIN GAZETTE #152

SMOKE SIGNALS

CHAPTER SEVEN

Carpe Mañana*

*Horked directly from a bumpersticker produced in
Hillsboro, New Mexico — origin unknown.*

*"With its dominant ideology, the West declares its time is the
time. Not so fast. Its dominance is actually far from complete.
Its challengers are everywhere."*
—Jay Griffiths, *A Sideways Look at Time*

A couple years ago, an acquaintance left her newspaper gig in a small New Mexico town that can aptly be described as "constantly in borderline disarray" and took a similar gig in the heart of Colorado ski-resort craziness. Several months after her move, I called and asked how things were going. "It's amazing," she breathlessly effused. "Up here, shit actually gets done! There is no oppressive mañana consciousness to kill people's initiative." Yeah, I'm thinking: Wall-to-wall McMansion developments obliterating both viewsheds and wetlands, more golf courses than you can count, big-box-dominated retail shopping complexes in places once commercially defined by mom-and-pop enterprises and a resultant cost-of-living far beyond what mere-mortal working people can afford. Yay! Still, I found this young person's observations worth pondering.

Weirdly enough, one of the main reactions from my

perpetual-motion busy busy busy High Country resort-town chums when I announced I was moving back to Gila Country after 24 years in Colorado was an overly dramatic, overly drawn-out, smirk-laden, "Ohhhh, you're moving down to the land of mañanaaaaa... " This was always said, for maximum dramatic effect, with eyes (generally colored blue) rolling back far enough into their sockets, there was concern a frothing mouth and twitching body would soon follow.

And this from people who once actually lived and breathed the glorious concept of Mountain Time, people who moved to the land of vertical terrain at least partially so they could orient themselves to lifestyle concepts such as the "powder rule," which was an unwritten, but still culturally codified guideline-cum-fiat that stated, simultaneously ambiguously and unambiguously, if it snows, then don't expect [fill in the blank with statements like, "me to show up for work till noon" or "this business to open today"].

Of course, as Mountain Country started transmogrifying from definitively kicked-back to unremittingly amped-up, the once-almost-poetic powder rule started getting quantified, to the point it became the "six-inch rule," then the "12-inch rule," until, finally, predictably, the entire concept of closing up shop to ski (or mountain bike, hike, paddle, etc.) got lost in an avalanche of the same type and degree of punch-the-clock busy-ness most mountain people moved up high to get away from in the first place.

And what has Mountain Time become in the resort areas?

For the most part, its conceptual antithesis. These days, "frenetic" best describes the individual and aggregate pace of life in far too many parts of the High Country, an observation covering the socioeconomic gamut, from deal-making real estate people, to harried health-care professionals, to hyper-kinetic hospitality-industry employees, to overscheduled dirtbags (yes, in some parts of the Mountain Time Zone, even dirtbags lead hectic lives). The busy-ness of the resort towns these days often borders on comical. You've got these self-ordained movers and shakers and captains of the tourism and development industries who are always sprinting through the temporal vortices defining their existence clear down to the DNA level constantly hanging precariously by the last few molecules of their fingertips from a snot-slick cliff of tectonic-scale day-timers. These people are always running 15 minutes behind, and they always have a smart phone in one hand, an iPad in one hand and a laptop in one hand. They dash through life with a degree of franticness likely not seen in our species since we were running across the veldt furtively foraging for carrion, hoping against hope there were no saber-toothed tigers in the vicinity. And even when these busy busy people finally arrive at whatever it is they're late for — again — their maximum sustainable train-of-thought is like point-two seconds, because they will invariably be interrupted by yet another cell phone call, during which they will, in all likelihood, be reminded the kids are waiting to get picked up from soccer practice, so they have to dash NOW, even though, because they were late to their meeting with you, you've not had nearly enough time to address, much less resolve, a single one of the 14 items you were supposed to have discussed in detail and developed action plans for.

This is how America moves these days, and many of the people who subscribe to this state of existence are the ones most likely to look down to the sanely paced lifestyle of New

Mexico and make disparaging comments about the mañana mindset. Is it unrecognized jealousy?

The Southwest may be viewed derisively as the Land of Mañana by people who translate that term to mean laziness or incompetence, but, in my mind, it translates to lifestyle sanity, a perception that, sure, occasionally results in one's vehicle being in the repair shop for — as but one random example, five goddamned WEEKS — but, more often than not, it translates to a fundamental lifestyle recognition: Some things are worth getting wound up about, while the overwhelming majority of things are not. Moreover, it translates to a reality, at least in this remote part of this remote state, wherein the sea-to-shining-sea commercial and residential developments that have turned many erstwhile splendid mountain places into cookie-cutter conceptual iterations of Metro Atlanta have not, and will never, come to town. (Well, maybe mañana.)

We don't have much in New Mexico to export to the greater, civilized world, the world where shit — literal and figurative — actually gets done. At least not much good. (We will be happy to send our meth addiction rates and teenage-pregnancy statistics to your quaint restored Victorian hamlet, should you find yourself in need of a little dark-side yang to counter your orderly, polished yin.) We have Hatch green chilies. We have the best art in the West. And we have a mañana attitude the resort towns need desperately, an attitude amounting to nothing more, nothing less than what once used to be called Mountain Time. Powder days would still be the norm down here, if only we had, well, you know, powder.

Actually, there once was some languid talk about building a snowmaking-dependent ski resort in the nearby Mogollon Mountains. No one seems to remember whatever became of those plans. Guess they just fizzled out. We might not have a roaring economy, but we still have the Mogollon Mountains blessedly unscathed. Of course, many of our downtown buildings are crumbling, but we'll get to that. Mañana.

— MOUNTAIN GAZETTE #159

CHAPTER EIGHT

The Dark Side

It was not the best of circumstances to be sitting in the Summit County Justice Center in Breckenridge hung over, for several reasons, not the least of which being that my lawyer had been adamant: "Whatever you do, DO NOT show up for your alcohol evaluation either drunk or hung over. They will know. That knowledge will negatively affect their evaluation. A negative evaluation might result in even more jail time." (Live and learn.) (Or not.)

The reason I was sitting in the Justice Center was, a few weeks prior, I had suffered through the inevitable indignity of going through what many consider a High Country right-of-passage: I had earned myself a DUI. Guilty as charged. Part I of the DUI process in Colorado is to have your drinking/lifestyle/drinking patterns evaluated by what ended up being a remarkably desultory mental-health professional, who, I learned later, was no stranger to X-treme Tippling.

In the first section of that evaluation, you are required to fill out a long questionnaire covering a lot of ground, from the hyper-literal, "How many alcoholic beverages do you consume per week?" (2,054) to the more conceptual, "Do you have negative feelings toward law enforcement?" (Only when they arrest me.) (Well, not *only*, but mostly.)

One of the questions dealt with hangovers. It was word-ed in such a way that, despite the hideous bottle flu at that exact moment defining my entire mortal coil, I managed to chuckle. "Have you ever felt fuzzy in the morning after drink-ing the night before?" That was, as far as I can remember, the only question on the evaluation I answered honestly*: "No!" I wrote, emphatically. Though there was no room for annota-tion, what I wanted to write was, "I — like almost every sin-gle person I have ever known in Mountain Country — have awakened after a night of imbibing with a heartfelt desire to immediately cut my feces-tasting tongue clean out of my mouth and throw it in the ditch. I have awakened wondering what horrible person it was who decided the night before to pummel my poor, poor aching noggin with a large piece of firewood. But 'fuzzy?' No, not ever. 'Fuzzy' would be a friggin' godsend."

At Happy Hour, I related my questionnaire experience to my amigos down at the Sluice Box, not realizing till it was too late, if there was ever an example of preaching to the choir, this was it, if you catch my drift. Anyhow, the subject of hangovers came as a result to fill a conversational vacuum caused by football season's recent conclusion.

Mountain Country is the only place I have ever lived where hangovers are such a huge part of the local fabric-of-life that there is almost zero in the way of social stigma at-tached to them, which, of course, is because heavy drinking is such a huge part of the local fabric-of-life at altitude. And it's not just obvious reprobates such as me and my drinking bud-dies. This reality bleeds into the demographic realm of those who shower more than once a week as well.

I remember covering a town council meeting for the local paper in a hamlet I will only describe as "being above 9,000 feet." On the agenda were several fairly substantial development applications due to be presented by well-coifed men wearing coats and ties who had driven many hours to attend this humble exercise in local corruption/insanity/ government. The mayor was 15 minutes late and, when he finally did arrive — looking like death warmed over, but not warmed over very much — he took the gavel in his hand, raised it slowly, tried to hit the little round wooden gavel target (whatever it's called), not only missed by a good six inches, but, while so doing, nailed his other, non-gavel-holding hand, sighed, dropped the gavel, dropped his head, lost his train of thought, tried to compose himself, failed, looked up with unfocused orbs the color of rubies and moaned, "Look, I'm just too hung over to conduct this meeting. Meeting adjourned," which — as a point of parliamentary procedure — was impossible, since the mayor didn't have his act together enough to have called the meeting to order in the first place.

In any other region in America, the next day's front-page story, under a 90-point banner headline, would have read, "Mayor too hung over to conduct meeting! Re-call election underway!" There would have been hell to pay for months. In this particular case, an entire roomful of people fully agreed you can't very well have a town council meeting with a hung-over mayor, so everyone — including the button-down developers — retired over to the Sluice to ponder the vicissitudes of democracy over pitchers and shots.

One time a couple decades back, we had one of those chirpy chamber-of-commerce directors who last about 14 minutes in a wild anarchistic mountain town before they de-

cide maybe it's a good idea to go back to grad school somewhere more civilized and predictable. This chirpy chamber
director, who was a nice enough lady, had heard some comments from those few chamber members who clearly did not
have a real firm grasp on High Country ways (read: newcom-
ers from less-funky realms) that their employees often arrived
at work feeling somewhat unwell as a result of the previous
night's indiscretions. The chirpy chamber director then decided to organize a seminar for local employees focusing
on the downsides of showing up to work so hung over you
smelled like the end result of a distillery that specialized in
fermenting alcoholic beverages from dog excrement. Stuff to
do with safety and efficiency and, for God's sake, basic human
decency and dignity.

Enough employers made their employees go to the seminar that people in the local bars had a very justified bone to
pick with the chirpy chamber director, who made the almost-
Freudian mistake of walking into the Sluice at the exact moment a couple of disgruntled regulars were lamenting the fact
that, at 9 the next morning, they were expected to show their
smiling faces in the banquet room of the local Holiday Inn,
where they would learn all about why they ought not arrive
at work in the exact condition that every single one of them
planned to arrive at the hangover seminar.

Fourteen shots later, the poor chirpy chamber lady, who
had spent the previous two hours desperately trying to ingra-
tiate herself to a confab of falling-down drunks who, not long
before, had all wanted purchase voodoo-dolls in her image,
was carried out of the Sluice, toes dragging behind her. From
what I heard from several of my chums, who were all particularly chirpy as they related the story, the chamber lady did not

fare so well at the hangover seminar, which was actually titled something like, "Showing Customers Your Best Side." At one point, she even had to hurriedly egress the banquet room to blow grits in a trashcan in the hall, much to the amusement of the attendees.

There are lessons to be learned from all this, of course: When in Rome, do as the Romans. If you choose to call the mountains home, do not pick and choose which aspects of the endemic sociology you consider good and which you consider bad. In for a penny, in for a pound. It is a wonderful thing to dwell in a place where the mayor can call a town council meeting mulligan because he attended a bachelor party the night before. Indiscretion is the better part of valor. Go with the flow. Have a beer on the back deck. Ogle the view. Thank your lucky stars you're not in a place that would go apoplectic if the perky chamber director ran a hangover seminar while hung over. Nothing wrong with a little institutionalized debauchery. Matter of fact, the world could use a lot more of it. Bottoms up. Pass the aspirin.

* While driving to my alcohol evaluation, I picked up a hitchhiker who was on his way to the Justice Center to begin serving a 60-day jail sentence for having been convicted of his second DUI. Upon hearing that I was at the early stages of dealing with my inaugural DUI, he laid much in the way of well-earned and well-intentioned advice on me, the first piece of which was to lie through my teeth on every single question on the alcohol evaluation. For reasons that still perplex me, I opted to follow his advice. The result of that decision was the mental-health professional saying she could not remember anyone performing so badly on the evaluation. "It's like you live in a state of denial that borders of delusion," she said. "Shit," I thought, "if she thinks thusly with me lying on all but one of the questions, I wonder what she would think if I had told the truth!" After being sentenced to Level-47 maximum-security alcohol counseling

as a result of my less-than-stellar alcohol evaluation performance, I realized I ought to have gone ahead and lied on the hangover question too.
Something about, if you're going to lie, lie fully. Later it dawned on me,
if there's anyone alive whose advice I maybe ought not have taken under
those circumstances, it's a hitchhiker on his way to serve 60 days in jail for
his second DUI conviction. Live and learn. Or not.

— MOUNTAIN GAZETTE #160

CHAPTER NINE

Destinations

One of the most enjoyable aspects of the tag-team reading/book-signing tour I did a couple summers ago with *Mountain Gazette* senior correspondent B. Frank was the Q&A sessions following our events (Durango, Telluride, Moab and Cortez). Though all four contained heapin' helpin's of challenging and original questions (as well as some finger-wagging admonitions and accusations), the one I personally enjoyed most occurred at the Spruce Tree Coffeehouse in Cortez, which is owned and operated by long-time *Gazette* tribe member Charlie Campbell.

Actually, it would be more accurate to describe the post-reading part of our visit to the Spruce Tree as a discussion. Because both B. Frank's book, "Livin' the Dream," and mine, "Bottoms Up," are personal anthologies consisting mostly of work previously published in MG, it did not surprise us that many of the questions posed during what we advertised as the "Graybeard Tour" were focused on the *Gazette* itself.

During our visit to Cortez, one young lady, for instance, told us one of her favorite things about the *Gazette* is, when we do our annual Gear Issue, we spend more time talking about old gear — and the bond people develop with their old gear — than we do about new gear. Which led the discussion to yet another distinct (maybe even unique, at least among so-called outdoor publications) characteristic of MG: We do not run (and never will as long as my hand is on the editorial tiller) what are known as "destination" stories — articles that tell readers how to access certain places and why they would want to.

While many destination pieces are found in regular departments specifically dedicated to them (*Backpacker* magazine's "Weekend Wilderness" and *Men's Journal's* "Travel" sections are examples), they are often thematically packaged into a full-length features teased on covers proclaiming such conceptually oxymoronic (to say nothing of moronic) things like, "24 Secret Tundra Trails Revealed." (I mean, first, doesn't every kindergartner know it's bad form to *not* keep secrets that are entrusted to you and, second, once a place is revealed, isn't it no longer secret?) What *is* revealed, more than anything, in those lame, pitiful excuses of whore journalism, is the utter hypocrisy of most of the magazines peddling such drivel in the name of — irony of ironies — some sort of outdoor-recreation/outdoor-preservation Higher Good. (Yeah, it's *always* beneficial for an erstwhile "secret" place to get tromped all to shit by the zombie masses for no other reason than they just read a 750-word Judas story in a magazine purporting to be a defender of the backcountry.)

Those gathered at the Spruce Tree that pleasant evening seemed to understand perfectly that, sometimes, it's hard when a magazine runs a story about, say, a journey that happens to take place in the Nutripper Wilderness, to not make mention of, well, the Nutripper Wilderness (which, of course, does not mean you have to give seemingly mentally catatonic readers (not really, but it sometimes seems that way, based upon the stories that some outdoor magazines run) foot-by-foot skinny about such basics as how to drive to the goddamned trailhead ... I mean, if you need detailed directions to the trailhead, you probably ought not be venturing forth into the woods unchaperoned). Still, to a person, all 30 or so people in attendance at the Greybeard Tour stop in Cortez wholeheartedly agreed — to the point of thankfulness — with *MG's* policy of not naming names when it comes to specific backcountry destinations.

But there is one important thing to note when making that observation: All of those in attendance were rural-dwellers. They all lived in a remote and lovely place that suffers negative impact (in their mind, as well as mine) whenever one of the local "secret trails" or "little-known places" is exposed in a magazine, newspaper or guidebook. I don't often rub elbows with urban dwellers, but I suspect they might feel differently about all this.

Of course, Cortez and the area surrounding Cortez, being home to Mesa Verde National Park and Hovenweep National Monument, is tourist-industry Ground Zero, a place, like many other Western locales, that would probably economically wither and die were it not for the regular influx of cash-bearing visitors, some of whom are undoubtedly looking for "secret" kinds of "destinations." I do not believe for one minute that the people gathered at the Spruce Tree that evening were of a unified mind that *all* forms of promotional literature ought to be consigned to the ideational trash bin. I think they *were* of a unified mind that the marketing of a national park is something quite different than penning a story for a glossy magazine that practically leads people by the nose ring, step-by-tenuous-step, to places that local folks learned about the hard way, the right way, the only way that for eons we all learned about those special spots now constantly co-opted by magazines, newspapers and guidebooks, as though they were nothing more than baubles for sale at a roadside tourist curio shop, baubles anyone with $12 and half a brain can buy with nary a second thought.

The subject of destination stories is germane to this, *MG's* first Favorite Mountains Issue. Several well-intentioned people suggested to me, in order to maximize this issue's "salability quotient," once we determined which particular favorite mountains were going to be included, however obliquely, we ought to ask our contributors to send along a detailed sidebar letting our readers know exactly how they themselves could visit these favorite mountains, what time of year they ought to go there, what they ought to bring and, of course, how to prepare for the potential dangers those mountains might hold. Well, great idea, but, were we to ask our contributors to pen such sidebars, most would tell us to go to hell, while others would soak them in such a degree of sarcasm and, in all likelihood, overt untruth, that by the time any hapless impressionable readers were done digesting the "factual information," they wouldn't know whether to book a flight to Fresno or Namibia. And right after they got done justifiably throwing bricks through my office window, our readers would likely use such detailed sidebars as warnings to now avoid whatever favorite mountains appeared in our pages. I passed on the factual information sidebar idea, primarily because I operate under the assumption, if our readers want to locate a "destination," they are fully capable of doing so on their own.

All this in my mind is important in ways transcending whatever tourist dollars a person might bring to a locale — even a cash-starved locale — in his or her quest for a secret destination revealed by a magazine likely produced in cities by city people for city people, negative consequences be damned.

Traditionally — before the advent and onslaught of every-freakin'-issue destination stories, and "hikes-of-the-week" features in big-city newspapers and entire libraries full of guidebooks — these were the main ways a person learned of, and perhaps about, a new backcountry "destination":

1) Simply saying to oneself while one is out and about wherever, "I wonder what's up yonder?" then acting upon that wonderment, by way of an existing trail or via bushwhacking, or a combination of both.

2) Eyeballing a map, picking a "destination," then determining how to access the route and/or "destination", then acting upon that determination, again, by way of an existing trail or via bushwhacking, or a combination of both.

3) Being either shown or told about a place by someone. There are two subsets of this listing:

- Subset A: Being either shown or told about a place by a friend who has decided to trust your discretion, someone who is essentially taking you into his or her confidence, someone who either overtly swears you to secrecy or who assumes, whether stated or by implication, that you will likely eventually pass the information on, but only to someone you likewise have come to trust. This can be called discriminate passing of information.

- Subset B: Being either shown or told about a place by someone who doesn't know you from Adam. This can be called indiscriminate passing of information. Guiding services and organized hiking clubs generally fall into this category, as do strangers you meet in a bar who are perfectly willing after 14 beverages to tell anyone within earshot about the "secret" stash up on Mankiller Ridge.

Nowadays, this is the way most people learn of, and perhaps about, a new backcountry locale:

Via some sort of media, which includes guidebooks, destination stories in magazines or newspapers, videos or DVDs and what my friend George Sibley calls "nature porn" — which can include coffee-table photo books, calendars, posters and PowerPoint presentations (nee slideshows) and websites, among others. These are further forms of indiscriminate passing of information, but, unlike guiding services and hiking clubs, without the personal touch, for what that's worth, which is sometimes a lot, and sometimes not.

If you infer that I have placed these listings in an order that is not random, then you have inferred correctly. Even while understanding that a great many "destinations" are best left unvisited (I firmly believe that a new classification of wilderness ought to be established: CLOSED TO HUMAN TRESPASS), I long for the days when almost every person one met in the backcountry came to be there via methods 1, 2, 3 and/ or 3a. I know, I know, many readers might respond by saying this is yet another example of nothing more than longing for good ol' days that probably weren't as good as memory makes them out to be. Sure it is, if for no other reason than, back before destination articles and guidebooks came to rule the backcountry sociological landscape, there were a lot less people out and about tromping through the woods (which has the added benefit of being less-bad for the woods). But, as any true backcountry devotee knows, there's a lot more to this industrial-scale, institutionalized revealing of "secret" places that a personal preference for solitude.

There's a certain set of hot springs fairly close to where I live (hereabouts, "fairly close" means an hour drive on a paved road, an hour drive on a curvy, often-washed-out mountain dirt road, followed by three on-foot river crossings that at high water can be very dicey, followed by an hour hike along a formal system trail, followed by an hour hike along a trail best described as "informal." One needs to know where to cross the river, where the system trail leaves the river, and, most importantly, where the informal trail leaves the formal trail. This is a place I learned about in 1976 because several long-time local hiking buddies, after traveling with me in the boonies enough times that they trusted my abilities, perspectives and discretion, finally decided I was worthy. I visited those hot springs many times over the years, and only once did I ever tell anyone else about them. And, only once did I ever see anyone else at those springs. Then, one fine day, goddamned *Outside* magazine runs a fucking destination story on those hot springs. And, well, you know what I'm gonna say here, don't you? The next time I went there, the springs were overrun by dozens of city people. There were boom boxes and territoriality ("We were here first," one young piece of shit said to my buddy — a man who was born and raised in this part of the world — when we started entering the same pool he was sitting in with his comely, naked girlfriend. "No you weren't," we responded, as we lowered ourselves into the steaming water.) The litter factor had increased exponentially. Hippies had started establishing little shrines, even though these hot springs are located in a legally designated wilderness area. ("These wind chimes fit the overall vibe, man," one Rainbow Family-looking gent said, as I was removing said wind chimes from a tree.)

There is no doubt that hot spring was far worse off in ALL ways as a result of the destination story appearing in a national magazine. And this scene is repeated from sea to shining sea, wherever backcountry "destinations" are sold down the river by writers and publications.

So, why then do magazines run destination stories? I mean, if there's the slightest chance that destination stories might do more harm than good — both in the aggregate and in individual circumstances — wouldn't you think publications supposedly dedicated to the preservation of the backcountry would at least err on the side of caution? Well, they run them at least partially because they are easy to come by. There are exactly 422,354,237 aspiring writers out there looking for ways to break into print and put beans on the table via traveling through the boonies. (I should know; I was once one of them.) And, according to one young glossy outdoor magazine ad-sales hotshot — who, for the record, was rolling his eyes during the entire conversation (it's not always so easy being the out-of-step old-school, behind-the-times fuddy-duddy) (it's also not so easy to resist smacking the living shit out of glossy outdoor magazine ad-sales hotshots) — I talked to about all this recently, destination stories provide a low-hanging-fruit way to get advertisers to buy into the publications program, or, more accurately stated, to get the publications to buy into the advertisers' program(s). The more people who opt to access the backcountry, of course, the more people might be looking to buy packs and snow-shoes. And your average person — especially if he or she lives in the flatlands and/or a city — these days is not going to find him or herself setting out into the mountains or deserts sans clear understanding of where they might end up. They want to know *exactly* what they should bring. They WANT and maybe even NEED those step-by-step directions. They expect and desire their hand to be held. They can't abide even the thought — much less the reality — that there's even a slight possibility they might get lost or they might miss the scenic view of the lake. (And, if either of those events occurs, it will surely be the fault of the destination-story or guidebook au-thor.) One only hopes the psychic ramifications of this men-tality dawn on them somewhere, sometime.

Of course, magazines that run destination stories and publishers that print guidebooks have their own opinions on the matter, and those opinions generally operate on two self-perpetuating, masturbatory levels. First, there is what I call the advocacy argument, which means, the more people we can coax into the backcountry, the more people there will be who fall in love with nature, and, therefore, the more people there will be to vote for candidates who favor wilder-ness designation, and the more people we will have volun-teering for trail projects that, in all likelihood, we would not need were there not so many people now tromping through the backcountry. I would also stress I've met enough anti-additional-wilderness-designation people out in the boonies that I would classify this advocacy argument as at least partial bunk.

Then there is the education argument, which states, since almost every destination article and guidebook — explicitly and/or implicitly — dedicates significant verbiage to Leave No Trace ethics and backcountry safety and such, they are undeniably beneficial. And, while that might come across as a relative good, it is an absolutely specious contention. Sure, it's better for those folks you encourage to visit, say, erstwhile little-known hot springs in New Mexico to at least be appraised of Leave No Trace, but, in the interest of the surrounding environment, it's better NOT to point droves of people to those hot springs in the first place.

I understand I am beating my head against a wall here. I understand most "destinations" are located on public land, and, therefore, the guidebook-toting, destination-story-reading masses have as much right to know about them as I do, no matter how they gained their knowledge, superficial though it might be. I understand magazines and book publishers have the right to print whatever they want for whatever reasons they want. I understand I'm not necessarily the brightest bulb on the tree and I oppose/eschew destination stories and guidebooks at least partially because I want the destinations I am already familiar with to remain mine, all mine. I understand how fucked-up that attitude is on about 20 levels.

Basically, I understand full well I am herein tilting against windmills while simultaneously swimming against a tide that will surely one day suck my dispirited ass out to sea. I know I'll never, ever be able to convince my publications brethren to stop running destination pieces, as those pieces these days are too intertwined into the DNA of outdoor media. The only way things will change is if people make a vow now to stop reading destination stories and to stop buying guidebooks and to go about learning of, and hopefully about, backcountry "destinations" by setting out with the sole goal of seeking their own secret places via one of the traditional methods, by wondering aloud as you look up a valley you know nothing about and asking yourself: "Wonder what's up there?" And then, when you find out, realizing, when it comes to backcountry "destinations," mum's the best word.

— MOUNTAIN GAZETTE #170

CHAPTER TEN

Monsoonal

It's a strange and wonderful thing when the first few trick-
les of (hopefully) imminent monsoon season (like mountains, seemingly predictable weather patterns often tease us
with false summits) hit generally fairly parched Gila Country.
That joyful climatic circumstance is even more poignant because those first welcome splats of precipitation follow what
in the Southwest is known as the "Foresummer" — the hottest, driest and windiest time of year.

I should mention straight off: Despite whatever stereotypical mental images those not familiar with Gila Country
might have (*all* of which are completely inaccurate), when it
rains here, it is truly something to behold, in both relative and
absolute terms. My very first night in Silver City, back in July
1976, I was curious why the curbs in downtown are all like 45
feet high. That very night, I received an answer, as the heavens
opened up and before I could even begin to ponder the notion of what to me was a new and intriguing concept called a
"flash flood," Bullard Street suddenly became the first Class-4
main drag I had ever seen. My eyes nearly popped out of their
sockets as I witnessed scads of household appliances, herds
of mooing livestock, uprooted cottonwoods, Ford pick-up

trucks, women, children & wheelchair-bound old people and barrels of perfectly good whiskey all being swept down the street to their assured doom in full view of the entire town.

A couple nights ago, my wife called to ask me to pick her up from a local bar (a rare flipping of the designated-driver coin in our household) at about 10 p.m. because it was deluging and she did not want to risk having her mascara run. (Given the ferocity of the downpour, her mascara would have run clear down past her skivvies and into her shoes.) During the return trip to the Casa de Fayhee, I stupidly turned onto Yankie Street, which is literally a fundamental component of the town's not-exactly high-tech water diversion system. I'm not talking about a drainage ditch *alongside* Yankie Street, or a sewer under Yankie Street. Nope, I'm talking about the street itself, which, many years ago, some planning engineer genius decided to build directly on the bed of Yankie Creek, which, like most New Mexico waterways, is admittedly decidedly short on liquidity most of the time. While inching our way up the hill, with runoff literally pouring over the hood of the Outback (my wife's Outback, I should stress), I was wondering whether we were about to become characters in some Weather Channel documentary focusing on what NOT to do when it's monsooning in a desert town. "No matter the temptation, don't do what this hapless Silver City couple did," the narrator would say, dolefully, while shaking his head and trying to hide a snicker. "As anyone with half an ounce of brains ought to know, don't drive up Yankie Street when it has received like 75 inches of rain in the previous 11 seconds. If you do, not only will you get washed down near Lordsburg — a fate some would consider far worse in and of itself than death by drowning — but you'll justifiably be the butt of derisive jokes for three solid generations."

In all my years living in the Colorado High Country, only a few times did I ever witness a rainstorm that approached the level of ferocity of the *average* downpour in Southwest New Mexico during monsoon season. In the High Country, you sit there thinking, as thunder's reverberating all around you, how weird it is to be up as high as the birthplace of lightning. Because of the altitude, you get the feeling that you are a visitor to the realm of storms, and, therefore, whatever storm-related fate befalls you, you basically deserve it, like, if you weren't living and/or recreating higher than people were ever meant to, maybe you wouldn't have gotten zapped. In these parts, the storms come down to street level, as through they are purposefully, almost carnivorously, stalking the good folk of our humble hamlet. I mean, here we are, sitting on our front porches, smoking a bowl and sipping a beer, when, out of the blue, here comes an Old-Testament-like monsoonal weather front, salivating, licking its chops, looking for an otherwise innocent drunk person to scare the living shit out of and maybe even kill. And here's another difference between High Country monsoonal weather patterns and those found in Gila Country: In the mountains, storm fronts almost always arrive on the scene from the West; hereabouts, they literally come from all directions, and sometimes from several directions at once, to keep us on our toes (a result of being within meteorological striking distance of the Gulf of Mexico, the Sea of Cortez and the Pacific Ocean). In Gila Country, storms are sneaky bastards, ready to ambush the unwary, which pretty much includes most of us most of the time. But, as my buddy Pedro is wont to say, "At least they are *warm* killer tempests" — which is true; here you can actually comfortably stand out in the rain and not die from hypothermia in a matter of minutes, a reality that does not necessarily mitigate the "killer" part of Pedro's observation.

But, at the same time, the instant the first drop of rain impacts long-desiccated terra firma, the entire area becomes verdancy incarnate. Everything inclined to turn green does so, in about 15 minutes, in a National-Geographic-special, time-lapse-photography sorta way. Cactus-covered hillsides suddenly look like postcards from Ireland. Riparian zones become so lush they bear more resemblance to Central America than the image most folks have of southern New Mexico. And hordes of crickets spring to life and add their vocalizations to a natural symphony that also includes cicadas the size of house cats and the tweetings of the 200-some-odd song bird species that call Gila Country home.

As I was lying there in bed the first night after the monsoon rains came this year, listening, through no choice of my own, to the millions of chirping crickets apparently living not only in my yard, but right under my bedroom window, I could not help but be impressed with every aspect of Nature that has somehow found a way to adapt to harsh environmental circumstances. I wondered how all these critters manage to survive the nine or 10 months of the year when local precipitation is anything but guaranteed.

By the second night, I was thinking, in addition to playing their part in the symphony of life, the millions of chirping crickets now living directly under my bedroom window were also helping to drown out the usual nocturnal auditory emissions that define life in any New Mexico town: revving Harleys, emergency vehicle sirens, firecrackers, gunfire, barking curs and loud rap music emanating from low-riders with faulty exhaust systems.

By the third night, though, I found myself lying there trying to figure out a way to get those millions of chirping crickets to SHUT THE FUCK UP so I could get at least a little bit of shut-eye. I found myself thinking, in between mentally concocting several dozen sure-fire methods for torturing crickets, that I would happily trade straight up the otherwise splendid components and results of monsoon season for a world sans chirping. Fecundity, be damned! The pox on the adaptability of Nature! Fuck nature!

Toward first light, just as the crickets were handing the Fayhee-irritation baton over to the cicadas and birds, my sleep-deprived, delirious mind began to drift toward the subject of zoolinguistics (thanks to my buddy Stephen Buhner for straight-faced laying that word on me, as I was drinking beer and wondering aloud what on earth one calls the study of non-human languages; he's the only person I know able to answer that question, but it wouldn't exactly stun me if I learned he was practicing some spontaneous neologism, which is OK, because it's way better than anything I would have pulled out of my ass).

One of the main ecological features of a place that experiences true monsoonal weather patterns is almost every creature — from pond slime pretty much up my reprobate drinking buddies — has to fit the entire procreative process into a single season, before things start to dry out again and everyone seeks out a cool, dark corner to occupy for the next 200 or so days. Ergo: Since the chirpings of the crickets are unabashed mating calls (yes, I watch the Discovery Channel), those particular creatures, of course, have little choice but to chirp their fool heads off, no matter that yours truly is trying mightily to sleep off his latest indiscretions. Even though I often find myself this time of year perusing the web for products like "Crickets Be Gone!" and "Crickets Away!", I fully understand, having bellowed out a mating call or two in my time, as well. Though I often find myself pondering the admittedly very un-environmentalist concept of eradicating every one of those chirping little buggers within earshot of my bed, I at least grok the notion of begging for sex. Thus, I extend conceptual mercy and make no effort to act upon my species-specific genocidal fantasies.

In an attempt to turn insomniac lemons into productive pondering lemonade, I got to thinking the other night about what it is those crickets are actually saying when they chirp. OK, we know, as I said before, they are "mating calls." And we know, or at least I think we know, it's mainly the guy crickets doing the calling, a grim reality that has made its way clear to the top of the evolutionary ladder, to the very watering holes I visit. But what would their outwardly monotonous chirp-ings translate to, say, in a mountain-town bar? To the human ear, those chirpings seem to be the very definition of repeti-tion — the exact same noise over (midnight, unable to fall asleep) and over (2 a.m., still wide awake) and over (4 a.m., thinking again of hunting down a 55-gallon barrel of "Crick-ets Be Gone!), ad infinitum (fuck it, time to get up).

By and large, those chirpings are either mono- or bi-syllabic. So, as far as my 3 a.m. somnolent lizard brain thought process can tell, those male crickets are either say-ing, "Snatch," or else, when they add in that romantic, albeit unvaried, second syllable, they might be saying "Snatch, *please!*" Or "Snatch, *now!*" Or perhaps, within those one or two lower-life-form syllables, there might be enough in the way of inflection that, to the ear of a potentially receptive female cricket, the repetitive chirpings amount to, "Hey, baby, I've got the biggest cricket sausage in the whole yard!"

But, perhaps, the human ear is simply un-attuned to what's really being said. Perhaps those crickets are reciting lyrical love poems in Cricket-ese and Indo-Gryllidae that would rival a Shakespearean sonnet. Maybe what horny female crickets hear are not simple chirpings ("Snatch, now!"), but, rather, a cricket Frank Sinatra crooning "Strangers in the Night."

(My friend Julie thinks the crickets are saying nothing more than "Wake up!" — and, since she is a card-carrying Earth Goddess-type, she probably speaks several dialects of both Cricket-ese and Indo-Gryllidae. Shit, like many wild New Mexico ladies, she probably carries on conversations with the damned crickets!)

Thing is, it's my guess each species has its own vocal equivalent of a cricket's chirping contention that he has the biggest sausage in the entire yard. Bull elks bugle, cats yowl and middle-class white guys on bloated cruise ships grunt while trying to dance the limbo after seven margaritas. Once your mind starts wandering in that direction (that would be at 4:17 a.m.), there's no way on earth to apply the brakes.

Though many young people might consider this some sort of urban legend, thirty years ago, guys in bars actually did ask women, by way of an opening conversational salvo ("chirp") what their sign was. (Best response I ever heard to that lame interrogative (and I stress this was not pointed in my direction specifically, though it's my guess it was pointed to all males of the species in general) was, "Stop." I'd like to imagine cricket females have similar wit and exercise similar discretion, that they don't fall for any ol' chirp.)

I remember sitting in a now-defunct Colorado High Country imbibery, listening to the comely barkeep, who told me, for the ninth time that very evening, some young buck newbie said to her, "We ought to go skiing sometime." ("Chirp.") "Don't these assholes have the ability to come up with anything more original?" she fumed, leading me to believe the problem was not that these guys were trying to pick her up, but, rather, that they were using stale chirps. "Uh, we ought to go, uh, *hiking* sometime!" I responded (I thought wittily!), to no avail. (I considered chirping something about having the biggest sausage in the yard, but, for once, was waylaid by some very uncharacteristic discretion that somehow percolated its way to my usually speak-before-thinking-oriented vocal chords.)

There's a certain mountain bar I've been in, shall we say, more than once. But almost all of my more-than-once visits have occurred during happy hour time; rarely have I been in that bar after 10 p.m., when the crowd becomes decidedly less ancient. Well, one night, I happened to be in the bar much later than usual, and I pointed my ears toward the various attempts at chirping on the part of the young males. The main syllables I discerned were, "Dude" (a particularly weird choice of chirp when pointed toward a female) and a "Beavis and Butthead"-type snicker, a flaccid "heh heh" that followed whatever the previous sentence was. "My mother was just in a car crash." "Heh heh." And, since many of these young men were seemingly having far better luck at drawing the attention of the proximate females than most of my more loquacious happy-hour-drinking chums, I came to understand, when it comes to attracting members of the opposite sex who are in their prime breeding years, maybe mono- and bi-syllables *are indeed* where it's at.

Before I attempt to extricate myself from this sleep-deprived meandering quagmire, let me say, for all I know, chirping crickets might get laid more than all my mountain buddies combined, which, now that I think about it, is nothing really to hang your evolutionary hat on. "But, do they ever find true love? Do they maintain lifelong relationships?" my very-drunk buddy Pedro asked when I related all this to him one night at the Burro Borracho Cantina and Lucha Libre Emporium.

"I don't think that's what crickets are really looking for," I responded, like I'm an entomological Dr. Phil. "Well, maybe the older crickets," I added.

"Yeah, but, by then, it's the female crickets who are doing the chirping," Pedro (three times divorced, I should point out) said, as I looked around the bar and noticed the only female (probably for miles) left inside the bar was the well-worn bartender, and she definitely looked like, if she never heard another chirp the rest of her life, she would die happy. (Pedro had shortly before chased off the last two female customers with a *real* successful chirp: "If you want to buy me a drink, I'll let you.") "And all the older male crickets are wondering if it was all worth it, if they ought to have just kept their mouths shut in the first place," Pedro sighed, to his mostly empty glass.

Hours later, as I lay there in bed, bombarded by the chirpings of a million aroused crickets, with the latest batch of monsoonal storm clouds gathering over Gila Country, I thought to myself, "Get it while you can, boys, for soon you will find yourself drinking at happy hour with fellow old farts

instead of carousing all night long for snatch!"
Heh-heh.

— MOUNTAIN GAZETTE #171

CHAPTER ELEVEN

Digitized

There are few Mountain-Country nightmares more universal, more ass puckering, than the notion of unintentionally/accidentally (and, ergo, generally sans control, because, if you had control, then you would either be doing this on purpose or, failing that, not doing it at all) skiing into trees. Avalanches trump that nightmare, sure. And getting caught upside-down in a hole while kayaking, falling or getting doinked on the noggin by a rock while climbing and maybe getting pulled for a faulty taillight after consuming something on the order of 47 tasty, frothy, carbonated beverages all make the Land-of-Vertical-Terrain-lifestyle oh-shit list. But skiing into the trees (as opposed, by a wide margin, to "tree skiing") holds its own, at least partially because a high percentage of those meeting their maker at altitude do so while interfacing at unfortunate rates of speed with aspens and blue spruces, neither of which give much when impacted by a flailing human life form whose last thoughts are likely focused big time on some frantic variation on the can't-see-the-forest-for-the-trees theme.

This reality is most certainly exacerbated when one's skiing skills can best be described as "mighty poor," because, after all, were one's skiing skills better than "mighty poor," then, in all likelihood, one would not find oneself leaving the trail fairway and barreling into the slopeside or trailside rough and, even if one did find oneself so doing, one would stand some chance of being able to rectify the situation before things got Really Bad on the physiology front.

You may feel perfectly comfortable classifying me as a "mighty poor" skier, which is a bit weird, as 1) I have spent one serious amount of time with leather boots three-pinned into touring skis, 2) most of that time has transpired in the backcountry boonies of the Colorado Rockies (i.e.: rugged, challenging terrain) and 3), while not hinting for even a moment that I'm fit to carry Billy Kidd's jockstrap or anything, I have participated in sports pretty much since toddler-hood and possess at least a modicum of balance, stamina and reflexes.

Yet, I have never really managed to translate a lifetime's worth of athletic acumen (albeit low rent) into anything even resembling competent skiing, even though my life has largely been spent dwelling in places where the drunkest guy/guy-ette at the end of the sleaziest bar can chug his or her 39th beer of the morning and go out and ski 2nd Notch or Zero Chute with stunning sangfroid. For many winters, I psychologically dealt with my oft-mortifying skiing incompetence by spending most of my winter outdoor recreation time tromping through the woods on snowshoes, which, in a way, worked just fine, because I am more than anything a walker/hiker/backpacker, and snowshoeing is the closest approximation of those activities when you live in a place boasting five feet of snow on the trails for half the year. But, well, here's the thing about snowshoeing: Even though it is a sport with many positive components, it just is not all that fun. Or at last not as fun as skiing, even if your skiing skills are, as I said, defined as "mighty-poor."

So, after a few years of laborious snowshoeing, I decided to put my energy back into touring. I never have much liked visiting ski areas, mainly because, when I have a few extra hours, I'd just as soon go where there are a few thousand less out-of-control Kansans and Texans. Fortunately, I have generally lived in places where I can access backcountry trails pretty much by walking out my front door.

Which is exactly what I did on the day I'm getting ready to tell you about here.

Dawn had yet to even fully break when I threw my Karhus over my shoulder and headed out to the kind of trail that people who dwell in lesser realms fantasize about visiting once a year on vacation. This is a trail I have traveled upon so many times — in all seasons, skiing, snowshoeing, hiking, biking — if I live to be 100 and never, ever visit it again, I will go to the grave with every curve and contour still seared happily into my cranial on-aboard navigation system.

It was mid-January and a tad nippy there at 6:45 a.m. Meaning, yes, the trail was a bit on the icy side. There is one skiing skill I do have (all things being relative, of course): I am fairly strong on uphills. I have decent endurance and I have developed acceptable technique with my fish-scale skis. Yet, the slip-slidiness of the frozen tracks made for slow going. Slow going, I should stress, on the ascent. I knew as I climbed the descent would be a horse of a whole nuther adrenaline-based color.

I turned around at the usual spot and pointed my boards down in the direction of what I then feared might very well be an impending mishap — a self-fulfilling prophesy in the making. Yet, as I said, this is a trail I can ski in my sleep. Though there were a few moments when my eyes splayed wide, I made it most of the way down without calamity. But I then did the thing you never do: I relaxed and let my concentration wander before I was technically and metaphorically out of the woods. At a place I know like the back of my hand, a place where I never had problems before, I found myself 1) because of the iciness of the trail, skiing way faster than I would have liked, 2) losing control just as I arrived at a big curve above a drop-off into an aspen grove and 3) using especially colorful language.

Before I could even properly soil my knickers, I was headed willy-nilly for those aspens, and there was seemingly nothing that was going to get between me and an imminent direct interface with a tree, except, perhaps, another tree. I had visions of the unflattering front-page story in the local paper — under a banner headline: "Mighty Poor Skier Perishes on Backcountry Equivalent of Bunny Hill" — and my buddies coming out to eyeball the Place Where It Happened. "How could *anyone* hit a tree *here*?" they would ask, shaking their heads slowly, as they made their way to the wake, where their solemnity would at least be assuaged somewhat by the free beverages my embarrassed widow would surely pony up for.

It's important at this point to stress, relative to the speeds real skiers routinely achieve in this ski-crazy part of the country, my forward momentum was laughable. I once covered a pro ski event at Keystone, and, from my perch mid-mountain, scant feet from the course, I watched downhill racers zipping by at velocities that made them seem less skiers than corporeal manifestations of the Doppler Effect. Later, I heard they were traveling at almost 80 mph! I was even more dumbfounded than usual.

Me, as I was headed toward that grove of aspens? I would be surprised if I had even achieved double-digit miles per hour, but 1) it seemed to me quite fast enough to result in measurable misfortune and 2) I understand from personal experience it does not take much on the momentum front to intercourse oneself up when one impacts a tree. Though I am not exactly proud to relate this, I know this because, a couple decades prior, I lived in Grand Lake, Colorado, where I was employed by the town to run its admittedly modest tennis program. (That was not a bad gig, let me tell you.) This will come as a stunner to many of you, but, one night, I over-imbibed at a long-gone watering hole called the Corner Pub. There was a fairly substantial line of pines between said bar and the one-room, refrigerator-less, bathroom-less, $100-a-month attic I then called home.

You would think one as practiced as I was/am in both the art of over-imbibing and the art of mostly accurate perambulation would have been able to miss those trees by a wide margin — especially when you consider I had to walk by those pines numerous times every day. And it's not like those trees went into sudden, unexpected camouflage mode. No, they were right where they always were, doing what they always do. Though I was not exactly sprinting, and though my drunkenness autopilot was surely doing its damnedest to make certain I was practicing some semblance of involuntary inebriated evasive action, I still managed to pretty much head-on collision one of those pines hard enough I remember looking into the night sky and wondering what my feet were doing all the way up there in the middle of the Milky Way. Thing is, amusing (at least to my drinking chums) though that mishap was, the main point here is that my shoulder was bruised and contused badly enough I could not swing a tennis racquet for a solid week.

As I began to accelerate my way that icy morning toward the grove of aspens, I was definitely going faster than that night in Grand Lake — the very night I became a proponent of aggressive, planet-wide clear cutting — when that malevolent killer tree jumped out of the darkness and knocked me on my ass for no apparent good reason. (There went my annual donation to the Arbor Day Foundation.)

Researchers of all things human-brain related surely have studied the perplexing reality that, sometimes, when shit is about to hit the fan, time slows way down and sometimes it speeds way up, and this inexplicable truth is not just a matter of how one person handles shit hitting the fan and how another person handles it. With any given person, it can go either way, depending on who knows what. Most times, with me, time speeds up, which means I don't usually muck up a potentially dangerous situation with extraneous thought. My wuss gland just kicks in of its own volition, and, in the context of skiing, that generally means I automatically go into slide-into-third-base mode, on my side, with skis up, in hopes of fending off whatever I'm getting ready to crash into with the largest and most powerful muscles the human body has to offer: the legs.

This time, though, time slowed way, way, way down. It was as though God had just sprayed the world, Agent Orange-style, with a big batch of Quaalude dust. The birds were now tweeting as though you applied light finger pressure to an old

LP, just to see if you could hear any subliminal references to devil worship. My breathing, which I knew had to be operating at a hyper-inflated, fear-induced rate, seemed instead like I had inhaled a bucket of molasses (in January). I felt like I could have composed a long and heartfelt good-bye note to my beloved in the time between when my skis parted ways with the trail and when I arrived air mail, special delivery, into the midst of those trees, with, I'm sure, a look of abject terror defining my countenance so vividly, when search-and-rescue finally peeled my mug out of the aspen bark, an indentation of my petrified visage would have been left behind like a Roman death mask.

With time moving at about quarter speed, I tried mightily — to the point I could both hear and feel my quadriceps separating from their attendant tendons — to engage the most aggressive snowplow ever initiated. Then, with all hope for a happy outcome slipping by fast, my lizard brain came up with a survival plan that, to this day, I cannot fully explain in any manner save the most basic transitive relation. What I did was this: While continuing to apply every ounce of positive energy I could muster to my largely ineffectual snowplow, I lifted my gloved left hand, which still retained, within its increasingly weak grasp, a ski pole, and pointed my index finger directly at the aspen, which, in fractions of a nanosecond, I would impact. I do not know why this felt like it was the right thing to do, but that's exactly what it felt like: The Right Thing To Do.

Back then, I was deep into martial arts training, the deepest I ever was and ever would be. One of the main concepts you try to grasp when you're learning how to bust your fist through concrete blocks without shattering every bone in your upper body is this inexplicable power called chi. Matter of fact, the generation and studied application of chi is probably the most important concept when you're learning any martial art. And the goal is to be able to call forth the chi that flows through us all, flows through every living and inanimate object under the sun, without really having to think about it. It's one thing when you're applying every ounce of your concentration onto an imminent attempt to bust concrete blocks while a dour-looking Korean Grand Master is scrutinizing your every movement, but it's an entirely different thing when you're out in the woods by yourself, about to ski into an aspen, which, as my buddy Milt said after hearing this story a few hours later, at least has softer wood than many other kinds of trees.

In that Quaalude-dust, molasses-breath slow-motion time, I focused every molecule of my internal energy into my extended index finger. I tried to use my noggin as a cosmic antenna to attract every gram of chi that happened to be in the neighborhood that particular frigid January morning. And, then, finally, I made contact with the tree, finger first, and finger only. All of the physics that applied to my there-and-then condition — momentum, inertia, gravity (of both literal and figurative varieties), equal-and-opposite reactions, all that shit — met head on with the chi spewing forth from my body, my existence, and zeroed in on one frail extended digit, which did not exactly "hit" the tree, but which, rather, met the tree, as though I was doing nothing more than reaching out to touch it, as I often do with trees.

And I came to a complete stop, like I was doing nothing more than pushing a doorbell attached to the side of an aspen out in the middle of the glorious Colorado High Country. It was like, all I had to do was push it, and doors to entire new worlds would open. Which, I guess, in retrospect, is maybe exactly what happened.

I would like to schuss my way to this story's denouement by saying I emerged from the woods physically unscathed. This I cannot say, because, powers of chi notwithstanding, physics still played a large role in the experience. My left index finger was, not surprisingly, truly trashed. I never went to the orthopedist, because, for some reason, it felt like a dispassionate clinical diagnosis would pollute the context of what turned out to be a poignant, non-clinical experience. But I'm sure there were at least two fractures, a dislocation and some torn soft tissue. For most of the next year, my injured digit pointed at about a 40-degree angle to starboard. But, like most things, it eventually got better and now, by looking at it, you would never know it was one day long ago used to push an aspen doorbell at the exact moment I was trying as hard as I could to gain access to a place I still wonder if I ever really, truly visited. Maybe I was just peeking through the window.

— MOUNTAIN GAZETTE #173

CHAPTER TWELVE

Adventure Orgy

PART 1: HOT AIR

My buddy Pedro winked in my direction, smirked a mierda-eating grin and nodded his noggin Bobblehead-on-speed-style when I entered the Burro Borracho Cantina and Lucha Libre Emporium. "Well, I did it," he said almost smugly as I approached. Despite every pre-purchase protestation I could muster, Pedro had just spent 242 hard-earned dollars for what he considered the ultimate Christmas present for his latest l'amour: a romantic two-person, early-morning champagne hot-air balloon ride outside Albuquerque. I shook my head so vigorously, I lost several gold crowns.

I had forewarned Pedro about the psychological, to say nothing of physical, perils of hot-air ballooning. It mattered not one whit that I spoke from intense personal experience on this subject. Pedro's mind, such that it is, was made up. That month's lady-friend, Darlene, had commented almost abstractly (and certainly drunkenly) the week before about how it would be nice *for once* to do something not involving sitting hour after hour on the exact same barstools they always sat on in the Burro Borracho. Not one to miss something as obvious as an impending case of significant-other-based boredom, Pedro immediately suggested that they embark then and there upon what must have seemed at that happy hour juncture like a National-Geographic-special-level journey to the unexplored hinterlands of Botswana: "We could go sit over in the booth," he said, expectantly. I'm not sure whether his sweetie's exasperated groan was based more upon the multitiered revolting nature of the Burro's lone booth, which is upholstered in the finest of beer-stained, sticky (don't ask), tattered naugahyde, and which is located next to the doorless entrance to the single most unsavory men's room in the entire history of skanky watering holes, or whether it was more general in nature. I suspect the latter. Either way, as the final air molecules of a theatrical sigh lasting well over 15 minutes passed the last molecules of Darlene's globbed-on bright-red lipstick, the local news came on the Burro's 1957 scratchy black-and-white, aluminum-foil-antennaed, yard-sale-procured TV, which sometimes gets one channel and sometimes gets no channels. As this discourse was transpiring, it was getting the one channel, which was at that moment running a happy-go-lucky feature segment on the annual Albuquerque International Balloon Fiesta, an event so famous in New Mexico, a high percentage of the state's license plates boast an image that looks exactly like a flimsy air-filled cloth sack falling like a rock out of the sky.

"Look," Darlene said, pointing toward the flickering screen. "Maybe we could do something like that!" At first, Pedro thought Darlene was pointing toward the famous old Corona beer poster with the three provocative, bathing-suit-attired nubile young ladies. "Sure," he said, "but where are we gonna get two other women?" he asked. "Maybe your two nieces!" "No, asshole," Darlene snarled. "On the TV." By the time Pedro managed to focus his one good eye on the TV, which, on its best day, is able to generate about half-a--lumens of flickery light, the local news had cut away to coverage of a high-speed chase in Tucson involving about 40 cop cars, three helicopters, a SWAT team and, eventually, a pair of mean-looking homies being handcuffed and hauled away. This really confused the livin' shit out of Pedro. "You want to engage in a high-speed chase with police and get arrested in front of a TV camera crew?" he slurred toward Darlene. "Cool."

At that point, Darlene departed in a snit, stating for all to hear that she was going to have a few drinks over at the Poco Loco, "where they know how to treat a lady" (the problem there being, she's been 86'd from the Poco Loco — mainly because of her almost-stunning lack of lady-ness). "What just happened?" Pedro asked. "She wants you to take her ballooning," I yelled over the din. I have lived more than half a century, and never once I have seen a visage so befuddled. It took me almost two hours to de-intertwine the Corona poster/police-chase/balloon fiesta cognitive dissonance transpiring between Pedro's pointy ears. I finally, exasperatedly, made him understand that Darlene had casually mentioned something about wanting to go floating up into the sky like the Wonderful Wizard leaving Oz.

"Damn! I've been wondering what to get her for Christmas!" Pedro said, his face verily brightening in the dingy light in the Burro Borracho. "I got a cousin up in Albuquerque who owes me some, uh, money. I'll call him to see if he can arrange it."

It was at this point I decided to forewarn Pedro about

the entire concept of venturing forth into the wild blue yonder in a craft both un-navigatable and completely lacking in the ability to glide to safety back to Earth should the shit hit the fan, which it always has, does and will.

This is what I laid on Pedro vis-à-vis my colorful, though modest, ballooning resume: I have been up in a hot-air balloon twice, which is exactly two times too many, as far as I am concerned. Both times, I stressed to Pedro, took place shortly before Christmas, a cosmic coincidence worth his studied consideration before placing a call to his cousin in Albuquerque. The first time, I was on assignment for a justifiably long-defunct alternative alternative weekly in Denver. The publisher, a drunken reprobate of monstrous proportions, had found himself (not exactly for the first or last time) downtown at Soapy Smith's, looking for some hapless soul to buy him a drink. His victim this time ended up being, of all the people on the planet, the owner of a commercial ballooning outfit, and the publisher said he knew just the person to go up with him into what ended up being the stratosphere, the idea being 1) we would running a lengthy blowjob story about the flight/company in our paper (which, truth be told (something we rarely did) was read by all of about two people) and 2) that in and of itself was reason enough, in the mind of the reprobate publisher, to expect the balloon guy to buy him about 14 drinks at Soapy Smith's.

"Good news," the bleary-eyed publisher told me in the morning. "I signed you up for a balloon trip this weekend," which I hoped against hope didn't mean what I thought it meant, that, rather, it might have something to do with dropping acid and being the live entertainment at a children's birthday soiree. No such luck.

This I did not personally consider good news. I do not *exactly* suffer from aviophobia, the same way I do not *exactly* suffer from claustrophobia. Still, the same way I am always mighty, mighty happy when I emerge unscathed from an MRI machine, a cave or a jail cell, I am always mighty, mighty happy when the plane or helicopter safely touches down. Though not debilitating, never once in my life have I gone up into any sort of aircraft unless there was palpable good reason — usually getting to a place otherwise not reasonably accessible via non-aerial modes of transport. The notion of voluntarily going up in a hot-air balloon for no other purpose save going up in a hot-air balloon flat-out did not, and still does not, compute. It had never entered my head, the same way parachuting has never entered my head, except as something to avoid at all costs.

But, being a professional and all, I showed up at the appointed time, which was literally just as a stunningly beauteous dawn broke upon the Great Plains southeast of Denver. Since it was mid-December, it was a bit on the nippy side, which apparently is optimum for ascension, as cold air is more dense than hot air, and, for reasons that escape me, that helps the balloon get off the ground and make its way heavenward, until it's just this little dot lucky people sitting in the warm comfort of their living rooms, sipping hot coffee, can barely see. I would be joining a young (paying) couple that had just tied the knot and were looking upon this journey into the hereafter, er, sky, as some sort of marital consummation. They were all giggly and smoochy, which made me even more uncomfortable.

The ballooning outfitter my publisher had met at Soapy Smith's was also the pilot. He was affable enough and evoked a sense of confidence, and, truth be told, once we passed the moon and started making our way toward the outer Solar System, I calmed down a bit and started enjoying the expansive, albeit frigid, view of the Front Range. "Where we headed?" I, being on the journalistic clock and all, queried. "Don't know," the pilot responded. "What do you mean?" I squeaked. "I can use the burners to make us go up and down, and I have a pretty good eye for where the wind is, but, for the most part, I have absolutely no control over the balloon. We go where Mother Nature takes us."

Ain't that an interesting little tidbit?

After seeming decades aloft, it was finally and thankgodfully time to descend. The just-married couple was cuddling and cooing and sharing a bottle of bubbly, the pilot was pointing out various mountains and I was leaning against one of the basket uprights. Suddenly, the pilot went frantic. He yelled at the top of his lungs for all hands to hold on tight. We were apparently going through some sort of high-speed meteorological anomaly taking place like 50 feet above the ground I oh-so-much wanted to be standing safely upon. "I'M NOT KIDDING!!!! HOLD ON TIGHT!!!! AAAAHHHH!!!!" the now-frenzied pilot screamed. I wrapped both arms around the support, very much like Tom Hanks did in "Cast Away" when his plane was going down (I don't know about you, but I started paying a lot more attention to those pre-flight safety briefings after watching *that* movie), and instantly became a convert to at least seven religions. Seconds later, we crashed into Planet Earth at both a 45-degree angle and at a very uncomfortable rate of speed, and we spent the next almost 400 feet (I paced it off later), getting dragged by the still-partially-inflated balloon, which was now acting like a fully unfurled spinnaker, the muddy turf zooming by just below my nose (yes, it was my side of the basket that was closest to the ground). A couple times, just for grins, the balloon pulled the basket back up into the air, just so we could smack down hard and get dragged toward Castle Rock yet again. By the time we finally came to a stop, the new wife was crying, and the new husband, whose visions of a nookie-laden night were dissipating before his very eyes, was trying mightily to console her. That marriage was destined to either be very short-lived or very long.

After I wrote the blowjob story for the justifiably long-defunct Denver alternative alternative weekly, I vowed to never ever even ponder the notion of setting foot in a hot-air balloon, which, you would think, would be a fairly easy oath to uphold. Well ...

The very next year, the editor of *Adventure Travel* calls me up and asks whether I would like to go to the southernmost Appalachians to write a story about this outfitter who offers what he advertises as "Adventure Orgies," wherein clients are taken on a different type of NON-AERIAL potentially deadly recreational pursuit every day for a week (whitewater rafting, climbing, horseback riding, hiking and, I shit you not, wild-boar hunting and mako-shark fishing). Being the starving writer I was, I said sure. It was once again the very week before Christmas when I landed at Atlanta's Hartsfield-Jackson International Airport. The plan was for the outfitter to pick me up, take me to the closest bar, where I would conduct a formal interview over many pitchers of suds, and then drive me to his mountain cabin for the night. The next morning, we were set to go rafting on the famed Chattooga, the very river where some of the whitewater scenes from "Deliverance" were filmed.

"I've got great news," Adventure Orgy Guy told me as we were driving out of the airport. "I've managed to squeeze in one more adventure for you! A buddy of mine has a hot-air balloon, and he said he'll take you up this afternoon!"

Yey!

Shit!

The first thing I noticed about the man who was going to take me up into the muggy Georgia air was, unlike the guy I went up with near Denver, who actually seemed like a fairly normal schmuck, right up until the point when he started screaming for us to hold on tight because we were about to crash, this guy seemed crazy as batshit from the get-go. Something about the way he cackled like a crow at his own bad jokes and the way he kept furtively rubbing his hands together, like he was trying to get something nasty off.

Because Georgia was experiencing an unseasonably warm late fall, there was not enough in the way of vertical-lift-inducing death molecules in the air for Adventure Orgy Guy, the crazy-as-batshit pilot and yours truly to all go up together. As I was about to volunteer to man the chase car, Adventure Orgy Guy patted me on the back and, with a bemused gleam in his eye, wished me not bon voyage, but, rather, good luck. So, it was me and the crazy-as-batshit pilot, and, before I could calculate a plan for changing professions, I was airborne, with nothing between me and the ground save a wicker basket, some thin balloon material and one crazy-as-batshit pilot, who, it turned out, thought the best way to amuse his guest was to buzz the tops of as many giant Southern hardwood trees as often as possible while saying things like, "I'll bet we can take some branches off the next one."

And here I am, holding on for dear life, feeling like Sigourney Weaver in "Aliens," like, all I had to do was stay back on Earth, and I wouldn't be here getting chased by deadly, drooling carnivorous creatures *yet again*. And, of course, just like my first time up in a hot-air balloon, we came down hard — hard enough that I bit my tongue almost clean in two. Then we tipped over so violently that my nose literally hit the dirt. Then, the wind caught the balloon and we got dragged through a field for a couple hundred feet. And that was the best part. Matter of fact, some hours later, as we were being detained by several local Southern redneck police officers straight out of bubba central casting, I looked back with fondness upon the those relatively pleasant moments when we hit the ground with a back-breaking thud and my tongue was cleaved and my nose was smacked into the dirt so hard, I had to breathe through my mouth, which was filled-to-brimming with spit-laced tongue-wound blood.

What happened was this: The field that we thudded down in was home to endless vistas of waist-high dry grass. When we tipped over, the flamethrowers that are part and parcel of every hot-air balloon caught the grass on fire, which spread fast, far and wide, right before my very eyes. The crazy-as-batshit pilot started freaking and yelling for me to exit the basket and stomp the fire out. Try though I might, the only thing I managed to do was gouge a seven-inch-long wound into my shin, which got caught up on one of the wing nuts holding the basket to the balloon frame.

Finally, through no fault of my own, I found myself ejected and lying dazed on my back in a north Georgia field that was pretty much by this point totally ablaze. There would be no stomping this fire out. The only thing to do was get up and run, except for the fact that we had a big balloon to deal with. Thing is, it damned sure wasn't my balloon. Fuck the balloon, and definitely fuck the crazy-as-batshit balloon pilot. Just as I was getting ready to high-tail it into the woods, a pick-up truck came careening toward us, and, before it came to a complete stop, two very agitated, overall-wearing, African-American men jumped out and pointed their double-barrel shotguns at the crazy-as-batshit balloon pilot and, well, poor, innocent me.

"Ya'll ain't goin' nowhere," I was told in no uncertain terms by my personal gun-bearer as I started eyeballing a po-tential escape route toward the closest trees — and as those famous banjo notes from "Deliverance" started playing in my head. "We done already called the poe-leece."

So, there we were, standing with hands up, like we were bring robbed by banditos in an old Western movie, when, sud-denly, a large white van pulls up. It was not the poe-leece or the fire department or even a representative of the local loony bin looking for an escaped crazy-as-batshit balloon pilot. No, par for my karmic course, that van bore a Chattanooga TV news crew arriving on the scene so quickly they seemingly were parked in the very field we set ablaze on the off chance that an errant hot-air balloon might fortuitously fall out of the sky and crash at their very feet, a news story from God, if ever there was one. And, worse, since the crazy-as-batshit pilot was still running around trying to stomp out the conflagra-tion, which by then, could have been accurately classified as a "wildfire," a cute young on-air personality sprinted up to me and shoved a microphone the size of a baseball bat right into my face. Only then did she notice I had a bloody bandanna hanging limply out of my mouth and two nostrils completely caked with dirt.

"So, uh, what happened here?" she asked me, clearly flustered.

My brain was sending a red-alert message to my vocalization apparatus to unambiguously cast all blame at the feet of the crazy-as-batshit balloon pilot, but the only sound that sprang forth from my wounded maw was a series of unintelligible, pitiful moans and groans. I removed the bandanna in hopes of increasing my articulation factor, which caused a torrent of blood to dribble down my chin and onto my shirt. The reporter recoiled in abject horror, as though she had just in the flesh witnessed a man in the last stages of death-by-ebola. She shrieked and retreated to her van and, despite the best efforts of her cameraman, could not be persuaded to re-interface with the contagious pestilence standing there in the middle of the burning field with blood gushing forth from his most-obvious orifice.

About 20 minutes later, the poe-leece and the fire department arrived, sirens blaring. It took more than an hour to douse the flames, during which time the two shotgun-bearing African-American men, the poe-leece, several firefighters and the crazy-as-batshit balloon pilot realized that they all knew someone who knew someone else somewhere sometime. If memory serves, there were several "y'alls," "all y'alls" and maybe even a reference to hominy grits with redeye gravy. Basically, a meandering, drawl-laden verbal journey through Southern social inbreeding that resulted in the crazy-as-batshit balloon pilot eating a modest-sized bucket of shit and promising to pay for the damage and make a small donation to the poe-leece/fire-department retirement/drinking fund. We were let go and I, bloody tongue, gashed shin and smelling like smoke, was left with Adventure Orgy Guy to continue upon our merry way.

Despite the fact that I had related all this to Pedro, he still felt compelled to go forth and procure that $242 romantic two-person, early-morning champagne hot-air balloon ride outside Albuquerque. It dawned on me later that all of the mishaps I had described, Pedro considered to be plusses. I realized, once he finally took Darlene up into the stratosphere, he would be disappointed, maybe even to the degree of wanting his money back, if he did not get to experience a crash landing, setting a field on fire and having shotguns leveled at him.

I wished him all the best.

A few days later, Pedro called. Darlene had left him, and he asked, "You want to go ballooning with me, bro? I already got the tickets. After all, this was your idea. Merry Christmas, amigo!"

— MOUNTAIN GAZETTE #174

PART 2: DELIVERANCE

The scheduled second segment of our Adventure Orgy, like I said before, was a full-day raft descent of the Chattooga River, which straddles the border of Georgia and South Carolina. This is the very section of river upon which significant portions of "Deliverance" were actually filmed. Adventure Orgy Guy assured me the gnarliest scenes from "Deliverance" were filmed on the Tallulah River, which, I'll admit, in my battered state, was something of a relief, for, you see, I had not even slightly recovered from the balloon incident. The deep gash on my right shin was oozing all manner of repugnant-colored fluids, my left shin was swollen so badly it looked like some sort of Frankensteinian mad scientist had grafted a partially decomposed watermelon onto my leg and my tongue was lolling involuntarily, like what you'd see coming out of a tranquilized rhino's mouth in a *National Geographic* wildlife documentary.

We drove to the quaint mountain town of Clayton, Georgia, where we met our two partners in river crime: a sports editor from an Atlanta TV station and none other than Billy Redden, who, at age eight, was the banjo-picking boy in "Deliverance," though, come to learn, it was not he who actually picked the haunting notes that, to this day, strike fear in the heart of any non-Southerner who ventures forth into the more rural parts of Dixie. The national eight-year-old banjo-playing champion crouched behind Billy Redden, whose arms were literally tied to his sides, and slid his arms through Billy's jacket and, without being able to see the instrument, picked the strings flawlessly.

It did not help mitigate any preconceptions I might have held when, before meeting Billy, who works as a professional river guide for Adventure Orgy Guy, I was told how he "auditioned" for the part of the (non-) banjo-playing boy in "Deliverance." "They went way up in the sticks and picked out the most inbred, retarded-looking kid out of the local elementary school. And there were a bunch to choose from. It was like an anti-beauty contest. Out of all the available material, they chose Billy. Then, just to make him look even more inbred and retarded, they shaved his head." Of course, based upon that vision, combined with actually having watched "Deliverance," I naturally assumed Billy Redden would be the walking, talking epitome of every negative Appalachia-based stereotype imaginable. I assumed he would likely be a perpetual drooler whose best attempts at fundamental articulation would mirror those of Jodie Foster when Liam Neeson first made her character's acquaintance in "Nell." Ends up Billy, by then in his 30s, while not necessarily the most handsome man I have ever met, was a totally great guy, witty and funny, and, if there was a drooler on the scene, it was I, due to my wounded tongue situation.

We partially inflated the two, two-person, 11-foot rafts right there on the sidewalk in downtown Clayton, where both Billy and Adventure Orgy Guy were well known. The 17,000 passersby — all of whom had a mouthful of chaw and were named Clem — who stopped for a chat (our raft-inflating procedures apparently being the most noteworthy event to have transpired in Clayton since the last summer's Hog-Sloppin' Festival) were surprised to hear we were headed for the Chattooga. "All y'all ain't gonna run Bull Sluice, are all y'all?" was a question pondiferously drawled by every single one of those 17,000 curious chaw-chewing Clems. And when Adventure Orgy Guy answered in the affirmative, every single one of those 17,000 curious Clems slowly shook his head, let out with a feigned nervous whistle, and said words to the effect of: "Well, best of luck to all y'all. Wouldn't catch us'ns trying to run Bull Sluice this time of year."

It will come as no surprise that these exchanges caught my attention, but I said nothing, at least partially because, due to my lacerated tongue, any attempts to speak all sounded like I was the guy tied to the chair in a million Hollywood movie torture scenes with the gag stuffed in his mouth. Try though I might to spill the beans about where the drugs and money were hidden and where the torturers could most easily locate my cohorts, all I could do was grunt.

Once we got on the river — me with Adventure Orgy Guy in one raft, Billy Redden and the Atlanta TV sports guy in the other raft — Adventure Orgy Guy, after much apparent mental cud-chewing, said: "You probably heard all 17,000 of those Clems back in Clayton asking about Bull Sluice." "Grunt." He proceeded to tell me Bull Sluice is one of two Class-5-plus rapids on the section of the Chattooga we were going to run. It had claimed literally dozens of lives over the years. Forgive me insofar as I am not familiar enough with death-based river terminology to describe this properly, but Bull Sluice is a very short and steep rapid — a waterfall, now that you mention it — which changes directions three times in about 100 linear feet — once at the top, once halfway through and once again at the bottom. You start out going over the waterfall at about 10 o'clock, then you've got to alter your heading to about 3 o'clock, then you've got to go back to 10 o'clock, all while you're attempting to negotiate a rapid that, even if it didn't have three major turns, would still be exceedingly dangerous.

"Don't worry though," Adventure Orgy Guy said, reassuringly (at least in theory), we'll be on the river a couple hours before we get to Bull Sluice, and, by then, you and I will be very comfortable paddling together. It'll be great!" (This from the man responsible for placing me in a hot-air balloon that crashed-landed the previous afternoon.) The plan was for Billy Redden and the Atlanta TV guy to portage around Bull Sluice. Adventure Orgy Guy and I would pull over above

Bull Sluice, walk downriver to shit our pants and devise an appropriate stratagem, return to our diminutive raft, clean our pants out, then tackle a rapid that might as well be named "Death Waterfall from Hell," after which I would either have to clean my pants out yet again or arrive at the medical examiner's office with Fruit of the Looms full of caca.

Since we had a couple hours to kill before we ourselves were killed, I opted to chill with the scene, which was wonderfully pleasant. Even though the first day of winter was literally 72 hours away, it was sunny and warm. We paddled by scads of overall-adorned, dentition-challenged men, who, stunningly, were also named Clem, sipping jugfuls of moonshine while tending to their stills. We passed veritable tribes of corpulent women — all named Bessie May and Shirley Sue — sitting on riverside front porches shucking corn and green beans and smoking pipes while stirring vats of possum gizzard stew (or something like that).

Yet the thought of Bull Sluice never completely left the back of my mind. Quite the contrary. Every time a squirrel farted on the riverbank, my eardrums translated the noise to the roar of an impending life-swallowing rapid. Until finally, inevitably, we came to the spot where the roar was no longer a figment of my squirrel-fart-based imagination. We pulled over and, as Billy Redden and the Atlanta-TV guy (who, as a casual aside, had already mentioned numerous times how heart-flutteringly joyous he was that *he* wasn't going through Bull Sluice (I believe his actual words were: "Hell, no, ain't no way you could ever talk *me* into going through Bull Sluice! Only a fucking moronic idiot from Colorado would even *ponder* the insane notion of going though Bull Sluice! Hope you've got life insurance" (or something like that))) started carrying their raft around the rapid, Adventure Orgy Guy and your humble narrator ventured forth to eyeball Bull Sluice with the idea of coming up with a plan not involving direct interfaces with mortality, or, better stated, did not involve direct interfaces with mortality for yours truly. My part of the planning process, as predicted, consisted almost entirely of shitting my pants when I laid first eyes upon the awesome power of Bull Sluice.

As Adventure Orgy Guy was pointing out the myriad ominous hydraulic intricacies of Bull Sluice, all the while stressing the many, many potential fuck-ups we, more than anything in the world, wanted to avoid, because, even the slightest, teeniest mistake at any of those many, many fuck-up points would most certainly result in a series of soulful obituaries in the Clayton, Georgia, newspaper, I came to a realization that, while not exactly stunning, insofar as "surprise" is a necessary component of the definition of the word "stunning," was at least a bit disconcerting. When you're an outdoor writer on assignment for a magazine named *Adventure Travel* to pen a story about a company that offers something called "Adventure Orgies," you are vocationally, if not dispositionally, obligated to live up to certain big-balled personality stereotypes. And none of those stereotypes include overt displays of pants-wetting wussiness when faced with a mere Class-5 death waterfall. Yet, here I was, experiencing an unmistakable tingling in my nether regions neither indicative solely of excitement nor enthusiasm. Rather, those tinglings were indicative of the type of vibe-based fear that, in some circumstances (circumstances that often include actually going forth with the proposed action), results in optimal physical performance, while, in others, can best be translated as the great undefined "something" telling you in no uncertain terms this is not the day to attempt whatever it is you are considering attempting. In short, there was no way my increasingly shriveling nuts were going through Bull Sluice that fine day. Mortifying though that realization was on several levels, it was actually a liberating moment. I mean, it wasn't like I then started racing along the riverbank, my arms held high, like "Rocky" running up the steps of the Philadelphia Museum of Art, shouting "I am a pussy, and I'm proud of it!" Still, it was nice to realize I had arrived at a point in life where, if I didn't feel comfortable running a very intimidating rapid, I wasn't going to let peer pressure convince me otherwise. The best stories are the ones you live to tell.

When I relayed, via a series of grunts and hyper-kinetic hand gestures, this non-negotiable reality to Adventure Orgy Guy, he seemed crestfallen, like any hopes of a positive story in *Adventure Travel* just disappeared.

I, of course, thought we would then portage our raft around the rapid and proceed upon our merry un-dead way. Ixnay. Adventure Orgy Guy beckoned Billy Redden to join him in the raft we had stashed upriver. "This way, you'll at least be able to get some photos of us going through Bull Sluice for your story." To say Billy Redden looked shocked would greatly minimize his contorted visage. Yet, Adventure Orgy Guy being his employer and all, he hung his head and dutifully made his way to the top of Bull Sluice. I stood below the rapid, camera at the ready.

A few minutes later, the little raft, which looked, against the fearsome immensity of Bull Sluice, like a toy boat bobbing in the surf of Oahu's North Shore, shot into the maelstrom. There was no visual run-up — one nanosecond, they were not there, the next nanosecond, 14 kinds of fearsome hell were breaking loose. They entered Bull Sluice OK, but, at the 90-degree dogleg in the middle of the rapid, Billy Redden got his paddle caught between two rocks, and the force of Bull Sluice ripped it from his grip so intensely that the banjo-playing boy from "Deliverance" came within a single ass molecule of being pulled from the raft at a place that all but assured his doom. It seemed at that frightening moment like his last above-water act was going to be a very wide-eyed, frantic arabesque penchee. The look on Adventure Orgy Guy's face was a mix of fear and resolute determination I will carry with me the rest of my days. He was down an engine in the middle of one of the most-notorious river rapids in the entire country, and, if he did not perform in extraordinary, superhuman fashion right then and there, fatalities were likely, which, while adding the potential for some spice to my *Adventure Travel* magazine story, would likely have negatively affected the overall vibe of the trip.

In the time it took me to snap off one photo, they were out of the rapid. Adventure Orgy Guy pulled it off and saved the day. He was magnificent. Their raft drifted limply to shore, its occupants spent in a way that all but assures many weeks of deep introspection. Billy Redden wobbled onto shore and staggered downriver a few feet, where he plopped down on a rock, lit a cigarette and muttered to himself, over and over, "I ain't never going through Bull Sluice again … I ain't never going through Bull Sluice again … " And I could tell he meant it.

The rest of the trip down the Chattooga that day was pleasant as can be. We drove back to Clayton, where we enjoyed a Southern repast so splendidly lard-laden and voluminous it served as poster child for all those nation-leading bad-health-based statistics that some out of the Deep South. And that repast was served, come to find out, by Louise Coltrane, who wrote the very first check that got the famed "Foxfire Book" series going. Both of her daughters were in Eliot Wigginton's Rabun Gap-Nacoochee School English class when he conceived what ended up becoming a world-renowned 12-volume series.

How cool is that?

On the drive back to Adventure Orgy Guy's cabin, I could tell there was something on his mind. After we knocked off most of a 12-pack, he finally said, "You know, you and I had been psychologically working our way up to Bull Sluice all day. I think if we had just gone through like we planned, everything would have turned out fine." The implication, of course, was, Billy Redden (a professional river guide, I stress) had paddled throughout the morning under the assumption he would be portaging Bull Sluice, and, if he had died, it would have been my fault. I've got to admit, that observation rubbed me a bit wrong on numerous levels. But I really didn't give it any further thought till I was back home, sitting in front of my computer, getting ready to write the Adventure Orgy story for *Adventure Travel* magazine. After all, right then, as we were bounding down the darkening Appalachia highway, beers in hand, there was much to occupy my thoughts. We had a horseback-riding trip planned the next day. My mind raced, pondering possibilities for mishap associated with straddling thousand-pound beasts with brains the size of peanuts. Those possibilities were limitless.

— MOUNTAIN GAZETTE #178

CHAPTER THIRTEEN

Bad Trip

AUTHOR'S NOTE: *I spent literally months and months working on a fairly-heavy (at least by my lightweight heaviness standards) Smoke Signals about the municipal government of the town in which I live last year passing an ordinance effectively putting the kibosh on panhandling within the city limits, and how that sort of shit causes some serious internal argumentative turmoil for a card-carrying liberal who happens to sometimes get a tad tired of getting hit up for spare change by people who seem young and healthy enough to work, except, of all the things I truly appreciate in life, it's the idea of people not wanting to work, but, were it not for people working, then there would be a lot less of the fundamental, and required, raw material necessary for most panhandling and how that sort of shit is emblematic of the gentrification vs. funkiness argument taking place in many New West towns these days blah blah blah. Alas, I never got to where I answered the questions that I couldn't figure out for the life of me how to even ask properly. So I decided to scrap that Smoke Signals and opted instead to retreat to more conceptually familiar territory. I decided to write about LSD.*

"You ever dropped acid before?" asked Winona, a bartender both young and sweet enough, her mere existence can persuade those of us otherwise inclined toward tea-toddling to take up serious and regular imbibing — and who boasts the added positive personality trait of at least pretending to be amused (or at least not offended) when lecherous graybeards such as myself flirt with her.

Winona's pleasant disposition notwithstanding, it was an out-of the-blue question loaded with enough potential doom, I ducked before even pondering what I hoped would be a retort filled to brimming with such a high degree of indignant denial that, had a lie detector machine right then been hooked up to me, all six little ink lines would have been so damned flat, it would seem as though I had died sometime last year.

"Uh, heh heh, why do you ask?" I responded furtively, while feeling surreptitiously under the barstool for miniature microphones. (All I located though was a wad of sticky god-knows-what.) I seriously considered asking Winona if I could pat her down just to make sure she wasn't wearing a wire. ("Sorry, Winona, but I'm going to have to ask you to unbutton that blouse ... ")

"Well, it seems there's a lot of acid around town these days, and I've never tried it. I'm thinking about giving it a go. I just figured, out of all the older people I know who might be able to give me some observations about what it's like to trip, you are the best choice."

Fortunately, Winona had to see to other patrons right then, because I needed a few moments to mentally process the apparent reality that I have reached a time and place in my life where twenty-somethings are hitting me up for advice regarding the use of illegal psychotropic drugs. Part of me wanted to feel as though I had been complimented, that I had become the kind of person who could be trusted to give sage words of wisdom to a lady so young, cynicism had not yet even begun the process of rotting her still-cherubic, halcyonic psyche. Another part of me, however, was borderline mortified It Had Come To This. Had Winona — a black-and-white photographer who takes her artistic efforts seriously — asked for my guidance regarding the long-term nurturing of the creative process or how to balance youthful free-spiritedness with the sad reality of having to make money, or, hell, even if she'd asked for any observations I might have regarding local panhandling ordinances, I would have puffed my chest out a just a little bit and thought, "Shit, growing old sucks, but, having a nice young lady seeking out your hard-earned wisdom about the really big issues of life is pretty cool." But, no, here was a bartender barely past puberty asking me whether she should drop acid.

Great.

Here's the thing (and here's the other thing: I had only a few minutes to chew my mental cud before Winona finished with the other patrons): There was a time when, if a cute drink-slinger had asked me such a thing, I would have effusively said, "Damned right! Go for it! And I'll be happy to join you!" But it has been literally almost 30 years since I last interfaced with LSD. And here I am, grandfather aged, sitting on a barstool, wondering if my advanced years, if nothing else, oughtn't compel me to at least pretend to recommend to Winona that she should seek out natural highs, like riding her mountain bike, and forego ingesting recreational chemicals. But, well, I didn't want to risk getting struck by lightning.

There was — not exactly for the first time in my life — an angel and a devil duking it out upon my shoulders.

"Well?" Winona asked, innocent eyes wide.

What I should have said was, "Do you want to risk turning out like me?" What I did instead was tell Winona about the very last time I ingested acid, in hopes she could draw her own conclusions. Which, in retrospect, was likely dodging the question, but not dodging it by much.

It was the summer of 1983. The previous winter, I had become an economic refugee of near-Bangladeshi proportions. I had been summarily laid off from my gig as a Silver City-based reporter for the *El Paso Times* during a period when unemployment rates were hovering about 15 percent in Grant County. Restaurants advertising for part-time grave-yard-shift dishwashers were getting 200 applications from people who had considerable more dishwashing experience than did I. For the only time in my life, I had to apply for food stamps. A childhood chum offered me a free place to stay in Denver, where I was certain I would surely land a high-paying writing position within hours of arriving. Such was not the case. By a long shot. Though I did land a few freelance-writing assignments, I hobbled through my first half-year in the Mile High City in such perpetual state of fiscal duress, I found myself bussing tables and selling blood plasma.

I became a serious devotee of the help-wanted ads in the *Denver Post*. One day, my potential economic salvation magically appeared: the daily paper in a place called Russell, Kansas, was looking for an editor. Kansas, I reckoned, actually bordered Colorado, so how bad could it be? Since I more than met the qualifications described in the classified ad, I placed a call to the *Russell Daily Udder* (I don't remember its true name). The publisher was surprisingly excited to hear from me. A little too excited, I remember thinking. He wanted me to come to Russell ASAP for an interview. "Uh," I told him, "I don't exactly have the money to get there." "So, you need a little gas money?" he asked. "Uh, I don't exactly have a car. I'd be coming by bus." That I was broke, carless and desperate enough to seek employment in the heart of the Great Plains apparently did not dissuade the *Daily Udder*'s publisher. Matter of fact, after outlining the salary and benefits package (which amounted to far more money than I had ever made before) and telling me I could use the company car as though it were my own and there was even a small company-owned apartment I could live in, he went ahead and offered me the job, sight unseen. The word "indentured" sprung to mind. Somewhere deep in my memory banks, a grainy "Twilight Zone" episode flickered. Desperate though I was, I told him I thought it might be a good idea for us to meet face-to-face before making any life-altering decisions. He wired me enough money for a round-trip bus ticket and, the very next night, I boarded a Greyhound bound for Russell, Kansas, the hometown of none other than Senator Bob Dole, who ran for president against Bill Clinton in 1996 on the Sacrificial Lamb ticket.

I did a fair amount of long-distance bus traveling in those pre-cheap-airfare days. Thus I knew you could tell within nanoseconds what kind of transitory mobile potpourri sociology you were about to be submerged into for the next however many hundred miles. It could go in any direction, from a bus packed with the craziest-assed Bible-thumpers imaginable sitting there handling snakes and speaking in tongues to a motley assortment of recently released prisoners looking to put as much distance as possible between them and their parole officers. This go-round, the bus contained — no shit! — an entire tribe of party-down freaks, a recreational coagulation of Rainbow Family hippies, dirtbag climber/hiker-types and Deadheads. It was an instant party involving about as much liquor as one bus could carry, an astounding quantity of weed and hash and, yes, enough in the way of blotter acid to almost make me forget that I was on my way to a job interview in Bob Dole's hometown two million miles out in the middle of an endless cornfield.

I was scheduled to fetch Russell at 4:30 a.m. The publisher of the *Daily Udder* had made reservations for me at a motel right across the street from the bus station, which greatly resembled an unpaved feed store parking lot. The plan was for him to pick me up at noon. I was the only person to disembark the Greyhound in Russell. As I made my way toward the front of the bus, the party continued unabated, and it near-bouts broke my heart on several levels that I would not be continuing eastward with my newfound chums.

For some damned bonehead reason, I had carried with me not my usual backpack, but, rather, an old leather suitcase my mom had scored for me at a yard sale. As I started down the bus steps, the suitcase got ahead of me, and I tripped over it, performing a very well-executed somersault, and landing right on my ass in the unpaved feed store parking lot/bus station. I stood up quickly, acting as though nothing had happened, regained what little composure a person can muster under those undignified circumstances, and staggered toward the motel. But out of the darkness came a voice. "John?" the voice asked. Surely an auditory hallucination, I thought, and proceeded upon my merry way while brushing dust off my pants. "Is that John from Denver?" It was once again the hallucinogenic voice from the darkness, asking me if I was, of all goddamned people, John Denver. Then: "JOHN!!! JOHN FAY-HEE?" This time, I turned around and there stood the publisher of the *Daily Udder,* who, it turned out, simply could not abide the thought of his next editor arriving in Russell, Kansas, at 4:30 a.m. without someone there to meet him. Which is very thoughtful and all, but, well, I was tripping my brains out, something, I wondered, if maybe I ought to tell him, just in case my behavior was not up to its normal polished snuff.

The publisher was so excited at my arrival, he decided this would be a perfect time to take me on a very detailed driving tour of Russell. Over the course of the next (I kid you not) 90 minutes, he showed me every square inch of the newspaper office, including the broom closets, which I must say, were among the very best broom closets I had ever laid eyes on. Impressively clean and orderly. Knowing I played tennis, he showed me Russell's two unsurfaced asphalt courts with droopy chain-link nets. He showed me his house. He showed me every school in the county. He showed me every church in the county. Then, saving the best for last, he showed me Bob Dole's boyhood home, Bob Dole's high school home, Bob Dole's mother's home and every street corner where Bob Dole ever scratched his nuts. And the whole time I'm sitting there nodding my head and saying "Wow!!!" over and over again, and inside I am screaming "AAAAHHHHH!!!!" at a million decibels, hoping against hope an asteroid will fall out of the sky and obliterate the entirety of Russell, Kansas, so I don't have to endure another single motherfucking nanosecond of this endless tour of Bob Dole's hometown out there on the Plains.

Finally, 42 torturous, excruciating years later, the publisher of the *Daily Udder* thank-godfully dropped me off at the motel, saying, "Get some sleep … we've got a big day" … and, instead of crashing, I paced the room frenetically, wondering if there wasn't maybe another Greyhound bus going through sometime very very soon that could take me anywhere but Russell, Kansas. "Leavenworth Prison? Fine, just get me outta here!" Shortly before noon, I ventured forth into the harsh midsummer sunlight of central Kansas, still tripping hideously, to wait for the publisher of the *Daily Udder* to pick me up for our "big day." As I'm waiting in front of the motel, I see a long line of massive cottonwoods, all leaning about 30 degrees eastward. I'm wondering what might cause an entire row of giant cottonwoods to all be leaning thusly. Then I notice the wind hitting me, and I notice that I too am now leaning over at about 30 degrees eastward, same as the cottonwoods. I felt roots suddenly growing down from my feet and extending deep into the Kansas topsoil. When the publisher picked me up, I was hopping from foot to foot trying to keep those roots from taking hold.

The publisher of the *Daily Udder* takes me to a Kiwanis Club meeting at, of all places, the local high school cafeteria, where our midday repast consists of high school cafeteria food — clean down to the grisly Salisbury steak and instant mashed potatoes and brown gravy and crunchy canned peas and carrots being splatted onto our trays by corpulent desultory women wearing badly stained white cafeteria employee attire who look like they have not left their stations there in the cafeteria for decades, like, if you removed their ladles from their hands, their arms would reflexively, robotically continue the ladling motion until they eventually expired.

I had no more idea then what a Kiwanis Club actually is than I do now. All I know is the guest speaker was a local high school junior who had placed 477th in the Kansas 4H oratory competition, and his subject was something like new and improved ways to slop hogs. He proceeded to deliver the entire speech (which, I'll say for the record, was well received by the people I would likely be socializing with if I decided to relocate to Russell) right then and there at the Russell, Kansas, Kiwanis Club meeting, in the Russell, Kansas, high school, over plastic trays heaped with grisly Salisbury steak and crunchy canned peas and carrots. Just as I noticed all of my little peas and carrots were starting to perform military marching maneuvers on my tray, I heard my name spoken. The publisher had just introduced me as "the next editor of the Daily Udder." I was asked to stand and say a few words. Would these people understand how easy it is to get caught up in a bit of good-natured recreational acid-dropping on a Greyhound bus? Would they understand marching peas and carrots? Would they understand how badly I awaited the arrival of the killer asteroid that would smoosh them all into oblivion? I doubted it very much. What I did not doubt was my need to get the hell out of Russell, Kansas, muy pronto.

Back at the newspaper office, the publisher handed me the keys to the company car and said he hoped I would drive it back to Denver to retrieve all my shit so I could begin my new life in Russell as soon as possible. The escape possibilities right then were as limitless as one tank of gas could carry me. Those keys were so shiny and seductive there in the harsh mid-summer Kansas sun, I felt like Gollum staring at the One Ring while standing on the lip of the volcano. At what juncture would the publisher of the Daily Udder call the cops and report his company car missing? A week? Two?

In the end, I begged off, saying I would need some time to think his generous (which it was) offer over. But I could tell by the look on the publisher's face he knew I wouldn't be coming back. It seemed like he had been down that road before. Maybe not specifically with a tripping freak, but with others who took one look at his little town, a town he obviously loved and was very proud of, and said thanks but no thanks. He deposited me at the bus station/feed store parking lot and the next morning I was back in Denver, broke as ever, wondering if I had learned any sort of salient lesson from my short-lived exodus to Russell, Kansas. On the one hand, I could easily have looked at my journey to Russell as an example of a desperate man doing nothing more than trying to survive, something that has defined our species forever and ever (at least the grown-up members of our species, which I clearly was not). Or I could have looked at my journey as a repudiation of that mind-set, as a sign from the heavens I needed to set my sights higher, that I needed to be looking not east toward the Great Plains, but west toward the Rockies, where, two months later, I found myself living in the town where I met my wife and where, when you get right down to it, I met my life. Lesson learned indeed. And a salient lesson at that.

I did not venture to Russell, Kansas, again for more than 20 years. While driving back to Virginia for a high school reunion in 2004, the Russell sign on I-70 beckoned, and I decided to eyeball what might have been. Though clearly suffering from economic malaise, it did not seem like such a bad little town. The tennis courts had been re-surfaced. I'm sure the broom closets in the *Daily Udder* office were as orderly as ever.

I do not know whether the fact that I was tripping on that first visit a lifetime ago made me miss the real Russell, or whether it made me see the town as I maybe would not have otherwise, from a perspective where my dire fiscal situation was not necessarily ignored, but was not the driving force in my decision-making process. Did the acid enhance my view or skew my view? Did it encourage me to look at Russell through the equally unfair and inaccurate lenses of a telescope, a microscope or a kaleidoscope? Either way, that marked the last time I ever dropped acid. I made no resolution; I just felt like it was time to exit that highway.

After relating that story to Winona, I could not tell whether I had talked her into trying acid or out of it. She was smiling as she left to deal with other thirsty customers. It could go one way or the other. I crossed my fingers and hoped for the best.

— MOUNTAIN GAZETTE #175

CHAPTER FOURTEEN

Little Dog

It took two years for me to be able to even think of being open to inviting/allowing/encouraging a new dog into my life. It does not make me feel good to say this — given how many millions of dogs there are in need of loving, or even tolerable, homes — but I am pretty much convinced, based upon purely subjective first-person observations, each of us will likely share time on this plane of existence with but one true cosmic-level perro, and, for me, that was a German Shepherd/Australian Shepherd mix named Cali, who succumbed in October 2008 to the vet's needle after having suffered through a series of debilitating strokes after 13 splendid years as the best friend I will ever have. Cali was a near-perfect dog. An impossible act to follow.

Gay and I had finally bought a house that had a large fenced yard, so, for the first time in decades, I found myself in a position where I could provide appropriate acreage for a dog. I spent literally six months going to various pounds looking for the right canine companion. That was rough, walking through the kennel areas, sometimes talking to individual dogs that seemed like they could maybe work, taking an occasional few out into the yard for a walk to see if the inexplicable connection took place. Gut-wrenching as it was to bypass all those pleading, long-faced dogs who wanted so bad for someone to fill out paperwork with their name on it, in no case did a requisite bond occur, until I saw a pet-of-the-week photo of Cali in the *Summit Daily News*, which 1) I still have and 2) just to add an extra dose of good vibrations to the situation, was taken by my buddy Mark Fox. One frigid February day, I went to the shelter, walked directly to Cali's prison cell, took her out for a stroll on the nearby bikepath, and, by the time we returned, the shelter staff was already calling her my dog. I picked Cali up the next day, without my wife ever having met her. That very afternoon, I took her snowshoeing sans leash up French Gulch, and both boy and dog knew something very, very special was afoot.

Last fall, Gay and I started realizing, not only did we miss having Cali in the house (understatement of monumental proportions), but also we missed having a dog in the house. We had had a couple visitors since Cali died who had brought their dogs with them, and it always felt good to once again have that canine energy within the four walls of the Case de Fayhee. I started — very tentatively, even painfully, at first — eyeballing various rescue group websites dedicated to specific large-ish, trail-appropriate breeds — Labradors, Australian Shepherds, German Shepherds and Border Collies. I had a Lab as a kid, and decided to go that generally good-natured route. I also wanted a puppy, something with a fairly clean mental slate who, after a short period of time, would look at me as daddy as much as a regular provider of kibble. I exchanged a few emails with a rescue group in Albuquerque and made arrangements online to meet a pup on my way to Colorado for Christmas. It was a bit of a chaotic environment, since the pup-in-question was being fostered by a very nice lady who already had three large, energetic dogs. Even though I did not feel anything even approximating the connection I felt instantly with Cali, that was OK, because, truth be told, I did not expect to, believing, as I said earlier, that such bonds do not happen twice in one's life. But it seemed like we had the potential to at least like and respect each other, and, I thought, that's a good enough start. On the way back from Colorado, we stopped in and picked up a 27-pound, three-month-old squirming bundle of fur that seemingly consisted of nothing more than four splaying legs and a mouth that rarely closed — the latter characteristic being an attribute, Gay was quick to point out, that gave the dog and I something in common right off the bat. She was named Casey just the day before by her foster mom. Ergo: The name did not yet register with the dog bearing that name, at least partially because the *concept* of having a name did not yet register. We could have given her a different name, but we liked "Casey" at least as much as anything else we came up with. So, "Casey" it was.

One of the reasons I waited more than two years to get another dog was I really wanted to make certain I was not looking to replace the irreplaceable. I did not want to burden a dog with having to live up to Cali's image. The analogy I used was that of poor Brian Griese playing quarterback for the Denver Broncos after John Elway retired. I even went so far as to make sure whatever dog I brought home looked nothing like Cali. Cali was long haired and jet black, while Casey is short haired and blonde.

But, no matter how hard I tried, during Casey's first days with us, I could not exorcize Cali's ghost from the premises.

(Not that I tried very hard.) I reflexively found myself talking to Casey the exact same way I talked to Cali, using the same phraseology, the same tones of voice, half-expecting, hoping, that by so doing, maybe some of Cali's spirit would descend from the heavens onto and into this new pup, that she would automatically transmogrify from four flailing legs and a mouth that rarely closed and act the same near-perfect way Cali did from the get-go and for all those years. And I found myself getting exasperated when that did not happen. I mean, how goddamned foolish — on about 40 different levels —is that? How unfair is that for a pup who does not yet even know her name?

Two weeks after bringing her home, we took Casey to the vet's for her second round of shots, as well as an overall physical. While making the appointment on the phone, we told the receptionist that Casey was about three months old and "mostly Lab." When we arrived, the vet looked at the chart, looked at Casey, looked back at the chart, looked back at Casey and said words to the effect that he thought he was going to be examining a three-month-old mostly Lab, a dog I had assumed was a blank slate who eventually would reach something like 50 or 60 pounds of stoutness running through the woods, crossing rivers and leading the way while we ski full blast down Mayflower Gulch. You know: a bonafide mountain dog.

"This dog is six to eight months old," the vet told our stunned selves. "And, if she's got a lick of Lab in her, I'll eat a stick. She looks to me like she's mainly Cocker Spaniel and Beagle. That means she's probably about as big as she's going to get." I do not remember the last time Gay and I were both as mutually shocked. I mean, 9/11 made our jaws drop, of course, but nothing like the news we received about our new dog. Fuck! Not only did I not have a stereotypical mountain dog, I had something borderline foo-foo. Near-bouts a lap dog! Double fuck!

As soon as I got home from the vet's office, I emailed the rescue group from which I had adopted Casey, informing them of my mislabeled, defective goods. They told me, if I wanted to return her, I was more than welcome to do so, no explanation necessary.

Though the very thought of taking a living, drooling, chewing creature back to a foster home made me almost sick to my stomach, every single person I related this story to told me in no uncertain terms that's exactly what I should do, what I *must* do. Everyone I talked to understood the nature of the bond between man/woman and his/her dog, and, they all said, if such a bond did not occur within a month or so, then it likely would not ever occur. And they said, if I wasn't happy with who/what my dog was, then the potential bonding was automatically whammied even more, because, as we all know, dogs are perceptive, empathic creatures. There's no way Casey was going to take a leap (assuming she possessed the inclination, which is not an assumption that ought to be taken for granted) if she thought there was any chance of me backing out on the deal somewhere down the road. Sure, people said, a perfectly acceptable long-term relationship might very well evolve, but the kind of attachment that de-fined — sigh! — my cosmic link with Cali would have been obvious by now. But, hey, retorted I, I am of the belief such things don't happen twice in a train-wreck life like mine. "If you believe that," said one chum, "then that's the way it assur-edly will be." Basically then: It is almost impossible for something to happen I believe deep down *cannot* happen — which is not only a problem, but perhaps one of insurmountable proportions.

Let me expound upon this human/dog link notion. For those many of you who know what I'm talking about, my likely clumsy attempt to articulate it is unnecessary. Since it is the only such situation I have ever experienced, I have no choice but to frame this in terms of M. John and Cali. Shortly after adopting her, Cali and I aggressively (and sometimes frustratingly) went together through official dog/human training classes. And, while there were often miscommunications regarding the ambiguous complexities of the various commands, it was apparent from the very first second we ever went out into the woods together Cali very badly wanted to know what I wanted of her. We may have had a few disagreements as to the best ways to go about communicating those desires (she taught me some things and I taught her others), but there was never any doubt we would not only muddle our way through such sometimes-complex inter-species dialogue, but, eventually, we would do so in a way that did not even require verbal articulation. I could tell from her slightest behavioral nuance what Cali wanted or needed. And I could give her commands (I hate how that sounds), by the subtlest movement of my fingers and, often, by merely thinking the right thought. No matter our location, no matter our activity, no matter what else was going on around us, Cali's biggest concern on the face of the planet was knowing where I was and what I wanted. And vice-versa. And she knew, when I gave her commands, I was not just bossing her around for the pure fuck of it, but, rather, I was doing my level best to protect her and look after her health, well-being and happiness.

Which I was.

It did not take long to learn that such was not the case with Casey. Once we came to understand she was twice as old as we had thought, we simultaneously came to understand she must have come to us with far more psychic baggage than we had envisioned. There was no clean slate to work with. The rescue people we got Casey from had somehow obtained her from death row at the Artesia, New Mexico, animal Auschwitz. How that happened, and what her life was before she arrived at her foster home (several foster homes, actually) in Albuquerque, I cannot say. But there was no doubt her short life had had numerous iterations, some of which, judging from her sometimes-cowering, sometimes-obstinate, sometimes-aloof disposition, were probably not pleasant. Therefore, it seems highly unlikely that, even after a month in my house, she looks at me as anything save the next bipedal asshole who is letting her bunk down for a short period of time before she has to move on yet again to god-knows-where. Cali had only one home before she came to us, and, even though those people were forced to give her up, we knew she had a pretty stable, loving pre-Fayhee life. She never forgot her first owners dumped her ass at the pound, and, thus, she was extremely appreciative of her new life with me. Casey's road was bumpier, and, however that bumpy road affected her, she ought not be faulted.

I decided to try to look at Casey as though I had never known Cali, to become a blank slate myself. So, in addition to trying to put her personality into a broader context that includes what likely was an inconceivably shitty first few months, I found myself trying to focus on her good traits: She gets along great with my cat, who, truth be told, was not all that happy to see a rambunctious puppy suddenly tres-passing on turf that, since Cali's passing, had been hers and hers alone. Casey loves playing with other dogs at the dog park. She shits only in the least-visited corner of the back yard and has the easiest-to-clean-up shit I have ever shoveled, and I have shoveled some serious quantities of shit in my time. She really likes going out into the woods and is up for ad-venture. She is extremely nimble, negotiating rock faces like a mountain goat. She has been very good about not chewing up things like expensive hiking boots. And she's cute, sweet and pretty easily amused.

But she cries in fear when she dreams. And she doesn't wag her tail very much. And she cowers when talked to stern-ly after digging yet another hole in my garden. And she still doesn't know her name, or, if she does, she doesn't let on. And she still doesn't pay any attention to me when I talk to her on the trail. And I don't know at this point if I will ever be able to let her off leash in the woods, something that is a non-negotiable component of a relationship between yours truly and any cur traveling with me down the path of life. I have heard many stories from people whose dogs are inclined to run off time and time again, and that's just not an acceptable option — though I understand such an inclination can be at least partially mitigated by proper training. But "partially" don't cut it.

As these conflicting, stomach-wrenching thoughts swirl around in a brain that is overwhelmed by the implications of my newfound conundrum, Casey lies sleeping on the floor behind me. She just had another nightmare, but, after I lied down beside her and held her close and whispered her name softly, she calmed down a bit, and, even as she dozes, her tale wags just a little. Is her biggest sin that she's not Cali, or that she's not what I pictured? Either way, those are both sins so easily pardonable they ought not even be considered minor transgressions. Whatever sin there is undoubtedly lies not with Casey, but with me, a man whose ego effects the way he looks down at a little dog who needs more than anything to be loved and considered special, if not perfect.

I do not know what I will do with Casey, what choice I will make with her life, and mine. I have asked Cali to visit me in my dreams to give me some guidance, but, so far, she has not. At this point, my main motive for keeping Casey is how horrible I would feel if I took her back. I cringe at the thought of what her facial expression might be: Let down again. (Or: Hallelujah!)

Maybe if we both try really, really hard, we could make this relationship work out just fine, even if it is not magical. Then again, perhaps the process of working through our mutual issues would in and of itself make it magical. Eventually. One of the things Cali liked most about me was I did my best to let her be her. Of course, it had to be within the context and framework of me and my life, which was easy enough. If I keep Casey, I owe it as much to her as I ever did to Cali to let her be her. It's the context and framework of my life part that concerns me.

By the time this tale sees ink, I will have made a decision. I have to, because, at this juncture, Casey keeps looking at me. And, in her eyes, I can tell she's asking: "What then will your choice be?"

And I look back at her and ask: "What then will YOUR choice be, Little Dog."

ADDENDUM: *More than a year later, Casey still lies at my feet as I write. She's grown to 50 pounds. We hike together almost every day, no leash necessary. And she hasn't had a nightmare in a very long time. Turns out, she is special.*

— MOUNTAIN GAZETTE #176

CHAPTER FIFTEEN

Scar Tissue

"Your hand will grow bigger and your finger will grow bigger, but your scar will always stay the same size."
— Eddie (Jon Foster) to
Ruth (Elle Fanning) in
The Door in the Floor

From the sidelines, I can see where some folks might have considered it a somewhat unusual (if not blatantly tasteless) spontaneous-combustion-type en masse subject for discourse among a wide-ranging demographic amalgam of patrons — some of whom were regulars, some of whom were just passing through, some of whom had been drinking for hours, some of whom had just ordered their first frothy mug of suds — that long-ago blustery winter night at the Dillon Dam Brewery.

It began by way of a young dirtbag snowboarder-type half-embarrassedly, half-triumphantly crutching his way into the establishment, people sliding barstools to accommodate his perambulatory difficulties, someone soon asking whassup, the young man half-muttering, half-proclaiming the dreaded, but-weirdly-honored-in-the-High-Country syllables, "ACL su-

rgery," and a longer-of-tooth lady a few seats down slurring/
growling the predictable, "Well, yer damned lucky surgical
knowledge has improved," followed by the equally predictable pulling up of the pants leg, revealing the results of what
ACL surgery looked like 30 years ago, like someone had operated on her hurt knee with a herd of rabid wolverines. Then a
bearded geezer at a nearby table raising a hand with a 20-per-
cent digit deficit rate and chiming in with a similar back-in-
the-day tale about the failed attempt to sew his pinky back on
after a negative interface with a non-OSHA-certified band saw.
"I think the doctor was as drunk as I was," the gent rasped. "It
seemed to me like he was trying to sew the damned thing on
upside-down. If he succeeded, I would have had four fingers
that curled inward, toward my palm like they're supposed to,
and my pinky curling upward. Guess that would have made
for an interesting party trick. In the end, he just gave up,
told me the pinky was too far gone and tried to throw it in a
trashcan. He missed and there sat my poor little finger, lying
bloody on the floor, looking very alone and forlorn."

And so it commenced, as bar confabs often do (and often don't). It was not long before the two-dozen or so folks
there gathered, in unified, borderline-soul-baring, pass-the-
story-stick-type fashion, embarked upon a verbal journey
centered — sometimes loosely, sometimes strictly — upon
the theme of scars, with at least as much emphasis placed
upon the stories about the scars as upon the scars themselves.
Kind of like ski-jumping, with points being awarded for both
distance and style.

Though clear recollection of most of the subsequently
told scar stories escapes me, there were of course some that
activated the long-term memory nodules. Among those,

there was a very large and gruff stranger of probably 60, who, despite his advancing age, could best be described as someone you would not under any circumstances fuck with. He wore a Vietnam Vet baseball cap, which, uncomfortable as this is to write, often is cause for automatically giving a person some eccentricity leeway. By the time this man, who was clearly bemused by the various tales being related about the kayaking mishap and the emergency appendectomy surgery while on a wine tour of France, cleared his throat, everyone automatically assumed he would then relate the tale about the vicious scar circumnavigating his entire goddamned throat and neck, as though he had once been hanged until not quite dead or maybe tortured with a cable. Instead, he spoke poetically about the time he was fishing up in Idaho on some magical mountain day and it was so quiet and peaceful and he'd been trying for hours to land this one trout and how he was becoming more and more exasperated and how he got sloppy on a cast and actually managed to catch a dry fly on his own eyelid and about how he had to hike out to the trailhead and drive into town with a dry fly dangling directly in front of his pupil like one of those weird little bacteria floaters, except with a sharp hook attached, and about how close he had come to losing a viewpod questing for trout. He asked everyone at the bar to come over and look closely at the scarcely visible remains of the incident, all the while everyone's peripheral-visioning their way down to the awful scar all the way around his neck, which, it's my guess, is something the Vietnam Vet knew would happen. No one asked him about it.

And then, after harrowing tales involving an entire vat of French fry grease being accidentally spilled onto a young lady's forearm, resulting in a series of disfiguring skin grafts, and a machete wound suffered in the deepest depths of the Darien Gap three day's hike from the nearest clinic and the entire top of a guy's scalp being sheared off like something from a Larry McMurtry novel when he was thrown through a plate-glass window in a bar after an altercation centered around a lost game of pool and a large bet the man could not pay, it was my turn to ask for the story stick. After dropping my pants and bending over to expose the back of my right thigh, I told the story of climbing a tree behind the neighbor's house across the street from ours when I was 12 years old and living near the banks of the Saranac River in New York State's Adirondack Mountains.

It was a fine summer day, and I was feeling my 12-year-old oats in a way I could not have supposed possible a few months earlier. For, you see, the previous winter, my erstwhile run-amok self had suffered its first serious physiological setback. I had to be tobogganed off the slopes of Bear Mountain by the ski patrol after having pushed a surely modest schussing envelope a bit too far. At that time, I subscribed to the "turns-are-for-pussies" philosophy of downhill skiing (read: I had neither the skill nor the training to turn, and I masked my ignorance with a gung-ho attitude that had but one foreordained outcome), and that philosophy-made-manifest ultimately came with a price, even for a stupid fourth-grader. I tore the shit out of my left knee trying to impress my love interest (boy, was she ever impressed!) and spent almost six months in a full-leg cast. Though my leg was still skinny from atrophy, by mid-summer, I was finally able to move, and, more importantly, to once again climb. In my youth, I was half-monkey, fearlessly ascending quarry walls, water towers, roofs and, in this case, trees. I absolutely *loved* climbing trees.

I was not the only kid up in the tree when it happened. Verily, there was a slew of jabbering pre-pubescents hanging out upon the rickety planks of a makeshift treehouse probably 15 (OK, 10) feet up. A flimsy home-made rope ladder connected treehouse to terra firma, a ladder only capable of handling one kid at a time. When someone suggested maybe heading over to the nearby Saranac for a swim, the notion of an orderly descent was not much in evidence. I, as always, being the most impatient person in the group, opted to by-pass the ladder congestion and move downward via a series of thin branches. "Race ya," I said, confidently.

Even now, 43 years later, the sound of branches breaking sets me on edge. There was the snap, then my first interaction with time moving at simultaneously variable speeds — slow motion (slow enough that it seemed like I was floating my way earthward) overlapped with blurring rapidity (so rapid, it seemed as though space had folded me instantaneously to my bleak destination), then the instinctive peeling of my right leg off a recently hatcheted stump maybe three inches in diameter and two feet high. I heard the sound of skin ripping as I pulled my leg off the pointed top of that little stump. Just before a tsunami of red overtook my world, I looked down and saw a bisected hamstring flapping and a large section of my exposed femur. As shock mercifully asserted itself, I looked back at that little stump and saw a huge hunk of my flesh still attached, twitching.

It was a tense moment.

I learned an interesting lesson about motherhood that day. My mom, gone now for almost a quarter-century, had always encouraged me to be adventurous, wild, actually, and, to her credit, once the dust settled on this torn-open-leg situation, she did not waver in that encouragement. She was over at our house barbecuing. Though in my head I remember hearing screams, apparently none came from me. Yet, somehow, maternal Def-Con-1 was activated and, simply via mother/child cosmic connection, she knew something was sorely amiss with her first-born and came running as fast as her little legs could carry her to my side, gracefully arriving with a spatula in one hand and an admirably unspilled martini in the other. Because my mom was, well, uh, slightly unpredictable, we had a tenuous, often painful, relationship clear up until the moment she passed, an unfortunate reality that, naturally, will haunt me for the rest of my days. But never in my life, before or since, was I so glad to have someone at my side as I lay there, my life force oozing away into the grass. Even though I knew she was freaking out inside, my mom, child of the Luftwaffe's unrelenting attack on her native London, went into instant survival mode. She remained calm, made sure my sister was tended to, field-dressed my gaping wound with towels and organized transport to the hospital. Ever the fiscal pragmatist, she directed the driver, a neighbor, to take us to the Plattsburgh Air Force Base hospital, where we would receive free treatment, rather than to the municipal hospital, which was closer, but which would cost money. On the way, I, of course, asked the inevitable question, one that had more immediate palpability than it does for many kids at that age, as my stepfather, my sister's dad, had drowned three mere years prior: "Am I going to die?" "No, you're not going to die," my mom responded with a smile that was not only reassuring, but reassured. "You've still got lots of trees left to climb."

And then things went dark.

The surgery lasted almost 10 hours. It was nip-and-tuck regarding whether they would be able to save my leg. I must have semi-consciously overheard that part of the discussion among the doctors, because I awoke at one point and groggily reached down to see if my leg was still attached, which pissed the surgeon off. He yelled at me to hold still and told the anesthesiologist to re-knock my ass out. In the end, I got more than 200 stitches — a lot when you're talking about a little 12-year-old leg, which had to be entirely rebuilt from the bone clear out to the skin. Almost half of my blood seeped away between the sawed-off stump and the operating table. I spent the rest of the summer on my back. It was many years before the requisite Deep Thoughts visited me, before I learned enough about anatomy to realize how close that little hatcheted-off stump came to my femoral artery, how, if my downward course was altered by even a few inches, I would have taken that stump directly to my lower spine.

Whenever I first visit a body mechanic — massage therapist, physical therapist, acupuncturist, chiropractor, witch doctor, voodoo practitioner —which I've been doing a lot these days, it will not be long before I am asked about the scar on the back of my right leg. I can feel their reluctance to even touch it, just in case its root cause might be contagious.

I recently started receiving treatment from a new chiropractor, because, basically, I am, at age 55, a flat-out physiological mess. I have a bad left heel, a lingering right ankle sprain, a totally trashed right Achilles tendon, a bulging L4/L5 disc, tendonitis in my left elbow, arthritis in my right index finger and a right shoulder that, even after two surgeries, still operates at about 50-percent capability. An orthopedist once told me, after hearing my corporeal curriculum vitae — thousands of miles of long-distance backpacking, two decades of competitive tennis and years of martial arts training — I could not have intentionally mapped out a more negatively impactful trinity of hobbies had I premeditatedly tried. Ergo: I have long assumed my lifestyle choices are simply catching with me and I will likely limp my way through what's left of my years, surviving off of old memories instead of hobbling my decrepit way toward new ones.

This chiropractor, after torquing my many maladies, the way chiropractors do, asked about one I had not mentioned. "What's the story with this big scar on the back of your right leg?" So, as I have done so many times in my life, I told him about the fall and the exposed femur and the 200 stitches. I added that it hadn't bothered me since the last of those stitches were removed all those years ago. He performed some neurological tests and hemmed and hawed and said, finally, "I think almost every injury issue you're experiencing right now emanates from that big scar. I think your body, your mind and your spirit have never recovered from that injury. It has affected the way you have moved through life ever since."

Great.

A few weeks after these words first hit print, it was my mom's birthday, her 75th, had she lived. It is a day, try though I might (and I don't try very hard), which invariably lends itself to ponderment of the internal-combustion/scrutinization variety. It is an annual Heavy Day in the Fayhee psyche. But soon after the chiropractor uttered his scar-based observations, it dawned on me out of the blue my mom would have loved being there for the bar-scar story scene at the Dillon Dam Brewery that long-ago blustery winter night. She surely would have told the story (of course) about her Caesariansection scar, which she received because of the desire of her eldest son to ingress this world feet first.

And I think she would have appreciated my own scar story, the one about how she arrived to save the day with an unspilled martini in hand. Her appreciation would have made my evening, to the point that, maybe, *maybe*, it would have helped some of that old scar tissue on the back of my right thigh to finally begin the process of breaking up and dissipating for good.

You know, maybe it's beneficial scars always stay the same size. They remind us of the roads we've traveled.

Ah, the wisdom that falls from the rafters of bars like little boys sometimes fall from trees ...

— MOUNTAIN GAZETTE #179

CHAPTER SIXTEEN

Big Bob and the Beer Math Saga

How happy is the blameless vestal's lot!
The world forgetting, by the world forgot.
Eternal sunshine of the spotless mind!
Each pray'r accepted, and each wish resign'd.
— Alexander Pope, "Eloisa and Abelard"

It all began innocuously enough on a hot summer day (at least as hot as they get in Summit County, Colorado). I found myself a tad parched after a nice, long hike up the Lenawee Trail, so I stopped in the Dillon Dam Brewery for numerous well-deserved recuperative beverages. I ordered up my usual pint of Dam Straight Lager, and the bartender, Natt Ross (1) asked when I was going to pony up for a genuine personalized mug, which, come to find out, cost something like $35. The benefit of doing so, I learned, was, from then on, I would receive 20 ounces of beer for the same price as a pint. Being a liberal arts-type person, I scrunched up my forehead and tried mightily, and unsuccessfully, to suss out just how many beers it would take before the $35 investment would be recouped. I jotted down some amateur numeric notations upon the backside of an at-hand coaster, tried utilizing fingers and toes, a la Jethro on *The Beverly Hillbillies*, and — sigh — yet again, regretted my pathological lack of attentiveness in high school algebra, or trigonometry, or whatever branch of mathematics it is that, in the right hands, is capable of solving such suds-based conundrums.

So, I threw in the towel and asked Natt, assuming, of course, a highly lubricated business operation such as the Dam Brewery would include such skinny in its employee-training program. Alas, I was greeted with nothing save a perplexed shrugging of the shoulders and an obvious statement: "M. John, I think we can all safely conclude, whatever the exact number is, you will soon come to exceed it."

Thus began the Beer Math saga.

Also at the bar that day was a tribe of senior citizens I am proud to call chums, and I believe the vice is versa. Though their ranks have thinned over the years, via an unfortunate combination of relocation and attrition, to this day, they are known as the Dillon Dam Brewery Old Farts Club, a non-organization of aging bro-brahs that meets at the Dam pretty much every day for happy-hour libations and shit-shooting. Unlike the stereotypical variations on the theme of regular cadres of senior citizens who hold down the fort at most small-town bars, this is a group of astounding ladies and gents (mostly gents) who, with one or two exceptions, serve as a composite of how I hope I am when I'm in my 60s, 70s and even 80s. These folks are all educated and erudite; they are all well traveled; they had interesting careers; they are jovial; they are great storytellers; and, at ages when most people are shuffling around shuffleboard courts in Florida, they are still hanging their hats in the High Country, skiing, hiking and biking at every opportunity.

It should come as no surprise that several sets of Old Fart ears perked up when my mug-ROI interrogative was posed. For the next hour or so, a gaggle of retired physicists, engineers, administrators, educators and whatnot, most of whom were at least partially in their cups, pulled out felt-tipped pens, grabbed proximate cocktail napkins and began scribbling, calculating and arguing. Now, I may not be smart enough to ascertain how many beers it would take me to re-coup my $35 mug cost, but I am smart enough to recognize a potential *Mountain Gazette* story when it slaps me upside the head. By the time happy hour was winding down (the witch-ing hour, as it were, for most of the Old Farts), I had in my possession more than a dozen cocktail napkins adorned with a vast array of Beer Math calculations, all of which were com-pletely different from each other. No two Old Farts drew the same conclusion, though all were equally vehement about the accuracy of their computations. It was only after I had gathered those cocktail napkins (all of which I still possess and likely always will) that someone thought to ask the ob-vious: "Hey, were we talking about regular prices or happy hour prices?"

The *Mountain Gazette* art director scanned in a handful of those cocktail napkins, I jotted down a couple silly obser-vations and we ran a half-page story, titled "High Country Beer Math," on the whole experience in issue #82. And that was that. Or so we thought ...

About 16 months later, out of the blue, we got a Beer Math Letter to the Editor (in MG #93), from Inmate #106669 at the Buena Vista (Colo.) Correctional Facility, who, while serving a 12-year sentence for, if memory serves, some sort of contra-legal fiscal liberation, had somehow received a copy of MG #82 and, since he worked in the slammer as a teacher of GED-level math to fellow prisoners, opted to take advantage of the real-life-lesson opportunities the Beer Math story presented. He asked his class to try to solve the problem. I don't know which was more sobering, that a *Mountain Gazette* story bearing my byline was being used in a prison GED class or the fact that this did not mark the first time MG had been on the receiving end of a submission from an incarcerated felon. (2) In addition to Inmate #106669 asking in his Letter to the Editor for a free subscription to MG, he took the opportunity to perform a Beer Math calculation of his own. His calculation essentially raised the boisterously stated algebraic ire of one Big Bob Kimble, a retired mechanical engineer of international repute, who wielded with great pride a well-honed, high-decibeled Southern drawl that would make even 10th-generation residents of the Mississippi Delta recoil in abject linguistic horror.

Big Bob responded to Inmate 106669's throwing down of the mathematical gauntlet by writing a long Letter to the Editor of his own (which appeared in MG #95). His letter, which included a series of very-impressive-looking calculations that filled an entire piece of graph paper, was addressed not to me, and it was not to the *Mountain Gazette* per se. Rather, it was addressed directly, personally, to Inmate #106669. And his letter essentially spat upon Inmate #106669's math skills. We received a good-natured response from Inmate #106669 stating, when he was released, he planned to visit the Dam Brewery to set things aright vis-à-vis this Beer Math contretemps.

And here we must exit the basic narrative to interface

with a long, but very germane, tangent.

Also in issue #95, right exactly adjacent to Big Bob's graph-paper retort of Inmate #106669's Beer Math calculations, we printed a 4,500-word Letter to the Editor from, yes, Inmate #106669 — which, for months to follow, generated many indignant response letters, mostly of the aghast "I-can't-believe-even-immature-assholes-such-as-yourselves-would-print-such-a-thing" variety — all of which showed more than anything we have printed before or since that people like me ought not be allowed to run a magazine without very direct adult supervision. In his 4,500-word letter, Inmate #106669 proceeded to share with us a group curriculum vitae for he and the rest of his prison posse, complete with a photo of five hombres who, under no circumstances I can even wildly envision, would you, or anyone you have ever known, mess with. The CV was all the more perplexing because, well, it was actually somewhat kinda marginally legit, as it was a component of the required pre-parole re-education program within the prison walls, part of which directed prisoners to send out actual resumes and applications-for-employment to real potential employers.

This group CV was soliciting employment as either bar bouncers/doormen or collection agents. It contained stunning details of each of the five people — including Inmate #106669 — and those details were, shall we say, captivating, in an obviously premeditatedly sociopathic sort of way. In summation, the group CV stated, via the pages of the magazine I then both owned and edited, to potential employers — including the *Mountain Gazette* and the Dillon Dam Brewery — if there's anyone you're having trouble collecting money from, hire us, and we *guarantee* they will pay up. The reason they will "pay up," the letter/CV further stated, was, according to Inmate #106669, "there are very few people who can beat any single one of us. There is no one who can beat all five of us." (3) Ha ha and all. But, not exactly lost in all of these gory details of felonious violence and such, but playing a definite backseat at the time the 4,500-word CV Letter to the Editor was written, were those seemingly innocuous five syllables: pre-release program. Yes, we learned in his rambling Letter to the Editor that Inmate #106669 and his posse were all soon to be set free as the wind.

At that time, the concept of Inmate #106669 venturing forth to the Dam to hobnob Beer Math skinny was still little more than an abstraction, but in subsequent communiqués over the next few months, I learned it was an abstraction with a very non-abstract expiration date, which was essentially looming. Until, finally, that date was translated to "I'll be at the Dam Brewery in two weeks at 3 p.m. Please make sure all the Old Farts are there 'cause I want to talk some serious mathematics."

Oh boy ...

So, there we were, at a point where I had to break the news not only to Big Bob and his Old Fart ilk, but also, in fairness and as something of a warning, to the management staff of the Dam, which included at the top of the heap the owner, George Blincoe. Now, George is one of my all-time-favorite people, but he is not a person who would think having a recently discharged ex-con coming to his establishment was in perfect sync with the "target demographics" component of his business plan. "George, I've got some GREAT news," I said, unable to look him squarely in the eye as those words were passing my lips. "You remember all the Beer Math stuff in *Mountain Gazette*? Well, I'm happy to report the con who played a large role in all that is coming to the Dam, not only to imbibe, but in his words, to get shit-faced! It'll be wonderful!" George did not exactly jump up and down with enthusiasm. Actually, I believe he had a bit of difficulty spitting out a nervous, disjointed, wide-eyed "uhhh … OK."

I am, embarrassing as this is to admit, an Investigation Discovery junkie and am by extension addicted to the various police/crime shows dominating that TV channel. Many of those shows have focused on people befriending cons and ex-cons, and I think it's accurate to say the overriding theme of those shows can be distilled into: whatever you do, you ought to avoid, under any and all circumstances, including but not limited to leaving the country sans possessions and moving to a mud hut in Burkina Faso, interacting with long-incarcerated felons. This concern was at least partially mollified by the fact Inmate #106669 had sent MG yet another well-worded Letter to the Editor, this one admitting to his crimes, apologizing to society for those crimes and promising with one hand on his hand on his heart and the other on a Bible to change his ways. It seemed sincere. That his 12-year stint in the BV Correctional Facility was not his first brush with the prison system mitigated my reaction to those allegedly heartfelt words somewhat. That he had a significant other and two young kids waiting for him re-un-mitigated them again. Besides, being a card-carrying (at least conceptual) pansy-assed pinko and all, I felt partially compelled to extend a friendly hand to someone who, when push came to shove, I was very interested in meeting.

"How will I know you?" I asked Inmate #106669 in an email. "Oh, you'll definitely know us," was the response. That the email included the word "us" made me gulp even more.

So, I arrived at the agreed-upon time, already having downed a few brews to settle my nerves. Over the course of the next two hours and 15 minutes, whenever the front door so much as wiggled in the wind, I leaned forward and seriously scrutinized whoever was entering. When Inmate #106669 finally arrived, I was reminded of the time my photographer buddy Mark Fox and I scheduled a newspaper interview with the Bud Light Girls, who were likewise tardy. Every time any young nymphets entered the interview venue — Eric's Underworld in Breckenridge (RIP) — Mark and I wondered if they might be the Bud Light Girls. When the Bud Light Girls finally arrived, we laughed at the thought we could have confused anyone else for them. Ditto when Inmate #106669 ingressed the Dam Brewery, with another gentlemen, who, turns out, was Inmate #106669's long-time cellmate (not one of the aforementioned posse members), a man who had been released a few months prior after having served seven years for beating up two cops. Also in tow was the spouse of Inmate #106669's ex-cellmate, a very pretty and personable lady.

Inmate #106669 was right as rain insofar as, when this threesome arrived, there was no disputing who they were. It was not so much appearance or action as it was simple bearing. Inmate #106669 and his cellmate would have been intimidating had they been life-long Hare Krishnas, which they assuredly were not. The vibe that preceded them and surrounded them and followed them like a dark ominous karmic wake was the very denotation of "Fuck with us at your own mortal and moronic peril."

No matter how tough you might think you are, you are a limp-dicked pussy compared to long-term-maximum-security-incarcerated ex-cons. Nothing compares to people who have spent significant percentages of their adult lives in tight quarters behind high walls containing not only the meanest, but the least-conscionable members of society.

My wife (who, as a casual aside, was *real* happy to hear that I was going over to the Dam Brewery to drink with an ex-con) and I once stopped for a couple beers at the Green Parrot in Buena Vista and found ourselves accidentally sitting at the bar next to a man who had been released from prison in Cañon City three hours prior. This guy was a pencil-necked geek who had been convicted of something like embezzling bingo money from his church. And, let me tell you, this was a man whose vibe was flat-out fearsome.

Many years ago, while visiting a particularly seedy watering hole in Reno, I ended up next to a guy who had just, the very week before, been released after serving 20 years for second-degree murder, a crime he gleefully admitted he had committed. (He stabbed to death a man he said had been treating his mother disrespectfully and, therefore, deserved to have his throat cut.) This guy was like four-foot-nine and I cannot think of the circumstances under which I would have physically engaged him. When he suggested it might be a good idea for me to purchase him a beer, I bought him two.

Neither inmate #106669 nor his ex-cellmate were pencil-necked geeks, nor were they four-foot-nine. They were both more than six-feet-tall, maybe 190, and flat-out cut.

We introduced ourselves, and I took Inmate #106669 over to meet, first, the Dam Brewery's very nervous management team, and then I introduced Inmate #106669 to the Old Farts. Inmate #106669 and the Old Farts hobnobbed good-naturedly about Beer Math for a while, but, since my ex-con buddies had arrived so late, it was soon time for the Old Farts to pay their tabs and move along, unscathed, much to my relief. Big Bob told me a few weeks later how much he enjoyed his levitous chat with Inmate #106669. The brewmaster of the Dam Brewery, the late and sorely missed Matt Luhr, had told the bartender he would pick up the tab for Inmate #106669, his cellmate and his cellmate's spouse, something I really wish Matt had run by me before the fact. Because of Matt's well-meaning, though misguided, generosity, my new friends opted to imbibe at what I would call an injudicious rate, and, believe me, my standards are not high in that regard. Over the course of the next few hours, we all got pretty hammered, especially the cellmate, whose demeanor, sad to report, started getting a bit surly and argumentative. Several of my attempts at sarcastic levity were not received as I had intended them. There were a couple of snarly "What do you mean by *that*?" retorts to my good-natured attempts to get through the evening without getting the shit kicked out of me.

About 9, Matt Luhr paid the tab and bade everyone a fond good night. I, too, said it was time for me to head home to Frisco, a parting of the ways that was somewhat awkward because I got the feeling Inmate #106669 was half-expecting an invite to bunk down at the Casa de Fayhee, an invite my wife had preemptively, and unambiguously, told me earlier that day damned well absolutely BETTER NOT be extended.

Though there had been some justified nervous tension, the M. John/ex-con/Old Farts confab went off without a hitch. The Dam Brewery was not destroyed, no patrons were pummeled, no women raped. Whew!

Then, the next morning, I got a voice mail from Inmate

#106669. "Man, I am *so* sorry for what happened. My cell-mate just got pissed. I don't know what to say."

The message ended without Inmate #106669 filling in any of the pertinent details, which made me think he was just joking. Still, I placed a call to the Dam Brewery and, much to my infinite chagrin, I learned, after I left, the cellmate had continued drinking and got up to leave without paying for his last beverages. When the bartender brought this to his attention, the cellmate said his tab was taken care of by Matt Luhr. The bartender said Matt had paid for everyone's beverages clear up till the point when Matt left. After that, the deal was off. The cellmate did not respond well to this and "caused a bit of a ruckus." The police were eventually summoned. And I had a series of red-faced apologies to make.

Several weeks later, I got a call from Inmate #106669. He told me his cellmate was dead. The cellmate and his wife had rented a recreational vehicle for their first vacation in many years. The cellmate could not contain his enthusiasm, so, the night before they were scheduled to depart, he went out into the RV, parked in their driveway, to spend the night. The wife woke up at 3 a.m. to find the RV totally engulfed in flames.

Inmate #106669 also brought me up to date on the status of the four other members of his prison posse, the folks he represented in that humorous, though foreboding, 4,500-word curriculum vitae Letter to the Editor *Mountain Gazette* had published. One had been murdered in prison. Another murdered the murderer and thus will spend the rest of his life behind bars. One other, after his release from the slammer, moved to Mexico, where, I believe, he is not necessarily living a totally above-board life. I don't remember what happened to the other guy, but I don't think it was anything good.

The Beer Math saga was fast losing its silly humor factor. Man, it's mind-boggling to see where shit that on the surface takes anodyne form can one day lead. The world is interlaced with trap doors descending into dark corridors.

Inmate #106669 and I kept in contact for a couple years. He was back with his family and seemed to be doing fine. He tried to talk me into going to Burning Man with him, but, since such crowd-infested events are not exactly my cup of tea, I begged off. He said he was going anyway and would like to pen a *Gazette* piece on the experience. Since I had long been enamored of Inmate #106669's potential as a writer, I hooked him up with a photographer I knew was also going to Burning Man, but nothing ever came of the assignment.

After a while, Inmate #106669 and I lost touch. I felt badly about that, but, as much as I truly liked Inmate #106669, I simply could not bring myself to fully extend a comfortable hand of true amigo-ship. Perhaps my hesitance stemmed from once having helped an ex-con, with near-disastrous results. A kid from my home county in Virginia, who I did not know well, had entered a local bank brandishing a rifle. The kid lived right up the street. Everyone who worked at the bank had known him his entire life. When he walked in, a teller recognized him and apparently said words to the effect of, "Hey, [Bill], whatcha doin' with the rifle? Goin' huntin'?" At which time, [Bill] pointed the rifle toward the ceiling, let go with several rounds, and demanded money from the very surprised staff. He was arrested less than an hour later, in his living room, gleefully making his way through a stack of bills amounting to about $2,000. He was apparently stunned he had been apprehended. (Unlike Inmate #106669, [Bill] was not a bright unit.)

While in college, I spent a summer back in Virginia and, as I was preparing to return to New Mexico for the start of the fall semester, this kid, who had served a couple years as a result of his ill-planned robbery, asked if he could accompany me, to try to start life anew in the great Southwest. My inner liberal said, "Sure." And accompany me to Silver City he did. It was a fucking nightmare. He smacked the shit out of one of my roommates, had trouble understanding the word "No!" when uttered by several of my lady friends and, I learned later, was probably involved in a rash of residential burglaries, with the goods being stored without my knowledge in my apartment, which I guess made me an unwitting accessory. On what turned out to be an emblematic final foray together up Boston Hill before he left to hitchhike penniless back to the Old Dominion the next day, we came face-to-face with an agitated rattler, and [Bill] reacted by losing his balance and landing, first, in a large prickly-pear and then in a large cholla. He had spines embedded from chin to shin.

I generally do not learn lessons well, but that experience stuck with me. Thing is, Inmate #106669 was not asking for any sort of help from me that I could see. He just seemed to want to be my friend. And yet I balked without having the balls to let him know I was balking.

A couple summers ago, B. Frank and I were traveling around the Four Corners area doing some readings. The first one kicked off at Maria's Bookstore in Durango. I arrived early the day of the reading and was killing time in Carver's catching up on correspondences. Stunningly, right then, I got an email from none other than Inmate #106669, who was, even more stunningly, living in Durango. His previous year had been a continuous tale of woe. He had $90,000 worth of uninsured construction equipment and tools stolen. His young son had accidentally burned his house to the ground. And he had received four DUIs (!!!) in two days (!!!) and had consequently spent the previous year in the county jail. Yikes!

Right next to my laptop was a copy of the *Durango Herald* with a story about our imminent reading at Maria's prominently displayed on the front page. Not surprisingly, Inmate #106669 showed up at the reading, and he joined us when we went across the street to the El Rancho for a bit of post-event fun and frolic. Because of the size of the group, I did not have the chance to talk to him much, and he seemed a bit disappointed. He asked me to join him for breakfast, but B. Frank and I were headed toward our next stop in Silverton that very night. The opposite direction, which, sad to say, is right where I felt like heading.

When I got back home a couple weeks later, there was a phone message from Inmate #106669. I never returned it. Am I an asshole? I am an asshole. God, I hate being an asshole.

Because I now live 600 miles away, I don't get to visit the Dillon Dam Brewery much anymore. Last fall, I was in Summit County, so I stopped in for few mugs of Lager (my $35 mug, #151, is still at hand … it has paid for itself many times over). At the bar were several members of the Old Farts' Club, including Big Bob. He wasn't looking so good. Seemed like his boisterous life force had dissipated.

"You'll never guess who I saw in Durango recently," I said.

"Who?"

"Inmate #106669."

He smiled wanly and we reminisced about the whole Beer Math saga.

When I left, I had a feeling it would be the last time I would ever see Big Bob. And it was. Ends up, he had been fighting pancreatic cancer and, shortly thereafter, he succumbed. Another piece of my personal High Country social milieu is gone. I am already starting to forget many of the old names and faces that defined my quarter-century at altitude. Self-centered way to view a friend's demise, I know, but there it is.

It broke my heart that I was unable to attend Big Bob's memorial service, which transpired, of course, at the Dillon Dam Brewery. But my buddy Mark Fox was there, camera in hand, as always. He sent me a couple of the photos he took for the *Summit Daily News*. Standing around a table laden with Big Bob memorabilia were many people I have long known, people I've consumed many beers with. They were all smiling. When I looked closer, I could see why: They were eyeballing a copy of *Mountain Gazette* #82, open to page 22. I could read the headline clearly. "High Country Beer Math." Directly under the headline, the topmost scribbled-upon cocktail napkin bore the name Bob Kimble. For the record, he calculated that it would take 55 mugs of beer to recoup that $35.

A bargain on many, many levels.

(1) One of the most-celebrated and successful endurance mountain-bike racers in the entire country. That he was slinging drinks at the Dillon Dam Brewery speaks entire volumes about life at altitude.

(2) A year before the Beer Math saga, we had received an uproarious review of the cafeteria food/ambiance of the Buena Vista prison by a

man named Zeezo, and, since (like Zeezo said in his cover letter),
he was able to view mountains (and wonderful mountains at that —
Mt. Princeton and Mt. Yale) from the prison exercise yard, he figured
his review was perfect for the *Gazette*. We agreed, and printed it, ver-
batim, much to the consternation of several of our more upstanding
advertisers. Little did those advertisers know what was soon to befall
our pages by way of the Beer Math saga.

(3) I learned much later that Inmate #106669 came within a whisker of having his impending parole revoked and being placed into solitary con-
finement as a result of penning that Letter to the Editor to *Mountain
Gazette*.

— MOUNTAIN GAZETTE #180

CHAPTER SEVENTEEN

The Bright
White Light

Those of us who have spent the majority of our lives traveling by hook or by crook through lofty and wild realms have many things in common. We have all been directionally discombobulated. We have all been tired and hungry and bug-bit and blistered and grungy beyond the belief of most supposedly civilized human beings. And we have all faced both objective and subjective danger, whether that danger has visited us on our backcountry forays via gravity, ice, roiling whitewater, flash floods, avalanches, wild animals, poor planning, bad decision-making, debilitating hangovers, stupefying intoxication, heat, cold, wind or, my personal sack-shriveling favorite, lightning.

The first time I hiked the Colorado Trail, back in 1991, I found myself camping near the old Beartown site in the San Juans in the midst of, not the Swedish Bikini Team, nor even the Bud Girls, nor even the Jagermeister Girls, nor even the Senior Ladies Bridge Club, nor even my most debauch, scumiest drinking buddies, nor even a crew of fellow CT thru-hikers. No, my life does not set up that way. What I found myself camping in the midst of was a large and boisterous Boy Scout troop that spent the entire late afternoon and evening

doing one high-decibel Boy Scout thing after another: reciting the Scout Oath and Law infinitum, working earnestly on
merit badge projects that required much in the way of hack-
ing, chopping and yelling and tying several screaming Ten-
derfeet to trees.

All of which is cool by me, for, you see, though this
may come as a surprise to many, I was about as enthusiastic
a Boy Scout as a young man could possibly be. I speak the
truth when I say I was the Senior Patrol Leader of what was
at the time the largest non-urban troop in the entire country — Troop 111, Gloucester, Virginia — one of the very
first troops chartered in the U.S. back in the old-timey days
of canvas tents and woolen undergarments. I actually came
within four merit badges of achieving Eagle Scout rank, and
likely would have pulled that highly unlikely event off, except,
out of the blue, I got diverted from my quest by a captivating recreational combination of a very sleazy and wild-as-hell
trailer-trash-type girlfriend and a new and intriguing sub-
stance called blonde Lebanese hash. Oh well. Still, though
my admittedly languid quest for Eagle Scout ended up being irreparably waylaid (as was, at about the same time, my
equally languid quest to graduate high school by anything
more than the skin of my chinny-chin-chin and thus get accepted at a college that boasted actual accreditation), it was
via Scouting that I was first introduced to camping, paddling
and backpacking.

It was also through Scouting that I first learned how to
roll a joint with one hand and to light said joint in all manner
of foul weather, among many other practical skills that were
not, but should have been, part of the traditional merit badge
curriculum.

While Troop 111 was perhaps a bit unorthodox — one of our patrols was the Zeppelin Patrol, named not after the dirigible, but, rather, after the band, while another was the Cougar Patrol, named not after the elegant feline, but, rather after the Chevrolet muscle car — my seven-year Scouting stint taught me how to speak fluent Boy Scout, which, as it had/has before and since in so many demographically awkward social settings, certainly helped break the ice at the Beartown site, which was good, as everyone there gathered seemed somewhat startled when my unkempt, hirsute, bedraggled self walked up, far too tired to venture farther, sorely tempted though I was when I eyeballed 20 or so tents in the otherwise tranquil meadow that was my night's pre-planned destination.

After the Scouts FINALLY!!! (HALLELUJAH!!!) began to settle in for the night, I enjoyed the company of one of the Scoutmasters at a dilapidated picnic table. As we spoke, a seriously mean storm swirled in from several directions simultaneously, and, in the gathering twilight, proximate flashes and deafening booms began to re-define what until then had been a relaxed vibe. The Scoutmaster, who had already told me he was a professor of meteorology — whose specialty was, yes, lightning — did not so much as flinch or wince. His calm demeanor was the only thing preventing me from assuming a teeth-chattering fetal position under the picnic table.

I believe I eventually squeaked out words to the effect of: "I guess you are well versed enough regarding the vagaries of lightning to know if we were in any imminent danger."

His response will stick with me forevermore. "No one knows enough about lightning to know if they are in imminent danger during a storm. All I know is, we are right now in the middle of a lightning storm, and nothing we do will affect whether or not we get struck. Lightning is defined by its unpredictability."

He went on to say, based upon a full career of peer-reviewed statistical interpretation, he had pretty much concluded just as many people get zapped by lightning while doing all the supposed "right" things we read about in mainstream outdoor-recreation-oriented magazines, while uncountable, unknowable numbers of people doing the supposed "wrong" things venture upon their merry way blissfully untoasted.

"It's almost like lightning has its own personality," the professor/Scoutmaster mused. "Most times, that personality is, though intimidating, fairly benign, even playful, in a sadistic sort of way. Other times, however, it seems vindictive, like it really *wants* to kill someone, like death is its goal, like the bolts are being purposefully aimed at people."

Great. So much for Nature being indifferent toward our fate.

After the professor/Scoutmaster hit the sack, with the flash/booms still pummeling the biosphere in every direction, I rolled a joint with one hand and managed to get said joint lit despite the wind. I kicked back, clad in Gore-Tex from head to toe, and pondered the Scoutmaster/professor's words from the perspective of my own personal greatest-hits lightning-based stories, from a perspective that at least entertained the notion that there's this all-powerful Sky Daddy consciousness — let's call him "Zeus" — way up high making mortality-based decisions about whether or not to sizzle such-and-such hapless person down here in the mortal realms or just scare the living beejesus out of him or her. And perhaps ascertain why.

#1

Though I grew up in the climatologically agitated area where the Chesapeake Bay meets the Atlantic Ocean, a place where almost every home sported a lightning rod atop its roof, the first time I ever pondered the concept of imminent mortality in the context of lightning was in 1979, during my thru-hike of the Appalachian Trail. At that time, the AT made its way through much of Connecticut by following the Housatonic River. Like most thru-hikers, my day-to-day itinerary was planned in advance by scrutinizing in detail the AT guidebooks. It was a bit on the early side when I arrived at my destination one day, but, since it was a pretty little riverside campsite, I opted to park it for the night anyhow. There was one tent already pitched at the far end of the cleared area, and, soon after my arrival, a head popped out. I know how this is going to sound, but I'll say it anyhow: That noggin belonged to a very homely woman who, I learned later, was a retired elementary school teacher who, I also learned, was a seriously proficient long-distance backpacker, having completed just about every noteworthy east-of-the-Mississippi trail I had ever heard of. But, her backpacking acumen notwithstanding, she was severely challenged on the physical-appeal front. Big time. And I guess I should point out that AT hiker standards in that regard are usually not very high.

As we chatted, a squall blew in. In those days, I did not carry a tent, only a small tarp, which I placed over a rope tied between two tall pine trees. As darkness descended and sheets of rain began to fall and thunder began to rumble in the distance, the homely elementary school teacher asked repeatedly, with quite a bit of enthusiasm, if I would like to take refuge with her in her diminutive tent, which she also shared with her hyper-kinetic, borderline Tasmanian Devil of a Sheltie. I politely declined, babbling something inanely Muir-ish about preferring to experience the heart of the storm on its own terms.

She finally gave up and retired to the relative comfort, if not safety, of her four nylon walls, while I hunkered down under my little tarp, which was being whipped mightily by the suddenly ferocious wind. I was soaked clear down to my skivvies in mere minutes, a reality that negatively affected my comfort level as it simultaneously positively increased my personal conductivity factor. Just as I began to second guess my decision regarding the homely schoolteacher's invite, a bolt flashed down from a sky that looked more like something out of *The Wizard of Oz* than it did anything I would expect from, of all places, pastoral Connecticut, and exploded the top half right off one of the tall pines lining the campsite. The simultaneous BOOM shook the ground. Before I had even begun the process of regaining what little composure I yet retained, another bolt exploded the top off another pine — this one closer to my tarp than the first. Then a third bolt exploded the top off a pine even closer to where I sat now urinating my pants. The strikes were progressing in a very orderly fashion right toward me, with just enough time between flashes and booms to allow me to consider how death by lightning would actually feel, whether it would be quick and painless, like flipping a life-force OFF switch, or whether it would involve lots of undignified screaming and writhing on the ground for 15 minutes in searing agony. While the former certainly held more appeal than the latter of those two hideous death alternatives, it also might include attempts at mouth-to-mouth by the homely schoolteacher, so I guess a little undignified writhing agony didn't sound so bad.

Then a fourth bolt exploded the top off one of the pines to which I had my tarp tied! The sizzling remnants of branches rained down upon me as fine as sawdust. The resultant thunder unceremoniously removed several fillings from my already-iffy dentition.

Then a fifth bolt exploded the top off the other pine my tarp was tied to!

Somehow, Edvard Munch presciently peered into the future, to the shores of the Housatonic River, for his inspiration when he painted "The Scream," for I'm certain that's the form my visage took as yet another round of blackened mulch fell onto my tarp. Matter of fact, I believe I sported "The Scream" expression for some weeks following.

When the storm passed, the homely schoolteacher slowly emerged from her tent, almost as shaken as I was. All she could see in my direction was a partially collapsed orange tarp, with two boot-clad feet sticking out, toes pointed skyward, like the Wicked Witch of the East when Dorothy's house landed on her.

"You dead?" she asked, very, very tentatively.

"I don't know," I answered. "Is this heaven?"

"No," she chuckled, "it's Connecticut."

She suddenly seemed radiant.

So, what was Zeus (who, I should point out, could have snapped his fingers and turned the homely schoolteacher into Elle Macpherson (or turned me into a non-dickhead, though that might have been beyond the capabilities of even an omnipotent deity), thus mitigating my moral conundrum before the fact) thinking during that squall? I had spurned what was probably a perfectly sincere invite from the homely schoolteacher to share her shelter during a frightful storm, an invite probably based upon nothing more than primordial genetic encoding that makes terror easier to cope with when you huddle close to a member of your own kind, in this case, another stinky AT thru-hiker. Yet I had turned that invite down because I wondered if there weren't perhaps ulterior motives at play. I made a probably unfair pre-judgment, and that pre-judgment was further bruised by my utter inability to look past this woman's unfortunate appearance.

But Zeus, though peeved enough to near-bouts scare me to death, apparently did not consider such inexcusable transgressions on my part to be capital offences.

OK. Lesson learned. Next time a homely woman offers me shelter in the storm, my ass is in, face first.

#2

My wife, Gay, and I were in the middle of an eight-day backpacking trip from Wolf Creek Pass over to Elk Park, through the heart of the San Juans. When you're hiking through the highest, most-exposed parts of the Rockies in the summer, you need to be aware of the prevailing weather patterns, which, as we all know, generally consist of clear mornings, followed by late-morning/early-afternoon cloud build-up, followed soon thereafter by fusillades of high-voltage blasts as far as the eye can see. Ergo, it is always extremely prudent to plan your itinerary with the idea of not being, as but one random example, in the goddamned middle of an endless sea of 12,000-foot exposed tundra at the exact moment the storm front that has been obviously building up for the previous several hours settles in directly above not only yourself, but, more importantly, your spouse. More to the point, though, it is important — and here I should stress this is one of those trail truths easily translatable to non-trail life — to not get so tied up with one's established itinerary one fails to scrutinize, and act upon said scrutinization when appropriate, the very dark sky under which one stands.

According to My Plan, we were supposed to be down to Weminuche Pass by lunchtime and, by god, that's where we were going to eat our lunch, come hell, high water or risk of what would clearly legally amount, as my in-laws were justifiably suing me in the very near future for wrongful death, to wife-o-cide. Despite Gay's trepidation, rather than seeking shelter, I marched us across one last exposed section of tundra, after which we would descend into the trees and the psychological salve the forest provides during a storm. More importantly, we would stay on schedule! With full packs and tired legs, we literally sprinted across the tundra, into the sparse foliage of the Krummholtz Zone, then down into the spruces. The trail was steep, rocky, muddy and very slippery. The going would have been treacherous under the best of circumstances, which, given the acrid smell of ozone permeating our nostrils, these assuredly weren't.

As I was starting to relax the teensiest little bit, I rounded a bend, just out of view of my wife, when a rogue bolt struck a tree not 50 feet in front of me. The percussion knocked me on my ass so hard there was dirt in my crack. I do not exaggerate when I say I was separated from my bearings. I did not know my name. I did not know where I was or how I got there. Just then, Gay caught up with me and, in the nurturing, empathetic way that defines the feminine gender, she asked what in the world I was doing taking a break at such an inopportune, to say nothing of uncomfortable, juncture. Her words scarcely registered. Hell, whatever language it was she spoke those words in scarcely registered. Then she looked at the smoldering remnants of what had been scant seconds before a healthy blue spruce and the love of my life exclaimed, while pointing, "Look, that tree just got struck by lightning!"

It's obvious what Zeus was thinking: If you're going to tempt fate, make absolutely certain your spouse is not in the line of fire with you.

But there was another, perhaps less-obvious, lesson I think Zeus was trying to drive home by way of that near-miss. That very day was our tenth anniversary, and the place we ended up camping (as per my writ-in-stone itinerary, I would point out) was one of the most wonderful we have ever visited, and we have visited beaucoup wonderful places. The wildflowers were in the height of bloom, and every inhalation was a veritable interface with a Paris perfumery. Though we of course did not know this before the fact, had we not dashed through the bowels of that storm, we would not have arrived at the best anniversary spot any couple has ever in the history of marriage enjoyed. I think Zeus was trying to drive home the point that, sometimes, one ought to tempt fate. And, if you make it to the other side, the rewards are often well worth the fear factor. Of course, that's easy to say when catastrophe was not part of the post-experience rumination.

Zeus, apparently fully understanding my cranial density, stayed with me on this one for several decades. I have passed that blue spruce — which, because of the lightning strike that almost struck me, had long since begun the inevitable process of decomposition — twice since I was knocked on my keister there in the middle of the trail. A week before these words hit print, Gay and I will have celebrated our 25th anniversary. Lot of water under the adventure bridge. But it has been a long time since we last sprinted through the tundra during a storm. Our life together has become borderline sedentary. I cannot help but wonder if we too have not begun the process of inevitable decomposition. Maybe it's time to go back out into the storm. I think Zeus would understand, approve and probably provide safe passage.

#3

In 1997, I hiked the 850-mile Arizona Trail from the Utah border to the Mexican border. The very night before I started, I camped near Jacob Lake with my late dog Cali. The weather had been so intense, the nearby town of Kanab, Utah, had received in one three-week period in August more precipitation than it had ever received in a single year in its entire history. A few weeks prior, 15 people got swept to their deaths in two flash floods in Arizona. Though I wouldn't claim it for a fact, I'm pretty certain, earlier in the day, my truck got hit by lightning as I traveled down the highway at 80 miles per hour. I saw the flash, heard the thunder instantly, and then it felt like the back of my pick-up was raised up, like when you're boogie-boarding and a wave passes beneath you.

Cali and I crawled into my Bibler just as the sun was setting. Then it came, like some shit out of the nastier, wrath-of-god sections of the Old Testament: A lightning storm like no other I'd experienced or even heard about. After more than an hour of lying on my back, teeth-clenched so tightly my jaw ached for days, I decided to start counting the flashes. I stopped at *800* — and a high percentage of those were of the multiple-simultaneous-strikes variety. The storm continued unabated for at least an hour after I stopped counting. It is no exaggeration to say that more than 2,000 strikes flashed in my immediate vicinity. I came within a whisker of panicking. It was everything I could do to resist dashing out of the tent and into my truck. But I knew — I just *knew* — if I did, I would get fried. So I stayed in my tent and had a chat with Zeus and his celestial ilk, something I only seem to do when shit's hitting the fan.

He said nothing, though I might have detected a snicker through the deluge.

When I finally left my tent the next morning, the air was post-precipitation sweet. The birds were tweeting. My dog ran hither and thither enjoying the earthly aromas.

I sat on the tailgate of my truck, PTSD'd, and the only thought swirling in my head, and it swirled and swirled and would not leave, was this: I realized how much I loved my humble little life and how blessed I'd been to have had a million million good, bad and ugly outdoor experiences and how it said something probably too profound for my lizard brain to comprehend, much less articulate, that, despite all those visions of the bright white light, I had always landed on my feet, sometimes bruised, sometimes battered, sometimes shaken, but mostly unscathed.

And, know what? Like those of you who have spent the majority of your lives traveling by hook or by crook through lofty and wild realms, I wouldn't trade a single interface with the bright white light for all the supposed comfort and safety the civilized world allegedly has to offer.

Later that day, I shouldered my too-heavy pack yet again and started yet another long walk into the great unknown.

— MOUNTAIN GAZETTE #181

CHAPTER EIGHTEEN

North by Southwest

"In the world of advertising, there's no such thing as a lie.
There's only expedient exaggeration."
— Roger Thornhill (Cary Grant),
North By Northwest

For the generation preceding mine, it was Pearl Harbor, December 7, 1941, the day marking the entry of the U.S. into World War II. For the generation before, it was likely October 29, 1929 — Black Tuesday — the day the stock market crashed and the Great Depression commenced. For my generation, it was November 22, 1963, when President John F. Kennedy was assassinated in Dallas.

You get the picture. All bonafide out-of-the-blue jaw-droppers that not only indelibly etched themselves into our national psyche but that caused both immediate and ripple-effect ramifications for many years to come. Game changers. Days that shall live in infamy, days when every single one of us remembers our immediate circumstances when the shit hit the fan.

We ALL know where we were and what we were doing on September 11, 2001, when the walls came tumbling down.

Moreover, as the 10th anniversary of 9/11 approached, and people began reliving and rehashing the events in bars and restaurants, at work and at the gym, on the trail and on the ski lifts, from coast to coast, I noticed everyone seemed to have a well-honed tale relating to 9/11 and how their lives fit into 9/11. This was more than just, "I was at school when I heard Kennedy was shot." The scale of 9/11 was so massive and widespread most of us are able to make some sort of six-degrees-of-separation-type connection with the events that unfolded that tragic day. We knew someone who worked in the Towers. We knew someone who was stranded in Boston for 10 days, unable to get back home to Colorado.

And, par for my personal course, my 9/11 experience was a tad bit off the mainstream radar.

My wife, Gay, late dog, Cali, and I were happily ensconced in a motel room at Mile 0 (our own personal Ground Zero, as it were) of the ALCAN Highway, in Dawson Creek, British Columbia, '96 Outback pointed toward the Northwest Territories, which we planned to cross into that very evening. This trip was essentially one of my life-long travel fantasies finally made manifest. Ever since I was an outdoors-leaning tike with a taste for *Sergeant Preston* dwelling in the farthest reaches of the wintry Adirondack Mountains — way closer to Montreal than any sizeable American city — I had wanted to visit the Northwest Territories, which had been much in the news the prior couple of years, as, in 1999, more than two-thirds of its terrain had been lobbed off to form the new territory of Nunavut.

Maybe reading about that non-violent political separation reignited a passion almost certainly based as much as anything else on the NWT's stunning expanse, which has always been further exaggerated in my many world atlases by the same Mercator projections that make Greenland appear significantly larger than South America, when, in actuality, it is eight times smaller. Those disproportionate projections aside, the vastness of the Northwest Territories — 1.25 million square miles before Nunavut's secession, 440,000 square miles after (Colorado — no small state — by comparison, is about 104,000 square miles) — combined with a population of less than 80,000 people (a mere 45,000 post-Nunavut), combined with a resultant wilderness factor found in few other places on the globe, all have long conspired to get my adventure juices flowing.

The fact that the NWT can be accessed from the real world via the family station wagon might knock off a few true-boondocks style points when compared to places like Kamchatka, the Congo Basin and Antarctica, but it also gives one the chance to actually drive to one of the last true examples of terra-near-incognita left on the planet within the constraints of a two-week vacation from workaday life.

So, in early September 2001, we began a round-trip tour north that eventually totaled more than 5,000 miles — the longest road trip in a marital life that had seen many long road trips. (Until then, the longest drive we had done was down to Honduras and back.)

It had already been a sorta weird trip. Several days prior, with Gay behind the wheel, we passed out of U.S. territory at Sweetgrass, Montana, and approached the Canadian border crossing at Coutts, Alberta.

As we neared the border, my mind predictably wandered back 21 years, to the last time I passed from the Big Sky State into the Sunshine Province.

My amigo Ed and I had procured an ounce of hash and had been doing our damnedest to ingest it over the course of a journey that had already seen us meander our way from Georgia — where I had just completed my thru-hike of the Appalachian Trail — to Montana. Though we had made an impressive dent in the hash stash, it had not sufficiently diminished in size to the point where we stopped referring to it as "The Big Chunk." We still had a lot of hash left on the day our extremely disheveled selves were scheduled to cross into Canada.

The unspoken unthinkable was starting to get thought and spoken: We had too much hash! — which marked the first time those words had ever visited my young cranial mainframe. Alas, we were going to have to either modify a travel itinerary months in the making or we were going to have to ... to ... dump ... the ... hash ... before crossing the border — a mighty depressing proposition. Rather than toss The Big Chunk unceremoniously into a ditch, however, we hoped to find some wayward hitchhiker(s) or fellow backpacker(s), and bequeath The Big Chunk to him/her/them.

I did something similar one time, and it made me feel undeservedly righteous. I was in China with my cohort-in-many-crimes, Norb, and, by way of a complicated trailside trade that included food, money and gear, we had managed to get our lecherous mitts on several very sticky black balls of opium, which, once again, we were unable to fully consume — try though we might (and we tried mightily) — before we had to cross an international border. So, the day before we were scheduled to fly back to Hong Kong — a place where one does not want to get busted carrying a pocketful of Kashgari opium — we found ourselves sitting in the hotel bar with a surfer-dude-looking Californian on his honeymoon who was lamenting his recreational druglessness. Norb and I looked at each other, simultaneously smiled and handed our countryman the last of our opium. (His new spouse, I should point out, did not seem pleased.)

Stunningly, Ed and I could not locate anyone appropriate to give our hash to, which shocked us, given, in those days, you could scarcely throw a rock in the woods without hitting some variation on the partying freak theme.

So, as Ed and I approached the Canadian border, a "plan" started gestating within the bowels of thought processes without a doubt extremely dulled by massive doses of THC. Rather than give our hash away, and rather than attempt to smuggle it across the border — which, even stoned nitwits such as ourselves knew better than to try — we would just smoke it all before leaving America! Great idea! The only flaw was, when we made this decision, we were only 30 miles from the border. Not much time to inhale what by then was probably 10 grams of moderately strong hash. So, we loaded bowl after bowl and smoked as fast as our respiratory systems would allow and, by the time we passed a highway sign informing us that Canada was a mere half-mile away, we were obliterated, and we still had probably eight grams of hash in our possession. The Big Chunk would not go away!

What to do?

Three choices: Pull a Bat-turn, throw the hash out the window or plow ahead, consequences be damned. Of course, we opted to follow the path of least wisdom, clear up to the point of no return. The hash was stashed in the pick compartment of my guitar case, which was in the back seat, on top of Ed's guitar case. Not exactly a sophisticated smuggling operation, but there we were. When only a few cars separated the Canadian border authorities and us, I looked over at Ed and dookied my drawers. Not only did he look as stoned as person possibly could be, but he was also sweating profusely, fidgeting uncontrollably and coughing his lungs out. He might as well have had the word "GUILTY" painted on his forehead with glitter nail polish. And I'm sure I looked no better. We were doubtless doomed. So, under the pretense of making sure the hash was secure, I surreptitiously moved it from the pick compartment inside my guitar case to the pick compartment inside Ed's guitar case. That way, if — when! — we got busted, I could at least pretend I was totally innocent, completely unaware the man I was traveling with — someone I thought was an upstanding citizen! — was in fact an international narcotics smuggler! How was I to know, officer?

The Canadian immigration officers took one quick look at us and told us to park in the Special Assured Imminent Arrest Area, where several uniformed officials, all of whom were wearing latex gloves, stood smiling and rubbing their hands together. They pulled every item out of the back of the car, wincing as they rummaged through piles of long-unwashed crusty skivvies and malodorous hiking socks. They went through the glove compartment with a fine-tooth comb. They looked under the hood and in the console and under the floor mats. The ONLY place they did not look was in the two guitar cases right there plain as day in the back seat. They likely thought, surely, even obvious stoners such as Ed and I would not be so stupid as to hide the drugs in a guitar case! After an hour of searching, they welcomed us to Canada through gritted dentition.

The Big Chunk made it all the way to Vancouver Island,

where it finally dissipated into hazy recollection on a beach at Pacific Rim National Park around a blazing campfire surrounded by all manner of singing revelers.

As Gay and I approached the border at Coutts, my home- and business-owning, long-married, semi-responsible self smiled at those memories. I could not help but look at M. John through the prism of time and place. It would be inaccurate to say I miss that irresponsible pack-toting hippie who used to bear my name. After all, I have plus-or-minus matured to be the person that young hippie wanted all along to be (mostly). Still, it's hard sometimes to overcome nostalgia, to wonder where all that youthful innocence went.

Little did I know.

Little did *any* of us know.

It was Saturday, September 8, 2001.

"Have either of you ever received a DUI?" the immigration lady, who, gender aside, looked like Gimli, asked.

"Well, yeah, now that you mention it, I have," I responded apprehensively from the passenger seat.

"Then I can not allow you to pass, because, in the eyes of the Canadian government, you are a felon."

Utter instantaneous deflation! Vacation plans mixed metaphorically torpedoed before they ever got off the ground.

Just as we were about to turn around, Gimli-ette said words to the effect of, "Well … we *might* just be able to make an exception for people who look as responsible as you two." Gay and I have done so much traveling, we instantly understood the words, the inflection with which those words were spoken and the words unspoken. We glanced at each other and prepared for a border dance we never expected in, of all places, Oh Canada. I was pointed toward an upstairs room already populated by several dozen forlorn-looking Americans. One by one, we were led into a small office, where we heard the exact same words from Gimli-ette: For $200, we could enter Canada. Cash only. No receipt. No guarantee next time we tried to enter the country, the same "opportunity" would be available. Understand? Yes, I understood fully. The entire process took four long hours, which totally screwed up the rest of our travel day. It was dusk as we approached the first town in Alberta, Milk River, which had a public campground, which we ended up sharing with most of those same forlorn-looking Americans, all of whom, like us, were $200 poorer.

By the time we arrived in Dawson Creek, a beautiful little college town, the bad taste of the border crossing had begun to dissipate. We were finally at that cusp point of any good journey, where and when you feel like, hey, we're actually here! We pulled it off! What could possibly go wrong now? We found a bar with a TV that had upon its screen, of all fortuitous things, a Monday Night Football game between the Broncos and the Giants. The Donkeys kicked ass, 31-20, and we returned to the motel happy about the result of the game, happy that, here we were, way the hell up in British Columbia, happy because, before we left the bar, one of the rather surly, Yank-hating locals we had been chatting with told us we didn't seem to suck as bad as most Americans. We felt an iota of national pride at that statement.

The only down side was we heard a cold-weather front was moving in, and, when you're that far north, that's news you pay attention to.

It was September 10, maybe 11 p.m. when we finally laid our weary heads upon our pillows.

Next morning, with Gay in the bathroom enjoying what was supposed to be her last interface with indoor plumbing for quite some time, I turned on the TV to check out the weather report.

You all know what I saw. Same thing we all saw. Even as I was trying to reconcile a mild hangover with the images flashing on the screen, the second plane hit. "Uh, Gay, I think you'd better check this out."

We watched for a few minutes before going down to the motel's breakfast room, which was filled with people staring slack-jawed at the images being replayed over and over. All eyes fell upon us when we entered the room. People started saying how sorry they were. We don't know how they knew we were Americans, but they all did.

And they were right. We were indeed, at that moment, more American than we had ever been.

It is fair to say we were a bit shaken, but, man oh man, I wasn't going to let the biggest non-self-inflicted attack on American soil in history stop me when I was six hours away from the Northwest Territories. With no small amount of trepidation, we lit out, passing by the last vestiges of civilization, fast getting to the point where the world was defined by wild. We saw bears, moose, raging rivers, endless lakes, thick boreal forests and vistas that did not end till they reached Hudson Bay. We were cut off from the world, and the last word we heard before the AM band went totally dead was, "War."

When we finally anticlimactically arrived at Fort Liard,

NWT, people streamed out of houses and businesses to ask us for the latest news, like somehow we had a proprietary communications link to the Land of the Free. A French-Canadian, whose English was poor, told us he had heard via short-wave radio the President was unaccounted for and most high-ranking government officials had already been taken to their secret bunkers.

Shit!

We stayed at a community campground by a lovely, placid lake. Ours was the only tent; everyone else had a hard-sided camper or motorhome. The host came by at dusk to warn us about recent bear activity in the campground. He suggested we remain vigilant. "I'm really sorry," he said before departing. I don't know whether he was sorry about the bear situation or what had happened to New York City and Washington. Maybe he was sorry we lived in a world where vigilance was necessary.

On September 12, we arrived at an end-of-the-world outpost called Checkpoint, which boasted about three rustic cabins and a café. The café had a small black-and-white TV with a grainy image and scratchy sound. We could barely make out the face of Donald Rumsfeld. He looked awful, which I guess is understandable. He was incoherently babbling something about the media being at least partially responsible for the attack on the Twin Towers.

When we arrived at the intersection of Canadian highways 1 and 3 — so close to the Mackenzie River, Yellowknife, the Great Slave Lake and Wood Buffalo National Park — names I have been uttering since I was a child — we could almost touch them, we sighed and, instead of taking a much-desired left, we took a reluctant right and pointed the Outback toward the Home of the Brave. It was a hard decision, not only because, given our remoteness, we were still pretty much in the dark vis-à-vis what was transpiring in the U.S. And not only because I was so close to some places I wanted so bad to visit for so long. And not only because I knew the chances of me ever returning to that point were slim, given that the next border Gimli-ette might not be amenable to a bribe. But because a part of me intuited what life in America was about to become, and those visions were not appealing. Rather, they tempted me to hide in the deep Canadian woods until the troubles had passed. And if those troubles never did pass, then at least my wife and I would be far enough away from the tumult that the chances of it directly affecting us would be slim.

Since the border was closed, we had conscionable opportunity to dilly-dally in Jasper and Banff on the way down. Not Wood Buffalo National Park, but not too shabby either. Everywhere we went, people would eyeball our license plates and go out of their way to express heartfelt sympathy. On the Icefields Highway, we parked next to a herd of scary-looking Canadian motorcycle enthusiasts. The biggest, ugliest, smelliest one walked over, extended a brotherly hand to me and said, tears welling up in his bloodshot eyes, "I hope you guys bomb the living shit out of them." I thanked him, but 1) I did not know who "them" was, but 2) I knew we would indeed end up bombing the shit out of someone, somewhere. It often seems that is the only thing we know how to do anymore. What happened to us?

When the border finally opened, we returned to the U.S. at Eureka, Montana, just west of Glacier National Park. We were the only car at the crossing and we were welcomed home by one of the biggest asshole INS agents I have ever dealt with, and I have dealt with a fair number. (I hate those guys.) I had pulled up about a foot past some stupid yellow line I could not see, and he red-faced verbally jumped my shit, which caused me to jump his shit back, which caused the supervisor to run out of his office telling all involved to calm the fuck down. In retrospect, I should have cut the asshole some slack, but I did not know INS was in the national crosshairs as everyone was trying to figure out how the hijackers entered the U.S.

By the time we got back to Summit County, the vitriolic, fist-shaking barroom arguments were already commencing full bore. I remember one lady in Pug Ryan's shouting me down after I mentioned, maybe, we ought to have our ducks in a huddle before we start sending troops abroad to who knows where in a raged-inspired attempt to avenge the 9/11 attacks. She was of the opinion people like me ought to just shut our goddamned traps and get with the national goose-step program — ready, fire, aim-like — whatever that program might be. My response was, predictably, in times of intense jingoistic flag-waving, getting with an undefined program just for the sake of national unity is the absolute *worst* thing a person can do because, at such times, that's when crazy shit like the Patriot Act gets passed by a compliant, confused and inept Congress.

And so it went. For months. For years. Clear up until the wounds started healing and people started composing their personal 9/11 stories and telling those stories to each other in measured tones-of-voice.

With two 9/11-based wars still raging on the other side of the planet, without the slightest hope of positive outcome,

I opted to pull up stakes and relocate very near a completely different border, the other side of which can be found the most-dangerous cities in the world — which was not the case pre-9/11. Two weeks ago, while passing through an airport security checkpoint manned by TSA people, I had my toothpaste confiscated. Last week, while driving down Interstate 10, I was pulled by Border Patrol for no other reason than ... who knows why? The National Guard is deployed south of my home. There are people seriously talking about permanently deploying regular military troops along a border that is now seeing erected upon it a 20-foot-high, million-dollar-per-mile wall that will never, ever work, and anyone who thinks it will is deluded.

Ten years after 9/11, it has come down to this: The higher the walls you build, the deeper your prison becomes. And that is no way to live.

— MOUNTAIN GAZETTE #182

CHAPTER NINETEEN

The Discovered

AUTHOR'S NOTE: *The events herein recounted occurred almost 25 years ago. Without a doubt, most circumstances, especially those dealing with airline safety, have changed.*

SECOND AUTHOR'S NOTE: *Be forewarned … there's one part of this story that gets a bit unsavory.*

> *"Butch Cassidy: Jeesh, all Bolivia can't look like this.*
> *Sundance Kid: How do you know? This might be the garden*
> *spot of the whole country. People may travel hundreds of miles*
> *just to get to this spot where we're standing now. This might be*
> *the Atlantic City, New Jersey, of all Bolivia for all you know."*
> *— Butch Cassidy and the Sundance Kid*

It was a law-of-diminishing-transportation-returns kind of sweltering Third-World overland journey. It began well before dawn in Santo Domingo on a jam-packed, barnyard-fowl-dense, 1960s-era, shock-absorber-free school bus designed to accommodate legs no longer than those borne by pygmy kindergartners, then degenerated in Barahona to the back of a jam-packed shock-absorber-free dump truck obviously used since 1945 to transport road kill, fish guts and a wide array of excrement to a fertilizer factory, then degenerated further still in Neiba, where we hired what in the Dominican Republic is called a "guagua" — small, antiquated Datsun or Toyota pick-up trucks in such states of dismal rusted-out, multi-colored, worn/mismatched-tired, dented, smoke-spewing disrepair that, had the orcs invented the internal-combustion engine, this is what they would have come up with — for the final 20-mile, two-plus-hour push along single-lane, shoulder-free, sinewy, unpaved mountain/jungle "roads" that managed to be simultaneously dusty, muddy, rutted, potholed, washboardy and populated by other guaguas being driven by people who seemed to be at least as drunk as the guy driving our guagua was, to our final destination: the diminutive and remote village of La Descubierta (translated: "The Discovered").

In other words: Very cool journey.

Still, by the time we were deposited in front of the humble headquarters for Isla Cabritos National Park, we were so beat-up and shell-shocked from the trip, we could scarcely stand straight. We were further unmoored and negatively physically impacted by the sobering reality that this marked the first time we had not been falling-down drunk since arriving three days prior in the Dominican Republic.

Norb, the expedition photographer, and I were, believe it or not, official guests of the Dominican National Tourism Office, a governmental entity that, because we were on assignment for *Backpacker* and *Adventure Travel* magazines to pen a few pieces on the outdoor recreation opportunities found in the DR, had given us a couple of free tickets on Dominicana Airlines. Everything was going remarkably smoothly until we boarded the not-exactly state-of-the-art plane in Miami. Most times, when jets with a capacity of several hundred passengers are "overbooked," it is purely an administrative term — more tickets are sold then there are actual seats and, therefore, "X" number of would-be passengers are told, sorry, tough noogies, but you'll have to wait for the next plane. This was not the case with our flight, which was overbooked by at least 70 people. But, rather than bumping those hapless folks, they were herded into the aisles, where they stood stoically as the doors were closed and the departure procedures initiated. Just as we were about to pull back from the gate, the doors were suddenly re-opened with a startling degree of exigency and everyone on the plane was ordered to disembark post haste. Surely, thought Norb and I, the FAA had got wind of the overbooking situation and had stepped in to rectify what was clearly an untenably unsafe set of airline-management circumstances. Then I looked out the window and saw a great many police officers and, captivatingly enough, several vehicles bearing the words: Miami-Dade Bomb Squad. Ends up, someone had called in a bomb threat for our plane. Perhaps a surviving family member of someone who had been lost when the last overbooked plane crashed into the ocean with no survivors.

Since we had already been officially passport-stamped out of the U.S., we were ushered into an isolated end-of-the-world lounge and ordered to sit tight till the bomb sweep was complete, or the plane blew up, whichever occurred first. No one knew how long the process would last. But, just as the first sighs of exasperation were about to pass my lips, in walks an airline employee pushing a beverage cart laden with several cases of cold beer, which, we soon came to learn, was being offered gratis as a small token of Dominicana's appreciation for our patience and understanding. Even better, though, just about every other passenger on our flight was some sort of crazy-assed Christian missionary, and the main manifestation of that craziness, as far as I could tell, was that they all turned their noses up at the several cases of free cold beer being wheeled out for everyone's refreshment. Yes, Norb and I were essentially the only ones drinking that free beer, which gave the crazy-assed Christian missionaries in our midst some palpable opportunities for warm-up/practice prayers before arriving in a country, as far as I know, had already been pretty much Christianized since back in Columbus days.

Here it is important to stress that this was not the first foreign foray magazine project dance for Norb and I. We had traveled together on assignment to the Far East, Copper Canyon and Central America. I should also stress that we are both also fairly focused, professional people. Before the free beer arrived, Norb was busying himself cleaning lenses and inventorying film and such, while I was jotting down notes and mentally sussing out The Plan, which, while woefully lacking in executable details, was, at least in theory, very doable: visit Isla Cabritos — at 130 feet below sea level, the lowest and hottest point in the Caribbean — then ascend Pico Duarte — at 10,164 feet, the highest and coldest point in the Caribbean. It's just, well, the bomb sweep ended up taking *four hours*, which was an awful long time to clean lenses and jot notes with a beer cart sitting tantalizingly scant feet before us. Needless to say, Norb and I ended up placing a sizeable dent in those several cases of free beer.

When the bomb squad finally signaled all clear, we verily staggered back onto the same plane, where, once gain,

70 or so overbooked passengers booked themselves standing-room-only-style into the aisles. As I boarded, I jokingly slurred to one of the stewardesses that Norb and I would like a few beers before departure to help calm our nerves, which were quite agitated, given our justified pre-determinisitic view that neither of us believed for a moment the tattered and overloaded plane we were on would do anything save fall from the sky in a million little pieces well before the landing gear was even fully retracted. My already compromised composure quotient was further impacted by the appearance of stewardess to whom I was speaking. She had remarkably detailed makeup on her eyelids that looked like, well, eyes. But not human eyes. Cat eyes, with slits for pupils. So, when her eyes were wide open, one looked into her, you know, eyes. Then, when she blinked, one observed what looked to be a completely different set of, yes, eyes. This was especially disorienting when she blinked only one eye at a time, something I believe she practiced often as a means of distracting passengers who might otherwise be bothered by the severe overbooking issue.

The over-orbed stewardess good-naturedly informed me there was no beer on this particular flight. I feigned shock and disbelief and fell into my seat, figuring, if there was one thing Norb and I were, it was drunk enough already. But before I had even fastened my frayed seatbelt with the broken buckle, a hand zoomed in from my peripheral vision, pulled down my seat tray — the one that's supposed to be fastened in an upright and secure position before take-off — and placed upon that tray a full unopened liter bottle of Bermudez rum, along with two cups full of ice, two cups full of lime slices and two bottles of cold mineral water.

"I only told you there was no beer on this flight," the multi-eyed stewardess said, beaming. "I didn't say anything about rum." This was an emblematic turn of events, as we would learn over the course of the next six weeks in the Dominican Republic, a country whose official slogan ought to be: There's no problem that rum can't fix, or at least mollify.

Had the stewardess not brought us that rum, it would have been the most intoxicated I have ever entered into a foreign country. But she did indeed bring us a bottle of rum, most of which Norb and I consumed during the two-hour flight. It was one of those jets that have three seats on each side, and to our right, next to the window, sat one of the crazy-assed Christian mercenaries who, during the entire flight, kept his nose buried in one of those miniature bibles, which, truth be told, I don't know if they're smaller because they contain less words, like maybe a Twitter form of scripture, or whether the print's really, really small. Either way, as we began our descent, the man, bowed his head and, with lips moving, started silently praying. We noticed almost every one of the other crazy-assed Christian mercenaries were similarly occupied. It was like watching a silent movie; every Christian lip was moving as though orating at an Alabama tent revival, yet no noise spewed forth, which, if you're going to be among a troop of crazy-assed Christians, is the best a heathen can hope for. Maybe they were going to the DR to minister to aspiring lip readers.

When our seatmate finally rejoined the land of the sane, he turned to us for the first time and said, "Gentlemen, do you have any idea where you're headed?" You want to talk about a loaded question, rife with any number of possible witty retorts, none of which either of us were able to even think of, much less articulate, unless you consider drooping heads and drooling mouths to be forms of articulation. Sensing our befuddlement, the man answered his own interrogative for our benefit, which we appreciated mightily. "You are about to land at one of the two or three most dangerous major airports in the entire world. The reason it is so dangerous, besides of course that it's surrounded on three sides by high mountains, is the power grid in Santo Domingo averages five or six outages a day, and the airport has no back-up generators for the control tower or landing lights, the latter of which, you may have noticed, because of our little four-hour delay in Miami, we will need, because it is now dark."

Exactly 17 minutes after we successfully landed at Las Americas International Airport, the power grid crashed and we passed through customs and immigration facilities illuminated only by flashlights, something we realized in hindsight, might have worked to our advantage, given that I'm sure we looked like the very dictionary definition of undesirable aliens.

We were not feeling exactly what I would call chipper the following a.m., but, still, we had an obligation to visit our benefactors at the Dominican National Tourism Office, to let those who had arranged for our free plane tickets know we had arrived safely. It was mid-July and near-bouts 100 degrees, with near-bouts 100-percent humidity. We dashed from shade patch to shade patch as we zigzagged our way through Santo Domingo's Colonial District.

When we arrived at the Tourism Office, it was lunchtime. Only one employee was thereabouts, a fly-swatter-bearing young black man who had lived in Brooklyn for many years and thus spoke fluent English. He sat beneath a slow-moving ceiling fan in a darkened room that was so miserably hot and stuffy, even the flies, of which there were many, refused to stir, preferring instead to simply park on the window sills, apparently hoping to soon be swatted out of their sultry misery. The tourism employee had perspiration rings so large they met at his solar plexus and, one would assume, back between his shoulder blades. Sweat droplets were forming on the tip of his nose and splatting onto the desk beneath with alarming regularity.

When we introduced ourselves, we might as well have been speaking a sub-dialect of Navajo. The tourism employee's face was totally blank. He had never heard of us either generally or specifically. The only person who *might* know — the Minister of Tourism — and this man assured us that the Minister would in fact *not* know, was gone for the rest of the month, and, truth be told, hadn't been into the office the entire previous month. We weren't exactly expecting a red-carpet reception, but we were expecting that someone, somewhere, knew we were coming. That this was apparently not the case was fine with us, given our shaky mental state. We figured at that point we would talk for an hour or so about our proposed itinerary, get some inside skinny and pick up a few maps and informational brochures. No such luck. Not only did the tourism employee not know a thing about our proposed destinations — both of which, I should stress, were located in national parks, something you would think the national tourism department would know a little something about — but he could not for the life of him understand why anyone would want to visit such out-of-the-way, under-developed parts of his fair land.

Whenever we tried to winnow some relevant piece of

information from him — about public transportation access to La Descubierta, where we could score supplies, are permits to visit the parks required? — he, without hesitation, returned to the only subject he seemed to know anything about, and the only subject that seemed of any interest to him at all in his position as the sole representative of the Dominican National Tourism Office right then occupying a seat in the center of the capital city across a desk from two professional magazine people on assignment to produce stories that would be eyeballed by literally hundreds of thousands of potential visitors: how one goes about pursuing nookie while enjoying one's time in the Dominican Republic.

In this regard, the young man seemed not only quite enthusiastic, but eminently qualified. We learned the proper techniques for determining whether Dominican women were approachable, how to initiate first contact, how to ascertain if they were in it for the money, the experience or the betrothal potential, how to negotiate satisfactory remuneration, how to actually transact that remuneration, which neighborhoods specialized in what, etc. etc. I am certain our visages verily defined the word, "dumbfounded." When we tried to explain to him that, in all likelihood, our spouses back home would be extremely displeased to read about our various snatch pursuits in *Backpacker* and *Adventure Travel* magazines, he recommended we immediately apply for quickie divorces — he could show us how and where — which would free us up to pursue some local material, which would doubtless prove far more understanding than those obviously uptight American women who bore our surnames.

Before we left, the tourism guy hooked us up with a credentialed local guide — young guy, well groomed, nattily attired in his official blue tour guide shirt — to show us around the Colonial District. Before we went upon our merry way, the Tourism Department guy whispered something we could not hear into the ear of the tour guide, who nodded earnestly and seemingly conspiratorially. Even though it was mid-afternoon and sizzling, we strolled around the various museums, restored fortresses and elegant, albeit decaying, edifices of the Western Hemisphere's oldest European city. We stuck our heads into the very jail cell where none other than Christopher Columbus had been imprisoned on his last voyage to the New World. Interesting enough shit. I took some cursory notes. Norb took a few cursory photos. But it was way too hot, and we were way too hung-over, to focus on work, and we could see our tour guide was growing impatient. "Wouldn't you rather visit someplace more … interesting?" he asked. "Maybe find some … refreshment?" Admittedly, we were getting a tad parched, the previous day's indiscretions suddenly seeming like ancient history. We said, sure, a beverage or two might go down easy. So, we started walking away from the Colonial District. And we walked and walked through increasingly deteriorated and threatening neighborhoods. We walked until Norb and I started wondering if maybe we were not right then venturing toward our very doom. Then, suddenly, our tour guide announced we had arrived. We looked up the sewage-drenched street one way, then we looked up the sewage-drenched street the other way. We looked up, we looked down. As far as we could tell, we had "arrived" at an oozing, malodorous ditch in the middle of one of the worst urban slums I have ever seen. Our guide grinned and pointed to a green door across the sewage-drenched street, and upon that door, in barely legible flaked letters, we read: HAMBURGER BAR.

Our guide walked over and, like a monkey-suited door-man at the Park Lane Hotel, opened the Hamburger Bar's creaky door and bade us welcome with a deep bow. We were greeted by an olfactory amalgam of stench that contained component wafts of tropical decomposition, malfunctioning plumbing, spilled beverages that were not cleaned up in a timely fashion (or ever), blood, sweat, tears, 10 or 12 types of body odors that we did not care to ponder further and, worst, the fragrant bouquet of perpetual hopelessness. Now, I've been in more than a few skanky brothels in my time — houses of ill repute often providing the only options for libations and lodging in many rural Third World hamlets — but the Hamburger Bar verily took the cake in terms of unsavoryness on every conceivable level, from uncataloged pathogens clear up the evolutionary ladder to the lurid excuses for art adorning walls caked with every variation imaginable on the grime/pestilence theme.

Since it was fairly early in the day, there were only three employees on duty, and our hearts bled at the sight of them. In the dimness, their ages were hard to peg, but they were young and attired in mismatched rags so unclean they might best be described as contaminated, maybe even toxic. They bore a hodgepodge of bruises, scars and needle tracks and, incongruously, smiles. They greeted us warmly and invited us to join them at a table they shared with three exceedingly hammered adolescent sailors on shore leave from the French Navy. Norb and I wasted no time getting straight down to the business at hand: We let those three on-duty brothel employees know, under no conceivable circumstances, including, but not limited to, the release of a deadly virus scheduled to wipe out the entire human population within the next two

minutes, would either of us be soliciting services more inti-
mate than superficial chitchat conducted at a distance great
enough to serve as a barrier to airborne bacteria. Being deco-
rous sorts, we framed this absolute statement in purely martial terms, so no insult would be given. We said, if such an ar-
rangement was cool, we would sit there and drink with them
for a bit, and we would pay for everyone's beverages. Truth
be told, the ladies seemed both relieved and flattered. They
made no advances toward us at all. They all turned out to be
very pleasant drinking partners.

And so we came to while away enough time there in the
Hamburger Bar with those three tattered ladies and those
three French sailors and our official Dominican tour guide
(who at one point disappeared into the back with one of the
ladies for 15 or so minutes) that, by the time we re-emerged
onto the sewage-drenched street, we had to do a space-time
continuum double take, for, while we were in the Hamburger
Bar, a cosmic cataclysm had transpired: the sun was no longer in the sky! It was gone, and who knew where? Yes, turns
out, we had been in the Hamburger Bar for more than seven
hours, during which time we learned that, the main reason
our guide — an official representative of the Dominican
National Tourism Office, no less — had brought us to this
particular sordid establishment instead of the myriad more
upscale sleazy brothels closer to the Colonial District —
where our hotel was located — was one of the ladies we were
drinking with hailed from La Descubierta, the jumping off
point for Isla Cabritos National Park. "My friend at the Tourism Office asked me to get this for you," the guide said. He
handed us a crudely drawn map, with public transportation
information all the way to the front steps of the national park

headquarters. That must have been what the Tourism Office employee had whispered to the guide, and that must have been why the guide disappeared into the back with one of the Hamburger Bar's matinee employees. And here we were, thinking that the Dominican National tourism Office was a slack operation! This, amigos, was efficiency incarnate, the way they managed to mingle both recreation and fact gathering into one neat experiential package.

You can imagine how we felt the next day, when we were scheduled to meet with the Director of the Dominican National Park Service, who, we were not exactly stunned to learn, not only knew next to nothing about the country's national parks, but had never actually visited a single one of them. He had no maps. He didn't think there actually *were* any maps. There might be guides. There might not be guides. There might be bandits, poisonous snakes, attack monkeys, mud, disease and noxious fumes spilling forth from the bowels of the earth. Or maybe not. Be all that as it may, halfway through the fact-free interview, one of the 12 mini-skirted secretaries on duty came in bearing three bottles of rum, along with the requisite cups of ice, soda water and limes. Guess how the rest of the day turned out.

And so we eventually arrived at the headquarters of Isla Cabritos National Park in La Descubierta — which we found only because of a map hand-drawn in a bar named Hamburger back in a Santo Domingo sub-slum by a prostitute who was apparently the official cartographer of the Dominican National Tourism Office — so grimy and so over-laden with gear, I'm sure Norb and I resembled those giant dirt termite mounds in Africa you sometimes see photographed in National Geographic.

The headquarters office was a modest house located in a backstreet residential area. The front room contained one desk lacking so much as a scrap of paper upon it and two bunk beds, made available to visitors, who, we got the impression, were few and far between. Before we had the chance to deposit our mountain of equipage, in walks a small man named Angel, the assistant administrator for Isla Cabritos. He seemed absolutely stunned at having to deal with tourists, much less camera-and-notebook-bearing tourists from the Great White North. The Director of the Dominican National Park Service had told us, somewhere around beverage number-14, that he would contact his charges in La Descubierta to inform them of our imminent arrival and to make certain all professional courtesy was extended to journalists of our international stature. (We might have slightly embellished our standing in the outdoor press just a bit.) Shockingly, that contact had not been made. Angel had no idea who we were, what we wanted or, more importantly, how our presence might impact what we came to learn was his responsibility-free life.

Since we had spent more money than anticipated on our journey from Santo Domingo (we were charged extra at every juncture because we had so much shit), our first order of business was changing American dollars into Dominican pesos, a task, we were informed, made more difficult by La Descubierta's banklessness. Good news, however: There was a local man who would be happy to sell us black-market pesos at a highly deflated rate. And, even better news, according to Angel, the man owned a bar! Great! Instead of converting dollars to pesos and pesos to beer, we could just go directly from dollars to beer! Our livers rejoiced!

So, par for our increasingly curvy course, we strolled

over to the black-market bar, which was just then opening for the evening. Come to discover Las Descubierta was home to exactly two watering holes: the daytime bar and the nighttime bar, an insightful exercise in community-wide organizational logistics. You'd have to be pretty damned drunk to screw those hours up.

Since the bar employees were still at the point of taking chairs off tables when we walked in, we were the only customers. We sat at a table both empty and large, rather than sitting at the bar, my preferred venue. Angel said we would need the extra space, because it wouldn't be long before the place was hopping. And he was right. Within an hour, every non-married female in La Descubierta descended upon that bar like locusts upon a cornfield. And every one of those females was dressed to the nines: there were bouffants and bangly jewelry and FM pumps and high heels and mini skirts and gawdy make-up apparently slathered on with full-sized paint rollers and veritable tsunamis of low-rent scent. And every one of those gussied-up fillies sat around Norb and I, forming a solar system of orbital estrogen. There were pretty girls and ugly girls; fat girls and skinny; tall and short; dark-skinned and light; shy and gregarious. Norb and I could utter an incomprehensible syllable, "Yug," or some such, and these ladies would hang on that syllable as though it were a personal blessing delivered by the Pope himself. They tittered and giggled while focusing on our every facial twitch. And did I mention they were all under 20?

"Uh, Angel," I finally asked, "so, heh heh, what's up with the 200 fawning nubile nymphets clawing at us?"

"They all want to marry you, so they can move to America," he responded in a tone of voice suggesting he thought I was perhaps a tad simple.

"Somos casados," I bellowed, in part to buy us some breathing room and in part to stress to these ladies we were not going to pay for everyone's drinks. A huge buzz-kill let-down sigh deflated the entire room, just as I realized what I had just said, which was supposed to be, "We're married" — as in, "Norb is married to a lady named Lori, while I am married to another named Gay" — was instead, interpreted as, "Norb and I are married to each other." My stuttering attempts to clarify the situation, by saying, "No somos casados," was fur-ther translated in the minds of those American-husband-de-siring Dominican lasses that my Spanish was poor and/or my thinking was muddled, rather than an indication of our actual marital status. Confusion reigned, which is normal operating procedure in the DR, but, even so, the partying vibe revved right back up.

Then the DJ took up his post. There are many positive statements you can make about Dominicans. They make great rum, beer and cigars. They are good chess players. They have organized themselves a very impressive national parks system. And they can flat-out dance. These people pop out of the womb dancing. The infants dance. The old people dance. The cripples dance. The nerds dance. Everyone dances all the time, aided and abetted by the fact that few are the moments in the DR when there's not music blaring from every struc-ture and automobile in the entire country. And it's rhythmic music. No trance, drum-and-bass or C&W shit here. It's all variations of the DR's endemic style: merengue. Music that enters your body less via your ears than via your skin pores.

It was not long before every single goddamned one of those proximate nymphets was lining up to boogie with Norb and I. But here's the thing: Not only am I the worst dancer who has ever drawn breath, but I also HATE dancing. My DNA carries nary a strand of funkiness gene. I am literally incapable of tapping my foot to a metronome. This is bad enough in my normal life, where I am generally adept at avoiding dance-laden environments. But, here I was, in a huge bar with music throbbing and a dance floor 12 feet away populated by 200 gyrating Dominican ladies, all of whom, according to Angel, wanted to bear my children. Wasn't long before the ladies of La Descubierta finally succeeded in pulling me out onto the dance floor, and, the exact nanosecond I made my first tentative twitch, trying mightily to match arrhythmic chromosomes to pounding salsa-infused merengue, all music-based movement within the four walls of that bar ground to a screeching halt. An immediate cessation of dancing. The DJ stopped spinning tunes. Mouths hung wide. Eyes popped. Hands were raised palms out in desperate hope of warding off an affliction that hopefully was not contagious. Visages that, an instant prior, had been gleeful now stared at me in abject horror. Birds fell dead from the sky. Somewhere in the distance, a dog wailed mournfully.

"Maybe if you drank more beer," Angel suggested, sympathetically, when I skulked back to the table, mortified. Well, there's a thought. Angel said he would talk to one of the nymphets about giving me dancing lessons. But apparently no one volunteered. Understandable. You can't teach stupid.

Sadly, what with the throbbing music, the giggling, gyrating damsels and the 447 beverages we eventually consumed, not much of the way of strategy-honing transpired that night, so we agreed to meet Angel for breakfast to see if we couldn't formulate a battle plan for visiting Isla Cabritos.

At this point, some actual facts might assist the narrative. Isla Cabritos National Park — the lowest point on any ocean island in the world — is located in the middle of Lago Enriquillo, a 102-square-mile endorheic lake that is the largest inland body of water in the Caribbean. Isla Cabritos, about eight miles by one mile, lies seven miles from the closest land, a point just north of La Descubierta. Lago Enriquillo is also home to about 15,000 endangered American crocodiles, which can reach 20 feet in length, and a great many of those bunk down every night on Isla Cabritos, where they are supposedly legally protected from poachers.

I mentioned earlier about how much gear Norb and I were carrying. Not only did we have full backpacks, necessary for our upcoming ascent of Pico Duarte, but we also had with us two one-person Sevylor inflatable kayaks, along with all the necessary kayaking accoutrements. The main reason we had those kayaks with us was because, later in our visit to the DR, we intended to descend the Rio Yuna, which we ended up doing a month later. We brought those Sevylors with us to La Descubierta in case we needed them to paddle across Lago Enriquillo to Isla Cabritos, though the thought of having our nuts sitting inches from the waterline in easily puncturable kayaks while making our way across a lake populated with 15,000 20-foot crocs did not exactly titillate us. We were hoping to procure sturdier aquatic transportation.

Angel told us over fried platanos and tomatoes the next morning that the park owned a Zodiac, which, for a nominal fee, we could rent. He also volunteered himself and the services of a cook, again, for a nominal fee. The only problem, he said, was the one outboard motor the park owned was right then in a state of disrepair, and he did not know when it would once again be functioning. So we hired a couple of motor scooters and made our way to the mechanic shop, where we found 1) three mechanics sitting around a table playing cards and guzzling rum straight from the bottle at 9 a.m. and 2) a boat motor spread around the facility in willy-nilly fashion in about 1,000 pieces. This was not encouraging, but Angel, after talking with the drunk, card-playing mechanics, assured us the motor would be purring like a kitten within hours. And so it went for three solid days, with the only progress being made on the motor as far as we could see being 1) the mechanics were even drunker than the day before and 2) the 1,000 motor pieces were spread around the facility even more.

There was very little to occupy us. We did a bit of day-hiking. We caught the few local sights. And we whiled away many hours in the daytime bar, and we whiled away many hours in the nighttime bar, where I was never once pulled back out onto the dancefloor.

La Descubierta's daytime bar was an interesting affair, less a public house and more a public works project that happened to sell alcohol in large quantities. The "bar" was actually a baño, a place where a rivulet that flowed through the middle of town was dammed and transformed into an ersatz swimming hole, which served as a bathing facility apparently utilized by every resident every day. As such, it functioned as a town plaza, with water, beer and the ever-present merengue being blasted continually through speakers the size of refrigerators.

Pleasant as those three days were, Norb and I were getting a tad antsy, especially because we were coming to understand the reason for our delay had less to do with a boat motor lying in 1,000 pieces on a drunk mechanic's floor than it did with Angel's 1) lack of desire to actually go out to Isla Cabritos and 2) his fervent desire to milk Norb and I for as many drinks as possible. So, at the nighttime bar, we announced we would be leaving first thing in the mañana with or without him. Again, the thought of paddling those flimsy inflatable kayaks across a lake filled to brimming with carnivorous reptilian teeth was cause for some concern, but we were resolute in our declaration to Angel. Astonishingly, Angel announced that he had recently learned the park boat would be ready for departure by sunrise.

I should have listened to his choice of words more carefully.

Angel arrived well before dawn with the Zodiac in the back of a truck. With him was a cook/fetcher/toter/slave, whose name I forget. We drove to the put-in and started loading gear. It seemed like something was missing, maybe even something borderline important. Just as we were getting ready to launch, my hyper-keen journalistic eye noticed, at the stern of the boat, right where the motor was supposed to be, there was no motor. I mentioned this to Angel, who just shrugged and said it was still lying in 1,000 pieces on the drunk mechanic's floor and, therefore, we would have to paddle those seven miles across the croc-infested waters of Lago Enriquillo, something we could have done three days earlier. Angel passed me a bottle of rum. Problem solved, or at least mollified.

The last piece of gear placed into the Zodiac was a foot pump, which the cook/fetcher/toter/slave attached to the air valve even before we set sail out into the heart of the food chain. This seemed unduly cautious, since the boat was clearly fully inflated. But in a lake full of 15,000 sets of razor-sharp choppers, maybe extra prudence was called for. As we started paddling toward Isla Cabritos, Norb and I could not help but notice there were only three of us actually paddling — Norb, me and the slave. Angel was sitting on the side languidly foot-pumping in cadence with our strokes, as though he were a coxswain at a very low-rent Olympiad. When I observed we could make better progress were he too to take a paddle in hand, he sighed and told us a stunning truth: the Zodiac had a pretty significant leak and, if one of us did not man the foot pump at all times, we would soon find ourselves submersed in the croc-filled waters. Few are the words that could have been uttered that would have bent us to our task more diligently. The nose of the Zodiac was suddenly pointed skyward and our wake suddenly became a rooster tail.

It took several hours to fetch Isla Cabritos. We made camp under a disintegrating thatched palapa, part of a long-abandoned meteorological camp deserted because no reliable fresh-water source could be established. Angel stressed to us in no uncertain terms that we needed to keep our eyes peeled for scorpions, of which there were apparently several varieties on the island, many of which lived in the thatch serving as the roof of the palapa. Suddenly, the crocodile situation took a psychic backseat.

At dusk, we crept down to the beach, which was filled to brimming with crocs. It was an exotic scene: glass-flat lake water, the verdant mountains of Haiti rising in the distance, several thousand crocs a stone's throw from our prostrate selves. And these creatures were, as advertised, huge. They rested with their mouths agape, which added to their fearsome vibe, though, in truth, while on land, they were very skittish. (Angel emphasized that, while in their native liquid element, they were assuredly *not* skittish.) The slightest sound, such as, but one random example, me cursing through clenched teeth because I just crawled across a cactus spine, had the crocs dashing back into the lake.

Once darkness descended, we returned to camp, where we made the mistake of shining our flashlights up into the thatch, which was literally crawling with scorpions. Norb and I moved our sleeping bags out from under the roof, something Angel advised against because, he said, occasionally the crocs were known to venture inland in search of carrion. Restful shut-eye did not come easily.

After breakfast — once again, fried platanos with tomatoes, a dish I still love — Angel showed me the old meteorological station outhouse. While so doing, he brushed aside the dry-rotted toilet seat, leaving me with a smooth slab of concrete upon which to sit and relax. I parked my posterior and let my mind wander for just a moment, self-satisfied, because, assuming we managed to successfully paddle the leaky Zodiac back across the croc-infested lake, Norb and I had pulled off Stage One of our Dominican agenda. I leaned back a bit and, as I did so, my left hand barely nudged the remnants of the dry-rotted toilet seat. I do not know what compelled me to look back. But look back I did, and what to my wondering eyes should appear, but a scorpion the size of a house cat sprinting out from under the seat remnants toward my exposed butt cheek, poison-tipped tail pointing like a lance at a jousting match.

I had to act quickly, lest my ass get skewered in a part of the world where mortality concerns might consequently come into play. Thing is, I was right in the midst of a digestively awkward set of circumstances. I had little choice, though, but to spring upward, ongoing bowel movement notwithstanding. Before examining what turned out to be some disgusting collateral damage, I turned back toward the toilet seat, where there stood the scorpion, its tail whipping back and forth menacingly and a look in its eye that bespoke a deep desire to leap onto my exposed noodle, which, I then realized, was dangling tantalizingly close to the massive arachnid's outstretched stinger. I retreated, tripped, because my pants were still around my ankles, and only then looked into those pants, the sole pair I had brought with me to Isla Cabritos. Given that I had been suffering a bit of stomach distress the previous few days, the sight was not pretty. As I scrambled to my feet in the most undignified circumstances I have ever experienced in my life, the scorpion watched me from the very slab of concrete upon which I had so recently sat in such comfortable contemplation. I wouldn't have thought that scorpions could grin. But they can. And this one did. And who can blame him?

I arrived back at the palapa naked from the waist down, my befouled Grammicis held out at arm's length. I was greeted by — shall we say? — perplexed looks. I cleaned myself and my pants as best I could down at the lakeshore while a snickering Angel stood watch just in case any hungry crocs with especially low culinary standards were lurking nearby.

Shortly after our otherwise uneventful return paddle to La Descubierta, I strolled down to the daytime bar one last time for a beer and a swim. We were scheduled to leave town at midnight on the red-eye guagua/dumptruck/pygmy-kindergartner-school-bus run back to Santo Domingo. Word of my unfortunate scorpion encounter had obviously preceded me, as I was greeted by barely suppressed giggles that soon gained momentum until the entire crowd was rolling on the ground, belly-laughing and trying to catch its collective breath. There was nothing for me to do but laugh along.

I suddenly did not want to leave La Descubierta.

Ever.

Toward late afternoon, I found a shady spot back in the woods and dozed. When I awoke, the daytime bar was closed. I sat alone, enjoying the rare quiet and solitude. But not for long. Just as the moon began to rise, females and females only began streaming to the baño. There were infants, toddlers, teenagers, pregnant women, young mothers and grandmothers. Someone turned on a radio, but kept the volume low. All those women entered the pool. There was storytelling and laughter and gossip and commiseration. Girls and women started washing each other's backs. As bars of soap began disappearing beneath the surface of the water, the ladies of La Descubierta started subtly moving as one to the rhythm of the radio, and the surface of the pool began undulating, almost imperceptibly at first, then gaining energy, with little waves lapping on the sides, until, at last, water started escaping the pool, wetting the ground. At that moment, in the murky light, with an entire town's worth of females submerged to their bosoms, there was no telling who was pretty or not, who was old or young, who had varicose veins or who had a protruding tummy. At that moment, they were all the loveliest things I had ever seen.

And there was my lecherous self, sitting in the shadows, pulse well past heart-attack level, sweating profusely, too fearful to move, lest I have added voyeuristic-pervert peeping tom to a resume that already included scorpion-dodging pants-shitter and woefully inept dancer.

I tiptoed over to the nighttime bar. Norb and Angel were there, wondering what had become of me. I did not tell them what I had just witnessed. All I knew was, for the only time before or since in my entire life, I *wanted* to dance. And dance I did. My spasmodic gyrations were certainly not things of beauty. But they were things of joy. And, before long, I found myself in the middle of the rhythmic throng, and we were all moving as one, even if for only one short night, and only a few short songs.

— MOUNTAIN GAZETTE #183

CHAPTER TWENTY

Holy Ghost

"God is in the rain."
— "Evie Hammond" (Natalie Portman),
V for Vendetta

"I don't believe in heaven
But I still believe in ghosts."
— James McMurtry,
"Childish Things"

"How come you called me here tonight?
How come you bother with this old heart at all?
You raise me up in grace,
Then you put me in a place where I must fall."
— Leonard Cohen,
"That Don't Make it Junk"

It was not totally my fault; rather, it was God's fault for making the weather so shitty that my wife, Gay, and I found ourselves seated at our respective barstools in Handlebars Saloon in Silverton for something like three hours longer than we had originally intended, and we had originally intended to be there for several hours to begin with. But, every time we entertained the thought of egressing the premises while still able to walk, or at least crawl, we could not help but notice the cold, grey deluge there on the other side of the front door was continuing unabated, sending us, what we thought, was an unambiguous communication from On High that we were supposed to remain right where we were, enjoying mug after mug of delicious blueberry beer in a warm, dry and convivial environment.

Finally, though, the storm moderated enough we could dash to our vehicle without getting drenched to the bone, so we decided to get while the getting was still mostly good.

Since my dog had been sentenced to the 4Runner the entire time we were inside Handlebars, I opted to zigzag her back to the Canyon View Motel on foot while Gay navigated my beloved Toyota, hopefully sans serious mishap. Within a few blocks, however, I started regretting mightily that I had not visited Handlebars' men's room prior to leaving. The clouds had lowered themselves to the point they could more accurately be called fog — an orientational reality that, combined with a BAC that likely hovered somewhere around 500, conspired to cause me a certain degree of directional discombobulation, which is a slightly embarrassing thing to admit in a town the size of Silverton, a hamlet I have visited, and staggered around in, many, many times before.

Finally, just as I was seriously thinking I might suffer a mortifying mishap, I noticed a footpath ascending into the brume. I sprinted up it as fast as my wobbly legs would carry me, eventually reaching a spot secluded enough that I felt comfortable taking care of what had become very necessary business.

It was then and there, while spraying a glorious arc above
Silverton as the universally comprehensible AAAHHH!!!
passed from my lips and echoed through the valley below, that
the hair on the nape of my neck stood up a bit and I started
getting the feeling every person who has spent much time in
the backcountry knows all too well: I am not alone. Someone
or something is watching me. And that someone/something
is close at hand. But I was enjoying my still-in-progress relief too much to pay that feeling, which ordinarily would put
me on instant red alert, much heed, because I would rather
have been mauled to death by a rabid grizzly bear than have
my revelry interrupted. As I stood there in the mist, however,
with dusk settling upon the majestic San Juans, the sense I
was not alone grew strong enough, and threatening enough,
that, even before my business was complete, I turned a bit
and glanced over my left shoulder to sneak a peek, lest someone inordinately crazed or something exceptionally big and
hungry be lurking nearby ("DIED WHILE URINATING" being a
completely unacceptable epitaph).

Something was. And it startled me so badly, next thing
I knew, I was tumbling ass over teakettle part way down the
hill I had just walked up, pants not yet re-zipped, finally coming to a stop only because I ended up like a supplicant on my
knees, which hit terra firma so hard skin was removed. What
had been standing behind me the whole time I was draining
was not some ax-wielding hick straight out of "Deliverance."
What was there was not a mountain lion, fangs bared, ready
to pounce on my pissing self. As my heart pounded and my
breath raced, and as I struggled to regain some semblance of
mental orientation and physical composure, which was not
easy, given the circumstances, what I saw standing there was

far worse. Jesus Christ!!!, I thought, it's, of all goddamned things, a giant, well, Jesus Christ!!! You want to talk about a man who was having some serious difficulty reestablishing any sort of grip on reality. The 200 recently consumed brewskis did not aid and abet my attempt to understand what the fuck a veritable Christzilla was doing stalking me into the woods. I mean, my recent transgressions were not really noteworthy enough in the grand scheme of sinful things.

Just as I was about to unleash a non-sequitorial ad hominem admonition to have mercy on my unworthy soul while I searched fervently for an escape route, the breeze picked up and swirled some of the fog away and things came into sharper focus. Of course! Though I had never before visited it, I remembered, above Silverton, is the Christ of the Mines statue/shrine, erected, according to the plaque, in the 1950s "… to ask God's blessing on the mining industry of the San Juans," a blessing that apparently did not work too well in the long run, since there is hardly any mining industry left in this entire part of the state.

I get back on my feet, zip myself up, dust myself off, look around to make certain no one besides my mightily perplexed perro witnessed my frantic tumble, examine the scrapes on my knees and walk back up the hill to face Christ of the Mines. This is not the first giant Christ statue I have ever rubbed elbows with. There's one outside Creel, in Mexico's Copper Canyon Country, that I've visited on numerous occasions. And then there's the world-famous Cristo Rey standing tall above Rio de Janeiro, which I have also visited. But those have always been full frontal assaults, undertaken in the brightness of day. Neither the Creel Christ nor Cristo Rey ever snuck up on me while I was relieving myself as the dusky mists swirled around. But, then again, who among us truly understands deitic humor?

My relationship with Christ started out so poorly that recovery, even after 50 years, has never been even remotely possible. I was six years old, and it's fair to say I was a bad boy rapidly getting badder. People understandably roll their eyes when I relate this, figuring that there are some Fayhee-esque memory-enhancement issues at play here (perish the thought!), but, at that tender age, I had already visited the back of a police cruiser twice — once when my exasperated mother, tired of my constant thievery, called the Air Police (we then lived on an Air Force base) and asked if they would frighten me in hopes that I would stop horking shit. They picked me up at the appointed time, drove me around, tried to scare me straight, then brought me home with a stern warning about "next time." And, next time, when I dumped fertilizer into the gas tank of our neighbor's brand-new Mercedes-Benz (don't ask, because the answer is, "I don't know."). The only effect those two experiences had on me was to raise my hipness quotient with my ne'er-do-well service-brat compadres, all of whom thought it very cool to have a genuine criminal in their midst.

As a result of my wayward ways and in hopes of not-so-subtly steering me in the right direction, my mom had hung upon my bedroom wall a fairly generic profile painting of Jesus Christ. Head and shoulders only. Bearded Caucasian hombre with long hair who bore a striking resemblance to just about every hippie I knew throughout my college years. Understated halo. Innocent, contrition-inducing eyes that verily shouted that this was a dude who definitely did not hork shit or pour fertilizer into the gas tank of his neighbor's new Mercedes. Every night, before the lights went out, Christ was the last thing I saw, though his poorly painted presence did not much influence my increasingly recalcitrant behavior. One night, though, the impression stakes were raised in a big way. I awoke in the middle of the night and there standing at the foot of my bed was not any variation on the usual kids' wild imagination monster theme — no Frankenstein or Dracula or even the dreaded Hand — but, rather, a life-sized, full-body extrapolated version of the Christ depicted in the painting on my bedroom wall.

It would have been one thing entirely if Christ had translated his holy visage to a loving but serious New Testament-type message that said, "Hey, buddy, you're heading down the wrong road. God loves you and you should change your ways. Think of your poor mother!" And it would have been one thing if he had sternly wagged a finger and yelled at me, Old Testament-like, that, if I did not get my shit together in a hurry, then the gates of hell awaited me. Either of those things wouldn't exactly have mitigated a glaring reality: There standing at the foot on my bed was, of all strange things, Christ, but, still, those actions would at least have been comprehensible and contextual, even to a boy who had not yet seen his seventh winter. However, what I faced there at the foot of my bed was Christ with fury emanating from his every pore and a dagger raised high above his head, getting ready to …

… stab me to death.

Despite the captivating raised blade situation, I crawled as fast as I could toward my imminent assailant. Maybe I thought Christ would be reluctant to stab me in the back as I groveled toward his holy tootsies. Maybe my then-pugnacious self figured, OK, *asshole*, you're going to stab me, I'm going to try to get a few punches in first. Either way, just as I got to him, Christ disappeared, pretty much never to again bother me with any manner of encore experience, good, bad or indifferent.

When I casually told my mom over Cheerios about Christ trying to stab me during the night, she smiled nervously and said I must be dealing with a guilty conscience, but the look on her face bespoke some very understandable serious parental concern. It was some years later that I wondered if my mom had not prayed to Christ to pay me a visit — much the same way she did when she called the Air Police to set me straight — to see if he couldn't maybe nudge me off the road to damnation/prison. I don't believe she would have wanted Christ to raise a dagger and try to kill me any more than she would have wanted the Air Police to beat me on the kidneys with truncheons. Then again, my mom was a hard woman, so who's to say?

Either way, Christ's visit to me that night had the opposite effect, and, for the next seven or so years, I was a hellion whose anti-social repertoire was fast growing to include serious destruction of private property, breaking-and-entering, burglary and arson. My mom's been in heaven for almost half my life now, and I've long wondered if she hasn't shared a cocktail or two with the Son of God, during which time the subject of his raised-dagger visit to her eldest child half a century prior maybe didn't come up. "Jesus Christ, Jesus Christ," I can hear my mom saying, "Maybe you could have been just a little less over the top!" "I know, I know," Jesus Christ would respond, shaking his head with a playful smirk. "Win some, lose some. Live and learn. But, look, Marge, he didn't turn out as awful as he might have," a point with which my Mom would surely have to agree, all things being relative, even, one assumes, in the hereafter.

Though I was christened a Catholic when I was a babe in swaddlings back in my native U.K. (the fault of my dad's Irish-lineage), my fractured family was not exactly what you would call churchgoing. While we lived in the northern Adirondacks, then in central Kentucky, we didn't even pretend to attend houses of worship. A couple times a year, I would be invited along by friends whose parents were troubled about the lack of theocratic structure in my life as they attended various Christian indoctrination camps, most of which, if memory serves, were of the snake-handling, speaking-in-tongues, fire-and-brimstone, twitching-on-the-floor variety. I would go for a week or two, then predictably revert to my natural heathen ways, wandering through the forests of a Sunday morning instead of prostrating myself in front of and singing really bad songs in praise of the scumbag who tried to stab me to death in the middle of the night when I was six.

When we moved to my stepfather's home turf in eastern Virginia after my seventh-grade year, my well-deserved independent Sunday-morning woods-wandering reverie was flat-out torpedoed all to hell: out of the blue, sans sufficient enough warning to develop any sort of tactical counter plan, we started attending church regularly — Ware Episcopal Church, the oldest Episcopal parish in the U.S. Truth be told, our lamentable religious conversion had at least as much to with networking opportunities as it did a sudden bloom of faith. As a new lawyer in town, my stepfather needed to make as many professional connections as possible, and, in Gloucester County, Virginia, at that time, Ware Episcopal Church was the place. The rule was simple: I had no choice but to attend Sunday-morning services, as well as rollicking Sunday evening gatherings of the Episcopal Young Churchmen, until I was 16. The exact nanosecond my 15th year ticked away, I stopped going with the family to Ware Episcopal Church. I didn't stop because I necessarily disbelieved any of the words uttered or sentiments expressed within those stifling Colonial-era walls. I just wasn't interested, the same way I have never been interested in hockey, though I still believe in the existence of the Great One. And thus it has since been. The only times I have ever entered houses of the holy in my adult life have been for unavoidable funerals or weddings. Well, there was also the time my younger brother played Joseph at the Ware Episcopal Church Christmas pageant. That I had to see with my own eyes.

All of which was neither here nor there as I zipped up and went to face the Christ of the Mines, which loomed above me, maybe 20 feet tall, with, like all monster Christ statues I have seen, arms raised and spread, like he was auditioning for a deodorant commercial. Or perhaps he was telling the multitudes, "I caught a fish THIS big!!! You can catch a fish THIS big too!!!" I tried to imagine either of those hands holding a dagger. I walked over and, right then, a passing bird splatted a load on the ground between yours truly and the holy ghost. I took that as a sign, and turned to return post haste to the land of the living. I then caught sight of what looked to be a simple pulpit placed not far from where I had just relieved myself. Like maybe people occasionally came up here to deliver sermons to the good folks of Silverton, who, I'm certain, appreciate the live entertainment. Upon closer inspection, it was a more like a desk, mounted on a post, with a transparent writing surface covering a storage area that included literally hundreds of handwritten prayers adorning everything from napkins and matchbook covers to notebooks so overflowing with text they took final form as palimpsests upon palimpsests. Though I felt like a peeping tom, I pulled that mound of pleas, praises, entreaties, promises and supplications out for closer inspection.

Here are some of the prayers I read as darkness fell.

- "I wish I was an angel."
- "Thank you for my blessed life. I hope in your light to continue walking with an open heart."
- "As I stand here in the quiet and peace of the early morning, looking around at your marvelous creation, I can't help but feel you are close. How beautiful are your works! Thank you for the works of your hand. The magnificent paintings you bless us with and the love and care with which you do it."
- "Help us win the Powerball or a big jackpot."
- "Help my back" (written on an Iron Horse Bicycle Classic card).
- "I'm not sure what this is so I'll be looking into it tonight. I was looking for a geocache."
- "In thanksgiving for our four daughters and getting us to town safely with a broken water pump."
- "We miss you, Paul and Desirea. Please help our hearts heal, Lord. Shawn is taking care of us. Thank you for him. Please help us restore our health and trust and faith in you. We lost our minds. I lost my head. I need it back."
- "I am the great-grandson of the man who built this monument."
- "Dear Jesus: Please slow down on the volume of stu-

pid and unnatural people you send to this planet."

- "Dear Lord, Please help me do math."
- "In a world where pirates are stealing and hurting others off the coast of Somalia, I believe you are pirates of hope and good. Thank you for the adventure. I am a reincarnated mermaid."
- "Thank you, Lord, for blessing me & help me get a wife."
- "Dear God, Hi! What is wrong with this world?"
- "Dear Jesus, Thank you for helping us climb the mountains safely through rain, hail and troubled travels. Bless Vincennes, Indiana."
- "Help my parents quit fighting."
- "Please, Lord let us find a way to get along, at least till we get home."
- "Hi God! What's going on? It must be cool to be high all day."
- "Pray for us. We need a lot of prayer. More than most."
- "Dear Lord, please bring my son back to believing in you."
- "Sorry about dead people."
- "Dear Lord, Thank you for ending my grandfather's pain."
- "Dear Lord, Tell my mom I miss her."

There is no doubt whatsoever, were one inclined toward the cynical, a lot of those prayers would make for easy targets, and, given my personal history with Christ, it was mighty hard to tamp down my auto-response jaundiced inclinations. But, just as my cynicism gland was getting ready to start secreting poison into my system, a rainbow broke out above

Kendall Mountain, and, well, the scene was just too damned pretty for even reflexive negativity. Instead, uncharacteristically, I pulled a credit card receipt (Handlebars: $73.82) from my wallet and decided to leave a small prayer of my own in that lectern full of scribbled notes, even though I believe it's fair to say that my experience communicating with the Big Sky Daddy is, shall we say, limited, and that inexperience initially translated to one of the few cases of writers' block I have ever faced. Ergo: My first thought was to write: "Dear Whoever You Are: Please unclog my current writers' block." That seemed a little blasé for my inaugural bar-credit-card-receipt-based prayer.

So I trended heavy: I thought about asking that all my fellow mountain travelers — the hikers, bikers, climbers, paddlers and skiers — be blessed and made safe during their backcountry forays. Thing is, it's hard to solicit blessings when you're not really sure what a blessing actually is. Like, is there a limited stock of blessing dust in heaven, so, if the hikers and bikers get sprinkled, are some of the starving kids in Africa left out? Or, is there plenty to go round, plenty for everybody? And, further, I started wondering why it's necessary for mere mortal schlubs like myself to have to ask that certain people or things get celestial blessings. It seems like blessings should rain down automatically from On High, if not onto all of us, then at least to those who need them most. What's up with this groveling shit?

So, I thought about just asking Sky Daddy to say howdy to my mom and tell her that, though I miss her, I'm doing just fine.

I thought about asking why the Son of God would raise a dagger in the middle of the night over a six-year-old boy, even a bad boy getting badder by the day.

I thought about selfishly asking for some sort of general-amnesty forgiveness for all my various misdeeds, especially the fun ones.

I thought about asking that the first words out of my wife's mouth when I return to the motel are: "Hey, big boy, get those clothes off fast."

In the end, I opted to cover numerous bases, to keep it practical and to keep it humble. "Dear nameless and/or named but either way faceless and stunningly ambiguous deity/ies: I thank you mightily for designing such a splendid place to relieve oneself and for making it so I was able to arrive at this place before my bladder burst. May you lead other inebriated souls to this spot. And also may you remind those of us prone to forgetfulness and/or poor planning to piss first before leaving the goddamned bar. Amen," I wrote upon that receipt. Not exactly worthy of inclusion in the Book of Common Prayer, but it's a beginning.

Or not.

And then I walked back down into Silverton, a town I consider to be heaven on earth, without looking back at the Christ of the Mines, and not knowing when, where or if the dagger would eventually fall.

> *"I know that I'm forgiven,*
> *But I don't know how I know.*
> *I don't trust my inner feelings.*
> *Inner feelings come and go."*
> — Leonard Cohen, "That Don't Make It Junk"

— MOUNTAIN GAZETTE #184

CHAPTER TWENTY-ONE

Crash Landing

"With your feet on the air
And your head on the ground
Try this trick and spin it, yeah
Your head'll collapse
If there's nothing in it
And then you'll ask yourself
Where is my mind?"
— The Pixies, "Where Is My Mind?" ("Surfer Rosa")

There's a stunningly fine line between a "misunderstand-ing" and an "incident." And the best time to try to suss out the relative lexical semantics associated with those two potential-powder-keg words is definitely NOT while you're on a 747 that has yet to achieve cruising altitude and is headed at 600 miles per hour out over the vast Pacific Ocean.

Unfortunately, I was in a Darth-Vader-depth foul mood and thus in no condition to be pondering the nuances of ety-mology. One second, there was relative calm. The next second, every head on the plane was turning fast toward the distant re-cesses of the coach section, as five flight attendants made their post-haste way to seat 58C. Guess who was sitting in seat 58C?

It was not my dour disposition per se that caused the flight crew to descend upon me. It was the underlying action of a well-dressed middle-aged Oriental douche bag in seat 57A. Almost as soon as my posterior was planted, I had started to doze off (read: pass out with my tongue lolling out of my head and drool pooling on my chest), but, before achieving total blissful insentience, I was jerked back into semi-consciousness by an agitated, albeit understated, conversation between my seatmates, a young married couple. "I thought this was a non-smoking flight," said the women to her husband. "It is. Maybe we should call the stewardess," the husband responded to his spouse. With great effort, I cracked one eye open and saw the aforementioned douche bag in seat 57A smoking a cigarette. This is when my ill humor asserted itself. "Dude, there's no smoking allowed," I snarled. His reaction, while holding his cigarette between his vertically extended index and middle fingers, European girly-man fashion, was to draw deeply, turn around, look me right in my solitary ajar orb and blow two full lungs of smoke directly into my face. It was total instinct when my hand shot out to grab the cigarette from the man's mouth. It was surely the result of fatigue associated with an arduous six-week trip that reached something of a climatic anti-climax with an ill-advised all-nighter that ended a mere hour before take-off that caused my aim to be askew. Basically, I overshot my target. Not by much, mind you, but enough that, in something of a physical manifestation of a Freudian slip, instead of snatching a smoldering cancer stick with my digits, two knuckles made solid contact with the douche bag's lips.

The douche bag did not react in an unruffled manner. Verily, he went ballistic, screaming maniacally in Chinese, blood seeping from his mouth, trying to climb over the back of his seat to have at me.

This is when all heads turned our way and when the flight attendants started dashing down the aisle, just as the beverage service was about to commence, a situation that added even more complication to our little contretemps, because, in all the excitement, the last flight attendant to sprint to my seat had forgotten to lock the wheels of the cart and, since the plane was still ascending, the cart rolled downhill at an impressive clip after her and, as she arrived on the scene, so did the cart, knocking her ass over teakettle hard enough that she found herself lying in the aisle howling in pain while holding a now-unfunctional Achilles tendon.

It was borderline anarchy. One stewardess is face-first on the deck, there's an untethered beverage cart running amok, there's an irate douche bag, blood now forming droplets on his pointy little chin, trying to climb over his seat to attack me and there are four other stewardesses trying to figure out just what the fuck is going on. And, just as it seems things can't get any more chaotic, all of a sudden, smoke starts filling the cabin. The irate douche bag's cigarette, something that had been lost in the shuffle, had starting burning a hole in seat 57A, cause for concern, sure, but an event that prompted the flight attendants to turn their attention away from yours truly, a man who, for all they could see, was doing nothing more that sitting placidly, almost catatonically, in his seat, while, one row ahead, was a crazed man jabbering agitatedly in a language no one comprehended with a bloody mouth and smoke rising from the seat he was trying to climb over. Between that and the stewardess lying writhing in the aisle, I mistakenly thought for a few seconds I was somewhere between sufficiently out of the limelight and the actual victim. But not for long.

Just as the beverage cart was lassoed, up strolls a Sam-Elliot clone wearing a captain's-type uniform. He pulls one of the flight attendants aside and, though their backs were turned to me, I knew full well the nature of the discussion. They were surely operating under a very reasonable assumption: The earlier in a problem-solving process small mistakes are made, the more those mistakes are, or at least can be, compounded and magnified as the problem-solving process progresses. This is called the accumulation effect, and it applies to structural engineering, physics and sociology, all of which are germane to the problem-solving process of getting a big-ass airplane full to brimming with a stunning demographic amalgam of people to stay in the air while crossing a vast ocean and while nudging its way toward the upper reaches of the troposphere. And here we were, early enough in the process of trying to fly a big-ass plane full to brimming with a stunning demographic amalgam of people across a big-ass ocean that the seatbelt sign had not yet been turned off. Now would be the expedient time to nip whatever troubles had arisen in seats 58C and 57A in the bud.

With visions of a Hong Kong jail cell visiting my dulled information-processing sub-routines, I thought I heard these words coming from the Sam Elliot clone and the flight attendant: " … turn the plane around … " I did not know whether those words were real or imagined. I did not know whether they were structurally declarative, imperative or interrogative. I did not know whether they took conditional form or were uttered in the subjunctive voice. All I knew was I was likely sitting in some heap-big shit.

My photographer buddy, Norb, and I had been sent by *Backpacker* magazine to the most remote corner of China's Yunnan Province, to cover/observe the first commercial rafting descent of the class-39 Yangtze River through 17-mile-long, 11,000-foot-deep Tiger's Leaping Gorge. We, being mostly sane, had no intention whatsoever to so much as stick a toe into the Yangtze through Tiger's Leaping Gorge. We, rather, planned to hike above the river, where we could more easily witness the inevitable carnage.

About two seconds before we were scheduled to leave for the People's Republic, those malcontents in Tibet who have lived for 50 years under Beijing's unconscionable repression decided now would be a good a time to revolt. Why they couldn't have waited another month, who can say? But, as a result of their actions, all of Tibet, and those parts of China proper bordering Tibet, were pretty much closed to foreign visitation while the People's Liberation Army went about liberating a whole bunch of Tibetans of their mortality. Well, guess where Tiger's Leaping Gorge is? Not to worry, we were told by the proprietors of Sobek, the company that was charging customers something like $20,000 apiece to risk life and limb in Tiger's Leaping Gorge. They would simply add our names to their special-exception permit list, which they had purchased from the Chinese government for $100,000, and all would be well.

So, we arrived in Hong Kong with a sense of ease that ought to have, right off the bat, worried us. We had two days before our departure to Kunming, the capital of Yunnan Province, so we immediately set about procuring last-minute supplies that would most certainly not be available in the rice-paddy-dominated People's Republic. Norb went his way with his list, and I went my way with my list. When we met up in mid-afternoon, Norb had good news: Not only had he obtained maps, fuel canisters and a Mandarin phrasebook, but, he said effusively, he had located the perfect watering hole in which we could slake our well-earned thirsts later in the day. "Yeah, I was just walking down the street, and a very nice man standing in front of a door invited us to come back." Good work, Norb. One less thing to worry about.

When we returned to the watering hole around dark, we were slightly taken aback when we had to descend two stories below street level to actually enter the bar, which was extremely dimly lit and which neither smelled nor felt savory. When our eyes finally adjusted to the gloomy murk, we saw we were the only patrons, it being a bit early, we supposed, for devotees of unsavory murk. There were several waitresses and a bartender (whose name, she told us, was "Money Cash"), all of whom, we came to notice by way of our finely honed journalistic skills, were topless. We, being the only available fresh meat, immediately became the focal point of every one of those topless employees, who quickly brought us a round of watered-down shots of indeterminate lineage, then a second round of watered-down shots of indeterminate lineage, along with several small bowls of stale potato chips. Two of the waitresses parked right next to us and asked if we would like to talk. I'm absolutely certain we came across like Gomer and Goober as we drawled words to the effect of "Ah, shucks, ladies, well, sure!"

We were soon asked if we would like yet another round of shots, which we declined, the fragrant bouquet of the second round not yet having quite dissipated. At that point, basically, 12 kinds of hell broke loose. There we sat, enjoying

numerous sets of exposed breasts dominating our immediate viewshed, while enjoying watered-down beverages, stale
potato chips and linguistically challenged conversation with
female employees whose native tongue we never did determine, the next snap of the fingers, there's three very menacing
burly bouncer-types, who we had not seen before that uncomfortable moment, up in our very confused faces, threatening to kick the shit out of us. From what we were able to
ascertain, you're not allowed to stop buying rounds of shots
for so much as a nanosecond. So, we apologized profusely for
our cultural ignorance and politely asked for the tab and, well,
I think it's fair to say Norb and I were somewhat stupefied to
see the bill was for $700! Fortunately for our stunned selves,
the tab was clearly itemized. We were charged $500 for two
rounds of shots, $100 for the potato chips and $100 in "conversation fees." I could not imagine what the bill would have
been had the shots not been watered down, had the chips not
been stale and had the topless waitresses conversed in a language we had heard of.

It was one seriously threatening scene, and that reality
was not even slightly assuaged by our adamant refusal to pay
that tab. We pulled out I think about $25, handed it to the
bouncer with the worst body odor, apologized yet again, and
started inching our way, back to back, toward an exit not as
clearly marked as we would have liked. The bouncers moved
in front of us. A split second before fists were undoubtedly
going to start flying, a little man, clearly the boss, emerged
from the shadows and intercepted us. "You two need to be a
bit more careful," he said. And, at that, one of the bouncers
opened a door so black it blended perfectly with the interior
décor, and we sprinted up those two flights of stairs onto the

sidewalk and ... directly into the waiting arms of two Hong Kong policemen, who had apparently been summoned the exact moment we articulated our refusal to pay our tab in full. It took us a solid hour to talk our way out of that one, but, in the end, the cops, like the little man in the bar, merely advised us to be more careful. In their own way, what the cops were issuing was a much-needed warning about potential dangers associated with the accumulation effect as it applied to Asian social physics. We were a tad too dim to pay much attention.

The plan was to hook up with the Sobek people in Dali, a lovely little mountain town eight hours by bus from Kunming. The Sobek people were right where they were supposed to be right when they were supposed to be there. That stunning positive alignment of the stars would be short lived. Sobek co-founders Richard Bangs and John Yost had some bad news for us: They had forgotten to include our names on the special-exemption permit — meaning, because Tiger's Leaping Gorge was, as I indicated earlier, closed to all foreign visitation (at least that which did not include a $100,000 check made payable to the Chinese Sports Ministry), we would be legally prohibited from venturing there to cover the impending rafting catastrophe. The liaison to the Sports Ministry said, maybe, we would be able to get some sort of off-the-books dispensation if we took a hand-written note from him to the Public Security Bureau — the dreaded PSB — in Lijiang, the next sizeable town up the road. While understanding the scribble he had jotted down might very well have been an admonition to the Lijiang cops to shoot us on sight, we boarded a bus for the lovely half-day trip to Lijiang, where we were informed in no uncertain terms by the local gendarmerie that we would not be allowed to venture any farther. We were at the end of the line, halfway around the world, a mere 60 miles from our destination. When we argued vociferously in favor of a reversal of their decision, we were handed a typed note in very polite English stating, unambiguously, if our most-honorable selves tried to go to Tiger's Leaping Gorge, we would be arrested, jailed and "eventually" deported.

Were it not for hefty quantities of fortifying beverages, that typed note would likely have signaled an ignominious defeat. But Norb and I have always been far too stupid to face defeat without doing something asinine to make that defeat even more undignified. We opted, after drowning-our-sorrows adult beverage number 41, to defy the PSB, to embark upon our own real-life experiment with the accumulation effect. Somehow, some way, we were going to make it to Tiger's Leaping Gorge.

We hatched a deceptively moronic scheme. We figured, after our conversation with the PSB, they would surely be on the lookout for us, which would be pretty easy, since there was only one road from Lijiang to Tiger's Leaping Gorge. Ergo: It would not take much in the way of law-enforcement acumen to catch us in the act. So we decided, come first light, we would sneak through the back streets to hook up with the road we needed to be on. Thing is, this was long enough ago that round eyes were decidedly unusual in small-town China. Almost immediately, people began streaming out of houses to eyeball the backpack-bedecked apparitions slinking their way along muddy alleys less wide than my desk. The concomitant chatter was not exactly aiding and abetting our attempts at moving under the radar. A few times, we both put our index fingers to our lips and said, "Shssssh," which, apparently in Mandarin, is the universal signal to jabber not only more, but more loudly.

Just when we thought the hub could bub no more, we passed in front of a goddamned elementary school, which literally disgorged before our very eyes. Every one of the 6,000 students had apparently, the very day before, learned two, and two only, words of English: "hello" and "good-bye." Minutes prior to our arrival, they had apparently been instructed that the way, and the only way, to articulate those two words was at maximum volume. The next day, apparently, was when the teacher was going to give them the actual definitions of those two words. Not that it mattered to Norb and I as we were trying mightily to tiptoe our way through the vocal cacophony, but those 6,000 screaming schoolchildren displayed no discernible pattern whatsoever in their ear-splitting use of "hello" and "good-bye." A third yelled "hello" the entire time we passed by, while a third yelled "good-bye," while the remaining third used both terms randomly, like they were trying to work out the lyrics to the old Beatles song. We were certain that the PSB cops we had talked to the previous day were right then sitting in their downtown offices, sipping tea and following our progress via the clamor.

In short, our attempt at subterfuge was counterproductive, and we could not for the life of us understand why there were not police cars right then pulling up, lights flashing.

Then, though, a miracle happened: We were out of town and on the road to Tiger's Leaping Gorge! Neither cops nor throngs of schoolchildren simultaneously greeting and biding us adieu were on our heels. Our joy was short lived once we realized the road upon which we found ourselves walking turned out to be less a highway and more a rutted dirt track into the Himalayas. The chances of catching a lift seemed remote. I will long remember the resolute way Norb and I, amigos since the 8th grade, looked at each other. We had come this far. We had survived a dark bar with stale potato chips. We had survived an onslaught of linguistically challenged youngsters. We were 60 miles from Tiger's Leaping Gorge. We had two days before Sobek was scheduled to run the Yangtze. We cinched our packs and started hoofing it.

Then, another miracle happened. In the distance, we heard a motor and saw a speck coming our way and getting bigger by the moment. A potential ride! We hooped and hollered ... right up until the vehicle got close enough we could see it was essentially an ancient Chinese guy riding what looked to be a lawnmower held together by prayer. We stood there on the side of the dusty track with our thumbs out, which, for all we knew, was the same as flipping the bird in those parts. The ancient Chinese guy stared straight ahead like, hey, if I don't acknowledge the hallucinations, maybe they'll just go away. Then Norb had a brainstorm: he pulled out a wad of cash, worth about 12 cents, and waved it as the ancient Chinese guy was passing. His attention was caught. He screeched to a stop and, next thing we knew, there we were, sitting uncomfortably on the frame of a Chinese riding lawnmower moving toward Tiger's Leaping Gorge at maybe 1.5 miles per hour — much slower than we could walk. Then, after about half a mile, the ancient Chinese guy pulls the lawnmower over and lets us know this is his exit, so, there were are, again, walking down the road, 12 cents poorer, with 59.5 miles still to go.

What we then did not need to transpire was indeed

what transpired. Before our packs were even fully re-cinched, Norb, whose eyesight has always been better than mine, started salivating all over himself while picking up his pace. "What have we here?" he asked, reaching out to grasp a roadside plant, which, of all fortuitous things, turned out to be as healthy an example of marijuana as I had ever seen. Now, given our undeniable extra-legal circumstances, it would have been prudent to completely ignore that plant while continuing diligently upon our already-challenging, if not impossible, quest to make it to Tiger's Leaping Gorge on time. Failing that, it would have been less imprudent for us to have snipped off a couple of the most-desirable buds and stash them in the deepest, darkest recesses of our packs for future reference. Sad to report, though not exactly surprisingly, neither the prudent nor the less-imprudent options defined our immediate course of action. Norb yanked the whole eight-foot-tall plant up by its roots and stuffed it lock, stock and barrel into his Mountainsmith. And, just as he was so doing, a large dump truck, which we had not noticed, our attention being diverted by the 14 pounds of free weed we just ripped from the ground, approached. Norb did not have time to tidily pack away the pot before the truck was upon us.*

Since the waving of the 12 cents worked with lawnmower man, we figured we'd try it again. And, sure enough, the truck stops and we are invited to ride in the back, which is populated by 15 or so snoozing gentlemen who seemed a bit bewildered by our sudden presence and more than a bit amused by the giant cannabis plant hanging out of Norb's bright-red pack. Ends up, this dump truck is going all the way to Dachu, the village closest to Tiger's Leaping Gorge. Though the ride was neither speedy nor comfortable, it was splendid. Our fellow travelers hid us under blankets three times when we were stopped at military roadblocks, and they were only too happy to share their exceedingly potent moonshine — which they called "champagne" — with us. We, in turn, rolled several joints, using pages torn from the grammatical-structure section of our English-Mandarin phrasebook for paper. Our traveling companions were fascinated by that phrasebook. After much earnest study, they pointed to a word, then pointed to each of us in turn in the back of the dusty dump truck, where we all huddled close, freezing our asses off. The word, which I will remember forever, was "toong-jir" — comrade.

Ten hours later, we were dropped off at Dachu's only guesthouse, where we slept fully clothed, ready to dash into the darkness at the drop of a hat should the PSB come looking for us. Next morning, we hired a rickety boat to take us across the frighteningly roiling Yangtze to the downriver gateway to Tigers Leaping Gorge! We were ecstatic! Our ecstasy, however, was fleeting, as, after only an hour on the trail, up walks from the opposite direction, of all perplexing and disheartening things, the entire Sobek crew.

"Uh, aren't you folks supposed to be *rafting* through this section ... tomorrow?" we asked.

"We decided it was too dangerous," was the almost-indifferent response. With that, they were off. Off too was the story we had traveled 12 time zones to cover. For the next four days, we did not know what would befall us when we emerged on the upper end of Tiger's Leaping Gorge, whether there would be a troop of PSB agents standing there ready to arrest us. And we did not know what would become of our story once the editors at Backpacker learned the Sobek people had sanely pussied out at the very last possible minute.

Those were not things we could control, so we pressed on, took pictures and, on those few instances when they did not sprint away from us screaming, chatted with locals. Lack of Sobek carnage notwithstanding, it was an astounding hike through one of the deepest canyons on the planet.

Two miles from civilization, we walked right through the middle of (and I am not making this up) a Chinese prison chain gang, dressed in ripped-up striped suits, breaking rocks with sledgehammers, just like in the movies. This was not a happy-looking lot, and the thought that, maybe in a few hours, we would be joining them in their labors almost made us run away screaming. But, when we arrived in the first town large enough to have bus service, not a single person paid the slightest attention to our presence.

We were free.**

We then spent a few days hanging out and celebrating back in Dali, before returning to Hong Kong, where we hiked the astoundingly arduous 65-kilometer MacLehose Trail up in the New Territories. We had four days before our return flights to the States. We hopped a hydrofoil over to Macau, so we could wind down by playing blackjack. As soon as the boat passed out of Hong Kong territorial waters — these being the days before Hong Kong and Macau reverted to Chinese authority — the doors were opened on ship's diminutive casino, which consisted of nothing more than a half-dozen slot machines. No sooner had those doors opened than the gambling-crazed hordes descended upon those one-armed bandits, which didn't displease me, as I've never been one for feeding endless streams of coinage into machines. For lack of better recreational alternatives, I stood and watched the voracious machine feeding frenzy, and, as I was about to return to the lounge, an exasperated gent abandoned his hopeless cause, leaving a slot machine free for the first time since the mini-casino opened. I sidled over to the suddenly unmanned one-armed bandit and fished a couple coins out of my pocket, even as the man who had just given up stood close by. I placed a coin in and pulled the lever. Nothing. I placed a second coin in and pulled the lever again. All manner of red lights started flashing and sirens started wailing. My initial instinct was to run like the wind, having come to the instant conclusion down in the lizard part of my brain that we were now under attack, or maybe the boat police were after me. Before I could react, though, there were about 15 fellow gamblers running over and patting me on the back as many, many coins much larger than the ones I had inserted starting gushing out of the machine and pouring onto the floor. Nothing like that had ever happened to me.

After the last coin dribbled out some minutes later, I counted my haul, assuming, since I was in foreign realms, that, upon scrutinization, I would realize the flashing lights and sirens were much ado about fiscal nothing, that my winnings would amount to 800 million of whatever currency it is they use in international waters between one British Crown colony and one Portuguese colony and that, in reality, it would total no more than 65 cents. To my utter shock and dismay, I had won $700. The man who had left the slot machine two plays prior, stood there and shook his head. "You are a very lucky man," he growled. "Skill," I responded, stuffing so many coins into my pockets, I could barely walk.

My luck continued in Macau, where Norb and I pulled one of the longest blackjack marathons I have ever even heard of: 72 hours, during which time we stopped only for a few quick, disgusting meals, consisting mainly of what, as far as we could tell, were snake entrails. By the time we returned bleary eyed to Hong Kong, we had each won more than $1,000. It is hard to express the degree of relief this run of good gambling fortune bestowed upon me, a prototypical, definitive, card-carrying starving writer. Though *Backpacker* had paid for our plane tickets, and would reimburse us for most expenses upon completion of the story, I did not know whether there even *was* a story, since the event I had been assigned to cover did not actually occur. That's the main reason we hiked the MacLehose Trail — so we would have a nice fall-back hike should the Powers That Be at Backpacker decide that the Tiger's Leaping Gorge story was no longer viable due to Sobek's decision to abandon ship.***

And that was it. We returned to Hong Kong for one last night before this demanding, interesting and rewarding adventure was over and done with. What could possibly go wrong?

Funny you should ask ...

We arrived in Hong Kong during the earliest hours of October 19, 1987, otherwise known as "Black Monday," the worst single day in the history of stock exchanges. By noon, Hong Kong, a place that survives off the electronic shuffling of dollars, pounds sterling, francs and yen the way most societies survive off food, water, shelter and oxygen, was in utter turmoil, and, by the time the closing bell rang, the entire colony was shaken to its core, because, in one short business day, the Hong Kong Stock Exchange, the third-largest in the world in terms of actual capitalization, had lost almost 50 percent of its value. By morning, when the shockwaves of

Black Monday rippled their way to New York, the Dow Jones would suffer its biggest one-day loss *ever*.

It was an interesting day to be in Hong Kong, especially for a person who looked at a couple days of successful black-jack playing in Macau as a monumental portfolio addition.

Even as people were running down Salisbury and Na-than roads, bumping into buildings and wailing in abject despair, Norb and I, being insulated from the vagaries of the stock market via our perpetual destitution, opted to deal with this international crisis-in-the-making by venturing forth into the Kowloon evening. Our destination was Ned Kelly's Last Stand, an Aussie-owned bar so popular with ex-pats and tourists that, if you did not arrive on the scene by happy hour, your chances of getting a seat were nil, and if you did not have a seat, there was nothing to do save stand in the middle of ill-defined passageways the wait staff traversed in their noble quest to slake thirsts. The bar was long and skinny, kind of like the watering holes on Whiskey Row in Prescott. Adding to an already skimpy amount of internal space was a large stage that, by dark, would be populated by an eight-piece R&B band consisting mostly of decidedly un-funky Filipino and Chinese musicians who had much in the way of articulation-based difficulties when they butchered songs like "Proud Mary."

We thought we were ahead of the crowd curve, but, since half the inhabitants of Hong Kong were enthusiastical-ly liquidly lamenting their newfound residency in the poor house, Norb and I arrived at Ned Kelly's too late to get seats. The only spot I could find to even stand was next to a 10-top horseshoe-shaped booth, which was completely filled with a group of very loud, young and drunk Aussies. The 10-top was the closest table to the swinging doors leading to the kitchen. Every time a waitperson passed through those doors, I had to suck in my stomach and hold my breath, lest I get knocked over. At one point, my attention was diverted ever so slightly by the chorus of, yes, "Proud Mary" (*"Lorring, lorring on the livel ... "*) just as a waitress from, of all places, Evergreen, Colorado, exploded through those swinging doors holding high above her head a tray so fully laden it seemed as though she were less a server and more a relief-aid worker on her way to Somalia with a food shipment designed to alleviate an entire famine in one fell swoop. I leaned back as far as I could, as fast as I could, and, as she passed, my center of gravity was no longer centered and, as a result, the smallest part of my ass made the slightest contact with the edge of the 10-top table and, as it did so, I could hear behind me 10 tall glasses of beer topple over in unison, like bowling pins.

The rowdy Aussies saw what had happened and were good-natured about it. Still, they were all soaked from the waist down, so they left to change into duds a bit drier. Bad as I felt, when the Aussies left, Norb and I found ourselves with ample seating. Shortly after we took advantage of the situation, a young Canadian, who was living and working in Hong Kong, asked if he could join us. He said he was meeting someone, an Englishman, who arrived in short order. The two men chatted conspiratorially and, under the table, a wad of folded bills was passed from the Canuck, who received in turn a small foil-wrapped packet from the Limey. Almost immediately, the Canuck asked if Norb and I would be interested in joining him back at his flat. "I've got something here you might enjoy," he said, without indicating exactly what that "something" might be. We said sure, and, minutes later, we were in a 40th-story abode about the size of my car, which the Canadian shared with one of his countrymen and two Hong Kongians.

The Canadian had purchased from the Englishman back at Ned Kelly's several grams of straight-from-the-source opium, which was debilitatingly potent. After one hit, Norb and I found ourselves fused to the couch, completely unable to so much as twitch, for the rest of the night. At one point, I tried with all my might to raise myself into something approximating a standing position and flat-out could not. Out of the corner of viewpods functioning poorly on both the focus and peripheral-vision fronts, I could barely make out a digital clock tick-ticking its way verrryyyy … slowwwllly… toward the hour Norb and I really needed to dash back to our hovel to get our shit, then make our way to the airport.

It would have been one thing if that were essentially the end of this long-and-winding story — we either made our flights or we did not and our wives consequently either divorced our despicable asses or they did not. But, well — shit! — that was *not* the end of the story, for, you see, the entire time we were parked comatose upon the Canadian's couch, one of his roommates, a yupster-type of Chinese heritage, had been … trying … to … commit suicide right in front of us. He had lost his entire family's multi-generational wealth during the Black Monday meltdown and wasn't handling the situation in any way, say, Thoreau or Gandhi would have sanctioned.

He had arrived shortly post-smoke, and, after exchanging pleasantries with the Canadian, he calmly placed his hat, briefcase and umbrella aside, screeched at the top of his lungs and dashed full speed to the closest window, which he impacted with the top of his noggin. *That* definitely changed the vibe of the evening. The window, fortunately, was closed tight and, though it cracked, it did not give way. Before anyone could react, or, in the case of Norb and I, not react, he had the window open and one leg was dangling 40 stories above the street. This man was not bullshitting; he was going out the fucking window. In one of the more heroic acts I have ever witnessed, the Canadian, who was surely as stoned as were Norb and I, was up and pulling his disconsolate roommate back into the land of the living. This suicidal savior dance proceeded apace every 15 minutes until the figurative roosters began waking a Hong Kong, which, in economic terms, was in utter ruins, and thus pretty much remained until China reclaimed its territory a decade later.

There came a point when Norb and I *had* to move, lest we miss our flights. With Herculean effort, we wobbled back to digs we had trouble finding, retrieved our filthy piles of gear, hailed a taxi and made it to the airport by the skin of our teeth. We parted ways, Norb headed for Sea-Tac by way of Tokyo, me headed toward Stapleton by way of San Francisco. And so I found myself in seat number 58C, with a gaggle of flight attendants and one Sam Elliot look-alike cabin crew member, discussing my personal fate, and, by extension, the immediate fate of my fellow passengers. The irate Chinese guy had been moved up to the front of the plane, the smoking seat had been doused with hot coffee and the stewardess who had been injured by the runaway beverage cart had been carried off to the unseen bowels of the 747.

Sam Elliot leaned over my seat. "You think we can make it all the way to San Francisco without further incident," he drawled with a bemused smirk.

"I thought of it more as a simple misunderstanding," I responded.

With that, I crashed hard, and, when I awoke, we were on final approach to the unseen conclusion to my own personal accumulation effect.

*We need not have worried about the potential legal implications of harvesting, possessing and using marijuana, which grew in profusion in China. The local authorities paid no attention whatsoever to Westerners smoking weed. Indeed, at one juncture, Norb and I were toking big time in the Stone Forest, a tourist site south of Kunming, when four uniformed Chinese police officers on vacation came upon us. They all laughed mightily (even as we were swallowing our tongues) and asked in broken English if the weed was good. We sheepishly answered in the affirmative. We passed the spliff to them, much as we would have done had a tribe of Deadheads walked up. They each took a couple hits, passed the spliff back, asked us to take their photo and went upon their merry way. I believe it's accurate to report that it took us a few minutes to regain our sense of balance.

**Midway through Tiger's Leaping Gorge, we met an American backpacker, who was in the process of putting together a guidebook to all of the areas in China closed to foreign visitation, of which, apparently, there were many, spread throughout the country. This guy, whose balls were undeniably big, spoke fluent Mandarin and had been in the People's Republic for almost a year. (He was the same person from whom we scored the hash we ended up bestowing upon the American man who was on his honeymoon, as referenced in Chapter 18, "North By Southwest.") He told us our first mistake had been visiting the PSB station in Lijiang. Our second mistake, he said, had been giving a flying fuck about what they told us after we made mistake number-one. Their job, he said, was to tell us we were not allowed to venture forth into Tiger's Leaping Gorge. Once that job was completed, they did not care if we followed their orders or not.

***Backpacker ended up publishing the Tiger's Leaping Gorge story, though, not surprisingly, they edited out all the parts about topless waitresses, playing blackjack in Macau, pulling up a pot plant on the side of the road and sneaking into a closed area. The finished piece, which bore little resemblance to my original manuscript, ended up being more than anything a goddamned destination-type piece, something I considered near-bouts criminally negligent, considering Tiger's Leaping Gorge was indeed located in a place legally closed to foreign visitation. I worried, once I learned the editors considered it too bravado-ish to include the parts about our illegal entry, that some readers might follow our footsteps. I would have felt horrible if they ended up getting arrested as a result. The more I thought about it, though, the more I realized, hey, if you're gonna take a trip based upon a Fayhee narrative, even, or maybe especially, one fatally butchered by incompetent editors, you get what you deserve — such being the nature of true adventure and all. We sold the MacLehose Trail story to *Adventure Travel* magazine.

— MOUNTAIN GAZETTE #187

CHAPTER TWENTY-TWO

Wild West

You certainly don't have to be a news junkie to know things in Border Country have been a bit dicey as of late. I mean, even dicier than usual. A recent Yahoo News entry, headlined, "Government border crackdowns on the rise," caught my eye. It leads with a couple tales about a recent municipal election in Sunland Park, New Mexico, the only American town that lies south of the Rio Grande. The story details allegations of extortion and financial kickbacks among town officials, and, more colorfully, that a mayoral candidate tried to force his opponent out of the race with a secretly recorded video of the other man getting a topless lap dance. (What is the world coming to when a mayoral candidate can't chill out after a long day on the campaign trail with an innocent lap dance?)

In addition, the Yahoo News story continued, former Sunland Park Mayor Martin Resendiz dropped a bid for Congress after admitting in a deposition that he signed nine government contracts while drunk. (Many of the mayors I've known personally over the years, I'd rather them sign documents drunk than sober!)

By the sixth paragraph, the story detours 70 miles west,

to Columbus, N.M. (more on fair Columbus in a moment), where authorities a year ago arrested the mayor, police chief, a town trustee and 11 other people who have since pleaded guilty to charges they helped run guns across the border to Mexican drug cartels.

I cannot say why those of us who choose to hang our sombreros near the southern border find ourselves more than anything almost indifferently shaking our heads, shrugging our shoulders and maybe even grinning a bit when we read such things. Sane people would justifiably pack up the Outback and head post paste to more socially normal environs (read: toward the great white north). But then you get into that seven-month winter thing that so many of us down here try so mightily to avoid.

Still, even the most avid Border Country/Southwest/desert-o-philes wince a little bit when we read such stories. We might try to limply rationalize the situation by saying things like, "Were it not for the crazy-assed 'War on Drugs,' things wouldn't be quite so bad.' Or we might say, 'Look, the border situation is not nearly as nuts as it's made out to be by non-border-dwelling politicians trying to pander to the lowest common electoral denominator." We might point out that, come what may, we at least have superlative green chile and incomparable year-round hiking and backpacking opportunities. Or we might observe that, insane though the border situation might be, at least we rarely lack for colorful media fodder.

Whatever your socio-political inclinations, whatever your proposed solution(s), there's no denying, when one approaches the frontera these days, whether for business, recreation or to commit major felonies, one had best cinch one's saddle on tight and, at all times, be ready to duck, run and bribe. It can easily be argued that things have always been plus-or minus-thus. And that may be plus-or-minus correct. Which doesn't change current operational reality one whit.

The closest legal border crossing to where these words are being penned is just south of the aforementioned Columbus, N.M., at Palomas, Chihuahua. About 80 miles from my front door. Columbus is the place where, in 1916, revolutionary forces under the command of Pancho Villa crossed into U.S. Territory (this being a mere four years after the Land of Enchantment became our 47th state) and launched an attack that resulted in the deaths of 10 civilians and eight soldiers attached to the 13th Calvary Regiment. That attack predictably spurred a response by the U.S. military that can charitably be called "not entirely successful."

Today, Columbus is one strange village, boasting a demographic mishmash that includes alternative-housing/ architecture devotees (read: people inclined to construct abodes out of materials that, in more-civilized realms, would cause shock and dismay on the part of building inspectors), Border Patrol agents, drug-and-gun-runners, tough-as-nails ranchers, retirees, eccentrics, loners, survivalists, religious zealots and, if the rumors are true, numerous higher-ups from the Mexican drug cartels who have moved north of the border to escape the violence they themselves have spawned in Old Mexico. There are a couple interesting restaurants, a few art galleries, a museum or two, Pancho Villa State Park (where I usually camp before pushing on into Chihuahua) and a cantina — along with much foliage boasting skin-penetrating spines, a healthy selection of rattelesnakes, oppressive heat and all the barking dogs, crowing roosters and blowing dust you could ever want in a town.

It was at the bar one day that I got a representative taste of the way things are in borderland limbo.

I used to work for one of the area daily papers. There was a 70-something man from Colorado, who was about to embark upon a four-year effort to hike the entire Continental Divide National Scenic Trail. The plan was for him to hike one state section per summer (New Mexico, Colorado, Wyoming and Idaho/Montana). The man was an avid Rotarian, and he planned on interacting all the way to the Canadian border with Rotary Clubs located near the CDNST route. (I believe he was trying to raise money for some good cause.) Since, stunningly enough, there was actually a Rotary Club in Palomas, the man opted to symbolically kick his 3,100-mile hike off with a gala at the famous Pink Store (a popular cantina/restaurant/gift shop a few blocks south of the Mexican border crossing), even though the official CDNST route was several dentition-jolting hours drive away near Big Hatchet Peak, over in the Bootheel.

I drove down to Columbus to hook up with the man and his somewhat substantial entourage/support team, with the idea of penning a piece for the paper, which is not too big a stretch, as the CDNST passes very near Silver City. (Verily, I hike upon it several times a week.)

Though certainly in fine fitness fettle, the man from Colorado, being a septuagenarian and all, rationally had hired a Sherpa in his mid-20s from Nepal to join him on his journey — for on-trail company, in case of emergencies and, I would assume, to help carry supplies. (I do not recollect how the man from Colorado made the acquaintance of the young man from Nepal.) Rather than risk problems getting the Sherpa back into the U.S., he left him in my highly responsible company at Pancho Villa State Park, where we planned to camp, while he and his fellow Rotarians sacrificed virgins over in Palomas, or whatever it is Rotarians do when they gather in lawless border towns.

This Sherpa kid was cool. He had summited Everest twice. His wife had also summited Everest, and, matter of fact, the Sherpa had actually proposed on the very top of the planet's highest mountain.

It was not long before we decided to make our way over to Columbus' sole watering hole. Even though it was only 4 in the afternoon on a Tuesday, the bar was full.

I had over the years made the acquaintance of several Everest summiteers, but I had never tipped brews with one. I was looking forward to hearing some death-zone tales. Sadly, the ambiance was not what you would call conducive to storytelling, even barroom storytelling. The reason was that the town's police chief was standing in the middle of the bar in full uniform. It was not his official presence, however, that drew the undivided attention of those there gathered. Rather, it was the fact the police chief was about as drunk as a person can be, and, lest you doubt me, this is a subject I have researched thoroughly over the years.

In addition, and very captivatingly, he was also loud, boisterous, obnoxious and, to add a little icing to an already very surreal cake, waving his sidearm around in a manner I believe most firearms experts would have deemed "unsafe."

The police chief's assistant was also there, and, though his visage bespoke minor concern with the way things were progressing on the potential negative incident front, it was obvious he felt compelled to serve as a wobbly wingman for his superior. Before long, both of them were waving their sidearms with one hand while holding shots of tequila in the other hand. Many toasts were given, and, in partial defense of the two inebriated law-enforcement personnel, only one of them — the chief — accidentally discharged his weapon, and, since the only thing that got shot was a ceiling fan, which, for all I know, deserved it, I guess I can't very well conscionably make any disparaging statements about local weapons protocols.

Still, the young Sherpa, who seemed somewhat taken aback by all this, and I decided that — who knows? — after another few shots of tequila, the police officer's aim might take a turn for the worse, so we aimed ourselves toward the door.

"Wait a minute!" the police chief slurred when he saw us leaving. "Where do you think you're going?"

"Uh ... "

"You're not going anywhere ... at least not until ..." (and here I must digress by pointing out that by now he was pretty much waving the recently discharged sidearm so close to my nose that I ended up inhaling gunpowder residue) "... you drink another shot of tequila with me ..." (and here I feel a need to digress yet again by pointing out that 1) I had not to that point done a shot of tequila with the police chief whose gun barrel was pretty much defining my immediate viewshed, 2) I dislike tequila so much that I never, ever drink that shit unless 3) I feel compelled to do so by someone waving a revolver under my nose) "... and I give you your get-out-of-jail-free card."

The bartender, an obviously once-comely lass, who looked 50 but was probably more like 40, sported one of those looks not uncommon to practitioners of her chosen vocation. Like, "You know, I should have taken advantage of that cosmetology school scholarship offer when I was 18 …" But she also seemed bemused by the proceedings. Without further ado, she handed me a shot of tequila, most of which was thankfully sloshed onto the floor when I traded saludos with the police chief and his underling. I choked the remainder down, said gracias and, once again, pointed my feet toward an exit that seemed to be getting farther away by the minute.

"Wait!" the police chief shouted. "Don't you want you get-out-of-jail-free card?"

"Well, of course I do!" I responded. "How could I let concerns regarding my immediate mortality allow such a patently absurd thing to slip my mind?"

I stood patiently as the police chief, who could barely maintain his balance, rummaged through the many pockets adorning his ill-fitting uniform. He was without a doubt earnestly searching for something palpable; this was not some sort of law-enforcement comedy routine, at least not one that was intentional. Finally, exasperatedly, he looked at me and said, "Hold this," and handed me his gun, which, I stress yet again, had recently been, albeit accidentally, discharged in a public place populated by several dozen potential victims/witnesses, in a border village literally crawling with hundreds of people sporting various types of badges within radio-able distance.

So, along about now, here's what's going on through my head: Even in a hamlet as off the grid of normality as Columbus, someone with a modicum of civic sanity had to have noticed that an otherwise innocent ceiling fan had been mortally wounded in the town's one watering hole. That someone very well might have made an effort to contact officialdom, which, of course, would have been the police chief and the one other cop in town who was on duty, both of whom were drunk as fucking shit in the bar and one of whom was actually responsible for killing the ceiling fan. When neither the police chief nor his personal Barney Fife could be reached, there would likely be further concern — this being a part of the world where police officers often suffer violent ends — and, then, the effort to contact some form of non-drunk on-duty law enforcement would be expanded to include the Luna County Sheriff's Department and local federal agencies, like Border Patrol, DEA, INS, ICE, FBI, ATF, the Army National Guard and the various and sundry other law-enforcement sub-species that patrol the borderlands in ant-like profusion.

I'm standing there wondering what would be the chances of one or more of those people busting through the front door of the bar, weapons drawn, and noticing in the darkened interior, a ratty-looking dirtbag, holding a service revolver in front of the town's police chief, who right then is searching diligently through his pockets in such a way that, to an outsider whose pupils had not yet adjusted to the dimly lit interior, might seem as though he's being robbed?

Finally, the inebriated police chief managed to find a business card bearing his name, his title, and the calming words, "Columbus Police Department." He held the card upside-down two inches in front of my eyes and said, if I were to find myself in *any* sort of legal trouble, all I had to do was pull that card out, and all would be forgiven. "It don't matter where you are or what you do," he stressed. I thanked him profusely for his generosity, took the card and once more began my long trek toward the exit, thinking, "Bueno ... now I can commit armed robbery in Duluth and, should I get caught, all I would have to do is pull out a business card handed to me by the shit-faced police chief in Columbus, New Mexico, and they'd let me go." (I look forward to the day when fate presents me with the opportunity to make that attempt.)

"Wait a minute!" the shit-faced police chief called out, as, yet again, the young Sherpa and I tried to depart. "I forgot to write 'get out of jail free' on the card."

So, once more, I was asked to hold his sidearm while he searched from collar to shoe laces for any manner of writing implement. He finally located a broken pencil stuffed, for reasons I did not dare explore, in one of his pants cuffs, took the business card back from me, placed it on the bar and scrawled words that for all the world seemed to be: "smsdkwersuwgd," his penmanship not being up to Japanese calligraphy master snuff.

The Sherpa and I finally emerged blissfully unscathed into the harsh light of the Chihuahua Desert. We stopped by the liquor store and purchased a couple six-packs and returned to Pancho Villa State Park to watch the sun set and to await the return of the Rotarian septuagenarian, who, for all I knew, had been kidnapped in Palomas by his fellow Rotarians, who were right then penning their ransom note.

At the edge of the park, there's a teensy little hill, which the Sherpa and I ascended with our beer. We sat on the rocky ground side by side, me still holding my get-out-of-smsdkwersuwgd card. From our humble perch, the Sherpa looked around, at the proximate Tres Hermanas Mountains, north to the rugged Florida Mountains, west to the Sierra San Luis, south into the heart of Old Mexico. All around was the most desolate part of America's most-desolate desert.

"I somehow thought America would be different," the Sherpa sighed.

"This is not America," I responded. "This is something else entirely."

"Why do you live here?" he asked, in a tactful tone.

"I don't know ... it just gets under your skin," I said, shrugging my shoulders the way dwellers of the Border Country often do. I don't think he understood. Right then, I think he was thinking about how, in a few months, he would be hiking through the Rockies, where the Wild West was long ago civilized to death.

— MOUNTAIN GAZETTE #189

Index

About the Author

M. John Fayhee, who worked as a newspaper reporter and editor for 15 years, was a long-time contributing editor at *Backpacker* magazine. His work has appeared in too many other local, regional and national newspapers and magazines to remember, much less list.

Since it seems in vogue these days for writers to show that they once got their hands dirty, Fayhee long-ago worked as a ditch-digger, house painter, land surveyor, tennis instructor, night watchman on a Mississippi paddle-wheeler and truck driver for a juvenile-delinquent rehabilitation entity that was seemingly modeled after a Stalin-era Russian gulag. Fayhee, whose travels have taken him to five continents, earned his Tae Kwon Do black belt in 1995. He has hiked the Appalachian, Colorado and Arizona trails, as well as the Colorado section of the Continental Divide Trail. He has stood atop the summits of 27 of Colorado's Fourteeners, but has since repented and promises to stand atop no more.

In 2000, along with two partners, Fayhee helped re-launch the iconic *Mountain Gazette*, where he still works as editor-in-chief.

After 24 years living in the Colorado High Country, Fayhee moved back to his old stomping grounds in Southwest New Mexico, where he lives in warmth and sunshine with his wife, Gay Gangel-Fayhee, his little dog, Casey, and his very weird cat, Tucker.

—PRESS—

RAVEN'S EYE PRESS
Durango, Colorado
Rediscovering the West
ravenseyepress.com

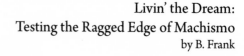

Livin' the Dream:
Testing the Ragged Edge of Machismo
by B. Frank

The Monkey Wrench Dad:
Dispatches from the
Backyard Frontline
by Ken Wright

Sometimes Creek:
A Wyoming Memoir
by Florence Shepard

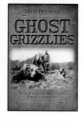

Ghost Grizzlies: Does the Great
Bear Still Haunt Colorado?
by David Petersen

How Delicate These Arches:
Footnotes from the Four Corners
by David Feela

Visit ravenseyepress.com
for a complete listing of our titles.

CPSIA information can be obtained at www.ICGtesting.com
Printed in the USA
LVOW041556240812

295829LV00009B/62/P